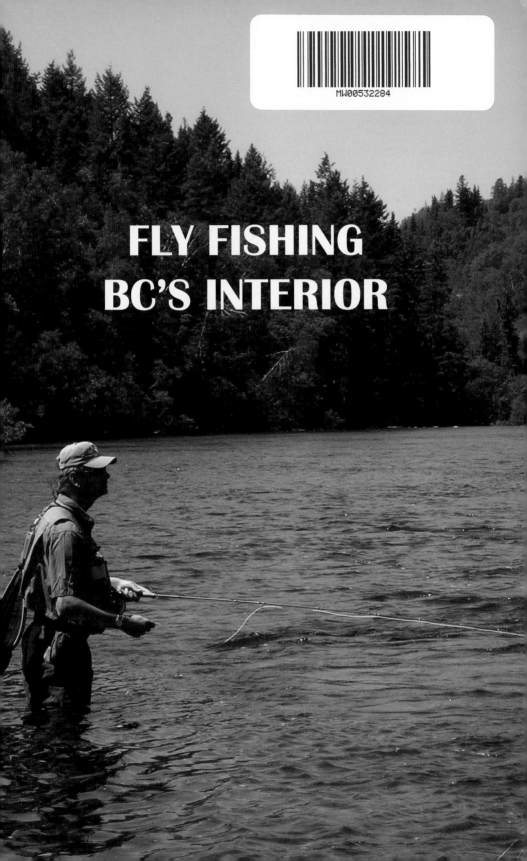

FLY FISHING
BC'S INTERIOR

Caitlin Press Inc.
8100 Alderwood Road,
Halfmoon Bay, BC V0N 1Y1
www.caitlin-press.com

Photos by Brian Smith: page 1 An unknown fly fisher on the Stellako River; pages 2–3 Mayfly Adult Dun; pages 4-5 Grizzly Lake East.

Text and cover design by Vici Johnstone.
Cover Photograph: Courtesey of iStock, photographer Jacom Stephens.

Printed in Canada

Caitlin Press Inc. acknowledges financial support from the Government of Canada through the Book Publishing Industry Development Program and the Canada Council for the Arts, and from the Province of British Columbia through the British Columbia Arts Council and the Book Publisher's Tax Credit.

Canada Council for the Arts   Conseil des Arts du Canada   BRITISH COLUMBIA ARTS COUNCIL
We acknowledge the support of the Province of British Columbia through the British Columbia Arts Council

Library and Archives Canada Cataloguing in Publication

Smith, Brian, 1947–
    Fly fishing BC's interior : a fly fisher's guide to the Central Interior
and North Cariboo waters/ Brian Smith.

Includes index.
ISBN 978-1-894759-35-9

    1. Fly fishing—British Columbia--Cariboo Region. 2. Fly fishing—British Columbia. I. Title.

SH572.B8S54 2009   799.12'4097117   C2009-901493-9

FLY FISHING
BC'S INTERIOR

A Fly Fisher's Guide to the Central Interior and North Cariboo Waters

Brian Smith

Caitlin Press

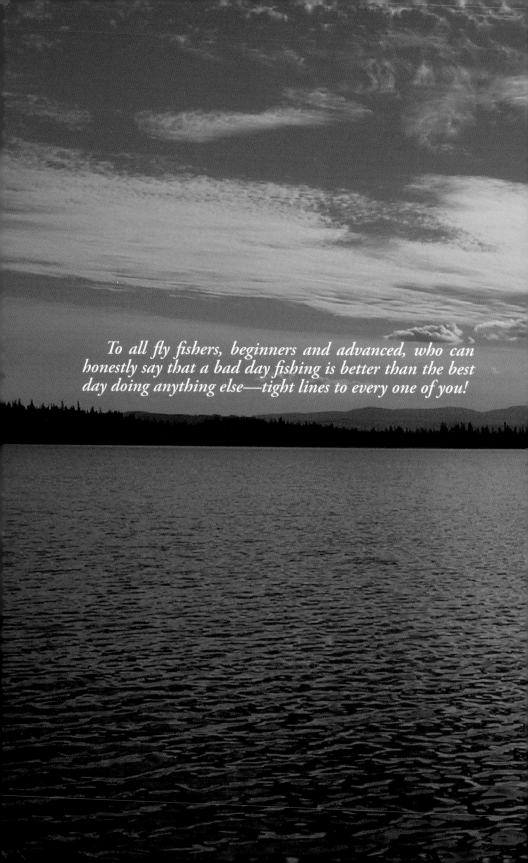

To all fly fishers, beginners and advanced, who can honestly say that a bad day fishing is better than the best day doing anything else—tight lines to every one of you!

Contents

Acknowledgements   6
Introduction   10
The Species   12
Times, Tackle, Safety   26
The North Cariboo   41
Nechako River Country   55
Prince George North   68
Against the Cariboo and Rocky Mountains   86
Thoughts on Fly Tying: Materials, Terms and Instruction   97
Chironomid   106
Midge   112
Mayfly   118
Damselfly   161
Dragonfly   165
Caddis   172
Stonefly   185
Freshwater Shrimp   192
Leeches   196
Water Boatman and Backswimmer   199
Terrestrials: Ants, Termites and Grasshoppers   202
Index   206

Acknowledgements

During my life, mentors have tended to be older men whose knowledge I value greatly. Other than my father, Ivan Smith, who showed me little about fly fishing but a lot about the values of hard work, integrity and family, there are a few individuals who have had a tremendous influence on me during my passionate hobby of fly fishing.

Jack Shaw will be remembered for his pioneer development of lake fishing fly patterns. Ralph Shaw (no relation) recently compiled and co-edited the fishing diaries of Jack Shaw, entitled *The Pleasure of His Company*. Bob Jones, the late editor of *Island Fisherman* magazine, former fishing editor of *BC Outdoors* magazine, and author of many good books and articles about fishing in BC and across Canada, co-edited Jack Shaw's diaries, and patiently edited several of my first magazine articles.

I am deeply indebted to Bob Graham for his editing prowess, geography background and photography of the fly patterns used in the production of this book, but mostly for his encouragement over the last two years.

My wife, Lois, and our two daughters, Brianna and Darcie, are fly fishers also; they each have their own equipment, and have never caught a fish on anything but a fly. I am indebted to Lois for unselfishly allowing me some freedom to do what I love secondly to her and the kids—my lifelong hobby of fishing, fly tying and, now, writing.

My sons, Kevin and Graham, have been fly fishing with me since they were old enough to sit up by themselves. Today, in their thirties, my boys are the epitome of what a fly fishing life can offer to youth—respect and honour for family and love for the outdoors.

Our fly fishing history in Central BC is perhaps lacking in big names, but not in character. Many have contributed generously of their time and knowledge to Central BC's fishery; I am proud to call them my friends, colleagues and fellow enthusiasts.

Throughout the years Bob Melrose has spent in the North, he has written a weekly column for the *Prince George Citizen*, conducted video classes at Kelly

Road Elementary School, held fly fishing schools in the lakes and rivers of our area, published several articles in *BC Outdoors* magazine and authored the segment "Grayling Waters" for Karl Bruhn's book *Fly Fishing British Columbia* (Heritage House 1999).

Lewis Johnson has guided many locals and tourists into our backcountry, fishing all of the lakes mentioned in this book and more, and has contributed greatly to the heritage of Central BC fly fishing through his 2002 self-published book *The Chronic Fly Fisher: Flyfishing the Central Interior of BC*. He has written short articles for the *Angler's Atlas* and *Canadian Fly Fisher* magazine and developed the website www.thechronicflyfisher.com.

Sheldon Moore, manager of Northern Troutfitters at his death in 2007, was proficient with all styles and methods of fly fishing and spoke his mind for the fishery of the North with a clear conscience and in a sensitive and caring way.

Blair Moffat of Northern Hardware believes that fly fishing is about more than catching trout; it's about the people you meet, friendships you gather and, mostly, the beauty of the North and its wilderness.

Twin brothers Bob and Gerry Knechtel, owners of Northern Trout Fitters Fly & Tackle Shop until February 2009, along with Casper Walraven, and Doug Steinbeck, were influential in the 1980s revival of Polar Coachman Flyfishers, the only organized fly fishing club North of Williams Lake.

Doug Brautigam founded Cariboo Fly & Tackle in Quesnel in 1992, and through his business guided many a wandering angler through the North Cariboo country, both in person and by sharing his vast knowledge of the fly fishing opportunities of the region. Doug has sold the business, but still guides fly fishers into the Blackwater River wilderness while working for Doug Mooring's business Cariboo River Fishing Adventures.

Marty Ashfield manages Bon Voyage Sports on the west side of Prince George, another valuable and knowledgeable resource for the fly fisher heading into the local backwoods region with a fly rod.

Lastly, I am grateful for the support, encouragement and photo contributions of my fellow members of the Polar Coachman Flyfishers Club of Prince George. My friendships and exploits with many of the members over the past twenty years have provided fodder for my writing, and fostered countless personal memories that have enriched my life tenfold.

Jack Shaw—b. Montreal, QC (1916–2000)

Jack Shaw passed from us in February 2000, but his legacy will be remembered through his pioneer development of lake fishing patterns during the 1960s, '70s, and '80s. Jack was gifted with great powers of observation and patience. He paid meticulous attention to detail in his studies of the insect life that lived and bred in his aquariums, and then transferred that knowledge to fish hooks to represent various life stages of his bugs. Before Jack's era, fly patterns around Kamloops were attractor origin—designs with names like Greenwell Glory, Black O' Lindsay and Yellow Sally. Fish liked them, and they still catch fish today, but fly fishers like Jack recognized that it was time to move toward better impressions. Leading the charge into uncharted territory, Jack developed patterns that the modern fly fishing generation continues to modify today. Chironomid, bloodworm, damsel nymph, leech, dragonfly nymph, caddis pupa, gomphus nymph, shrimp—all of these Interior patterns are prodigies of Jack's vise and thinking. He used natural materials and fabric in all of his imitations, a habit that I adhere to whenever possible.

I was fortunate to be a pupil in Jack's fly tying class of 1976 and we became good friends, striking a kindred-spirit relationship of thirty years that continued with his wife, Dorothy, until her passing in January 2009 at the age of 92. My wife, Lois, and I used to lunch with Dorothy when she visited her twin brother, Dick Lawrence, in Prince George. I miss Jack—he was in my thoughts and words as I worked through this manuscript.

Opposite: Staffan Lindgren—a fly rod and misty morning on Fishhook Lake, north of Prince George. *Photo Laurie Fiskie.*

Introduction

I grew up in the Lower Mainland and I am often asked by friends why I choose to live in the North. Winters are cold, summers are short, spring takes far too long to get here and fall is usually a lot like spring.

The fact is, Prince George is not in the North; it's in the Central Interior—the real North of British Columbia is a few hundred kilometres up Hwy. 97 from Prince George. I like to think of the divide at Summit Lake, a scant 43 km north of Prince George and only 12 km west of the Fraser River, as the beginning of the North. Heading north from Summit Lake, water flows to the Arctic Ocean through the Peace River drainage, but below that parallel, tributaries to the mighty Fraser angle their way southeast to the mother river and end at the Pacific Ocean in the southwest corner of the province.

It is freedom we relish up here: uncrowded rivers, roads and campsites, conservative thinking and independence. You can usually fish a favourite stretch of river alone, or paddle a pristine mountain lake for a weekend without seeing another soul. We think of 30-cm trout as pretty small potatoes; 50 cm a "nice" one. It isn't hard to put up with a little cold weather when you are a trout fisher, considering the options of where to reside in British Columbia as "Where can I work and have a life, instead of just work to live?"

This vast region north of the 52nd parallel holds amazing bounty for the outdoor person looking for peaceful places, harmony with nature and a variety of fishing experiences. There are few books on the market that speak directly to fly fishing the Interior Plateau of the North Cariboo and Central British Columbia or that offer proven patterns, how to tie and fish them and when to expect them to work on the water. I like to think of this book as a promoter for Central British Columbia waters. It is intended to be an introduction and showcase for some of my effective patterns that work for common insect hatches here in northern surroundings, and on any stream or lake elsewhere that supports fish habitat.

For Canadians of British and Irish origin like me—even though my family has been in North America for eleven generations—grappling with the thought that British Columbia is scarcely 200 years old is difficult to fully comprehend. The province's occupation began thousands of years ago with our First Nations people, aboriginals who welcomed us to this land and helped us survive the hardships of it. We owe them a great deal of respect for their contribution to our history in the BC Interior, for it was they who were here first.

The water I talk about in the North Cariboo and Central British Columbia is colder than Southern Interior water and generally not as fertile; therefore it doesn't grow fish as fast, but there is a lot more of it, and what is here is dynamite fishing water through a short spring and summer period of prolific insect hatches. The best part is the lack of fishing pressure, and subsequent aggressiveness of fish to the fly; seldom does a fly fisher need to resort to hook size 20 or 24 midge patterns to fool skeptical trout on a lake or stream—an oversized mouthful is often the best ticket. Most of our lakes and rivers contain wild original species, each strain evolving and adapting through centuries of survival.

The Central British Columbia area covered in *Fly Fishing BC's Interior* centres on Prince George, and includes geographic boundaries and drainages of Quesnel to the south, Vanderhoof–Fraser Lake to the west, Fort McLeod to the north and the Rockies to the northeast. Lying on top of the Interior Plateau in the shadow of the Rocky Mountains, this is a land of large lakes and rivers interspersed with muskeg swamps, endless pothole ponds and many kilometres of dirt road, where outdoor opportunities are endless, and visitors to some areas are counted by the handful during a fishing season.

We begin the fishing chapters with the earliest emerging insects on lakes, progressing by hatch expectation through a fishing season until freeze-up in November. Our journey switches back and forth, from still-water fishing from April through November to river and stream fishing at its peak from opening day in mid-June until October.

Living up here and choosing a fly-fishing life, I am motivated to go like hell during open-water season, and hibernate to the fly tying bench and writing desk during the winter. With so little time and so much to accomplish, a lot of water goes unfished and many words unwritten. These pages describe my favourite places—and among the words, the thoughts of a man who counts his blessings by the water and landscapes he has fished and seen, and his happiness by the friends and family who grace his path along the way.

Enjoy!
Brian Smith

The Species

The Interior Plateau of Central British Columbia is a vast and sparsely settled land of evergreen and deciduous forests, mountain valleys, marsh grasslands and abundant water. It begins near Williams Lake, extends north past Prince George, east to the Cariboo and McGregor mountain ranges and west to the Hazelton and Coast ranges near Smithers. Encompassing some two hundred thousand square kilometres of landscape, the lowest elevation of the Plateau is between six hundred and eight hundred metres, the highest around one thousand metres, which allows for predictable weather and hatch patterns for those venturing into the country with a fishing rod.

Cal Tant poses with a native bull trout, fly-caught on the Anzac River.
Photo Eric Franz.

The sustainability of the Interior Plateau relies on the health of a key geographical feature: the Fraser River, the major drainage artery of the Interior to the Pacific Ocean and one of the most prolific salmon rivers in the world. Of all waterways in the Interior Plateau, the Fraser River plays the most significant role in the fishery resource of Central British Columbia, though fly fishers rarely work the channels up here.

Beginning in Mount Robson Park as an innocent-looking divide in the Rockies, the Fraser heads northwest for about 300 km, picking up major tributaries: the Holmes, Goat, Bowron and McGregor rivers. It continues on this northwest course and then makes an abrupt turn southward 12 km east of Summit Lake. This change of direction is the transition point between the Arctic and Pacific Divide—south of this point, waters flow to the Pacific Ocean and north of Summit Lake, watercourses run to the Arctic Ocean. The Fraser then runs due south for a few kilometres, gathers the Willow and Salmon rivers and meets the Nechako River advancing from the west at Prince George. Continuing south of Prince George on the Plateau, the Fraser collects the Blackwater, Cottonwood and Quesnel rivers, three more significant tributaries that contribute to Central British Columbia's fishery. Resuming its southward journey for 800 km, it empties into the Pacific Ocean at Richmond.

The Interior Plateau is blessed with an abundance of fish species capable of reproducing naturally. The majority of our water systems have significant lake structure, enormous still-water bodies joined by rivers and their tributaries, which flow during all seasons. This wealth of free-flowing water allows indigenous fish to spawn successfully. Eggs mature naturally; young fry emerge and are nurtured to maturity in home waters, where they will reproduce to extend the genus.

Some fishers argue that coarse fish species like pike minnow, whitefish and suckers don't belong in water systems, but balance is an extraordinary act of nature. Left to their own resources and instinctive cycles, I believe ecosystems are capable of managing themselves without interference. Many of our wild rainbow trout strains in the North have adapted to balance the population of coarse fish that prey on rainbow fry; they have learned to prey on the young of coarse fish.

Fish Hatcheries in British Columbia

Our provincial hatchery program is the backbone of freshwater fisheries management in BC. Early in the last century, most of our desert-belt Southern Interior lakes were barren of fish. These lakes, however, exhibited many of the necessary ingredients for fish rearing—deep water, extensive shoals, rich nutrient and insect life and slightly alkaline pH factors—but they were devoid of fish. BC Fisheries biologists recognized the wealth they had in the resource, and began hatchery programs that now sustain a freshwater plan that is the envy of the world. Through its five operating hatcheries and many separate egg collection facilities, the province is able to produce over seven million fish annually, allowing for the stocking of more than eight hundred lakes and streams throughout BC.

The Clearwater Trout Hatchery north of Kamloops is the hub for Northern BC stocking programs, managing the plan for areas north of Clearwater between the Alberta and Yukon borders. This area encompasses wildlife regions of Thompson–Nicola, Cariboo, Omineca–Peace and Skeena. By rearing over three million fish annually, the hatchery stocks about 330 lakes per year with rainbow, brook trout and kokanee.

Pennask Creek, which supplies eggs to Summerland Trout Hatchery, has contributed to BC's hatchery program since 1928. The little stream receives more than twenty thousand spawning adults per year through the collection gate. Touted as having the world's largest natural run of rainbow trout, Pennask Lake is the origin of Kamloops trout, the strain used to replenish the high-country trout lakes of Bill Nation and Jack Shaw fame. As well, over 40 percent of stocked lakes in Southern BC receive Pennask Lake fry for their fishery programs.

The Fraser Valley Trout Hatchery in Abbotsford maintains a program that raises several trout species: rainbow, sea-run cutthroat, lake cutthroat and steelhead. The hatchery provides inventory for 150 lakes and streams in the Lower Mainland, Vancouver Island and the Southern Interior.

The Vancouver Island Trout Hatchery in Duncan rears the same trout genus as the Fraser Valley Hatchery: Tzenzaicut and Blackwater rainbow, Taylor River cutthroat, sea-run cutthroat and steelhead. Lakes and streams on Vancouver Island, the Gulf Islands and Queen Charlotte Islands receive the benefit of this hatchery.

The Kootenay Trout Hatchery near Cranbrook maintains several programs: the province's eastern brook trout plan, the Gerrard rainbow strain, kokanee, Premier Lake rainbow and the west-slope cutthroat inventory. This hatchery has expanded to include involvement in the white sturgeon recovery initiative for the Kootenay and Columbia rivers by building facilities to foster the spawning and rearing stages of this prehistoric species of river giant.

Rainbow Trout

Anyone who has caught one knows why the rainbow is the most sought-after trout species with a fly rod—they can leap higher than a boat, peel fifty metres of fly line and backing in several seconds and, when hooked, will fight to complete exhaustion. What more could one ask from a one-kilogram fish?

Experts believe that our rainbow and steelhead trout originated through the McCloud River progeny of California, arriving in British Columbia after the last glacial period twelve thousand years ago. The theory is that California trout migrated into BC through three systems to colonize lakes and streams left behind by receding glaciers: the Columbia River in the south and two sanctuaries in the north near the Queen Charlotte Islands that provided genus for Coastal and Central Interior regions. They adapted to their habitat through specialization, learned to survive and reproduce with the resources they were given and formed the nucleus of the fabulous trout fishery we have today. Kamloops, Pennask, Tzenzaicut, Gerrard, Blackwater and steelhead trout all came from the same California river.

Rainbow identification is differentiated from other trout species by several indicators: lack of red spots (brook trout), a pink lateral line (wild trout especially), a small mouth that does not extend past the eye and lack of teeth in the throat at the back of the tongue. Stream trout are heavily spotted above and below the lateral line, accentuated with dark-coloured backs for camouflage and prominent red or pink side stripes. Lake-dwelling trout are more silver, and their

A soon-to-be-released Blackwater-strain Rainbow from Dragon Lake in the North Cariboo. *Photo Kevin Crawford.*

spots contained mostly above the lateral line. Rainbow will leap and run violently when hooked; their cousins are more prone to run deep and fight with their heads down.

A trophy rainbow trout exceeds 50 cm in length and weighs about 3 kg. The average size, however, is 30 cm and typical weight is about 0.5 kg. Rainbow trout in some waters live ten to twelve years, their growth rate dependent upon abundance of available aquatic insect life, the number of ice-free feeding months per year and the amount of competition for food from fish of all species. In our Northern Interior climate, biologists claim that their life expectancy is five to seven years.

Spawning takes place in early spring during the third year. To reproduce successfully, rainbow require inlet or outlet streams that do not dry up or overheat in summer months and are rich enough in nutrients to support juvenile trout during their first several years of life.

Hatchery rainbows planted in lake systems that do not have natal streams instinctively go through the maturation process in spite of their inability to fertilize successfully. Colouration changes from silver to dark red, females become egg-bound and males' jaws become kipped. Females have a difficult time recovering from the process if they cannot dump their eggs onto a gravel bed. Much energy is expended to no avail during the reproduction process and it takes many months for them to recover from natural spawning urges, which they cannot

Danie Erasmus on Dragon Lake, where Rainbows like this one can be more then 60 cm in length. *Photo Brian Smith.*

control. BC Fisheries has addressed this problem by successfully introducing sterilization techniques into the stocking program. Hatchery-collected eggs are shocked after fertilization (3N designation in fisheries reports and regulations), resulting in sterility of both males and females. When these non-reproducing triploid trout fry are introduced to lakes that do not have natal stream reproduction characteristics, they can better concentrate on growth, being more beneficial to fish-retention programs offered by BC Fisheries.

Rainbow feed primarily on bug life that inhabits water depths of less than 6 m: larvae, pupae, nymphs, scuds, caddis flies, leeches and terrestrials. Eighty percent of their feeding activity takes place well below the surface; it is the remaining 20 percent of insect activity on the surface that fosters memories for the fly fisher. Besides westslope cutthroat (in my opinion), no trout rises more readily to the dry fly than the rainbow when conditions are right. Mayfly, caddis, chironomid, midge, backswimmer—of these dry fly opportunities, nothing brings the rainbow to the surface better than the annual caddis hatch occurring on the Plateau during June and July.

They will annually gorge on snails during periods of summer doldrums and low emergence activity, which makes for very tough fishing during these periods. Small non-salmonid (coarse) fish are targeted after the trout reach maturity during their third year.

Trout are no different than humans when it comes to food; they graze and forage, enjoy a variety of table fare and are opportunistic eaters. They get bored with repetitive hatches of chironomid, chironomid and more chironomid. Often, it is the emergence of a solitary "new" insect that triggers a change of feeding habit. The fish know what hatch is coming next, so it is important for a fisher to analyze the time of year, know about upcoming hatch expectations and to anticipate and recognize new emerging insects. The "new" hatch is the one the trout are looking for, and the one you will want to be fishing on most occasions.

To be successful in pursuit of trout, it is helpful to be familiar with the characteristics of the strain that you are targeting. Feeding habits, habitat preference and background knowledge of the prey are advantages that cannot be overlooked when fly fishing the lakes of our Interior Plateau. For this reason, BC Fisheries programs attempt to match various strains of rainbow trout to the lake type and structure preference of the fish.

Pennask Lake trout are characterized by light spotting on the body, with heavier markings toward dorsal and caudal fins. They prefer small high-country lakes, forage for food in deep open water rather than shoals and enjoy feeding during evening and low light conditions. Pennask trout don't compete well with other fish—they are best stocked into barren lakes, or those devoid of competing non-salmonid species. This strain is the basis for the BC Southern Interior stocking program.

Blackwater River trout prefer lakes that have extensive shallows and shoal areas for feeding, reminiscent of their river heritage. They are heavier spotted from head to tail than other rainbow strains, with their markings mostly concentrated above the lateral line. These fish enjoy feeding during the day, and dine on large insect specimens such as leech, dragon and damsel nymphs and coarse fish. BC Fisheries uses the Blackwater strain to stock lakes that have indigenous or illegally introduced coarse fish species present because they are genetically adapted to prey on these competitors. Because Blackwater rainbows exhibit migratory habits, Interior Plateau lakes that lack outlet streams are targeted to receive the strain. Blackwater trout are strong fighters, heavy through the girth and pack more weight per length than other rainbow species.

The Tzenzaicut Lake strain is similar to the Pennask strain, preferring cold high-country lakes, foraging in open water and most active at dusk. They are characterized by large spotting toward the posterior above the lateral line. Tzenzaicut trout will prey on non-salmonid species, a benefit to sport fishing when stocked in competitive coarse fish environments and, like their Pennask Lake cousins, Tzenzaicut rainbows possess great leaping ability and are known to be scrappy fighters.

Gerrard rainbow, originating in Kootenay Lake and Lardeau River, are popular for use in the Kootenay stocking program. They are piscivorous (fish-eaters) by nature, requiring cold, deep lake systems for survival. Native kokanee salmon are their main source of food. These are big trout, averaging a mean weight of 9 kg at maturity, and are used for stocking programs in some Cariboo–Central Interior lakes or streams.

Fraser Valley rainbow trout, originating from the McCleary strain and Trout Lodge Hatchery in Washington, USA, are important to the stocking programs of Vancouver Island, Kootenays, Fraser Valley and some Southern Interior lakes. These trout exhibit fast growth rates, and are well suited to high put-and-take urban lakes as the basis for their programs.

Bull Trout/Dolly Varden

Genetically, biologists conclude that bull trout and Dolly Varden are the same species—Dollies are bull trout after they reach 30 cm in length. They inhabit the coldest, most remote wilderness streams and lakes and do not reach sexual maturity until age four to seven, therefore they are easily threatened by over-harvesting and encroachment by man through logging and habitat destruction.

Native to fresh and salt waters of North America and eastern Asia, this char originally occupied ranges through all of the Pacific Northwest, but is now listed as an endangered species in the US. Because their primary food source is young fry of all species, there was once a bounty on bull trout and they were hunted to extinction during the 1900s in some US states.

Bull trout and Dolly Varden are identified by their oval-shaped bodies, whitish-pink spotting above and below the lateral line and white edges on the lower fins. As they reach maturity, the head flattens and the upper jaw curves downward.

Bull trout can live for ten to twelve years. At full maturity, they attain lengths of 60–70 cm in stream environments and weights of 10 kg in mountain lakes. They are connected to watersheds that have healthy salmon runs and are known to migrate up to 300 km from their native stream to partake in the protein meals of eggs and carcasses that result from the yearly run of Pacific salmon.

They prefer to live in waters that do not get warmer than 15°C. Spawning occurs in late fall when water temperature drops below 9°C, and fertilized eggs require an incubation period of four to five months, twice the length of time as rainbow. This characteristic leaves the char vulnerable to habitat destruction in our regions as most of our logging operations occur during winter months when eggs are incubating. They are not populous in their frigid native stream. A healthy river system a hundred kilometres long may only have nutrients to allow the survival of two to three hundred bull trout; of that number, only fifty mature fish are available for reproduction.

Julian Franz at Tacheeda Lake with a fly-caught lake trout. *Photo Erich Franz.*

Many of the mountain streams that I fish contain bull trout. I never target them but they sometimes scare the hell out of me when playing a small trout, as they come charging across the pool to intercept the struggling fish. I know fly fishers who target them using large mouse, muddler or minnow patterns tied on long shank hooks size 2–4. They are strong fish of a violent nature, difficult to handle when tackled by surprise with light fly rods.

Bull trout are a protected species in most regions of the province. Check local regulations, which change from region to region, before fishing streams and lakes that contain this genus of char.

Arctic Grayling

"Beautiful fish caught in beautiful places." That short statement by my friend Erich Franz summarizes the reason why people seek Arctic grayling. Native to streams primarily of the Arctic watershed, grayling used to inhabit territory as far south as Montana and Michigan but they have disappeared from those watersheds because of habitat loss and competition from other introduced species. Grayling now reside in country few people choose to populate: frigid, desolate land that can be frozen up to six months of the year. Their prime environment is the clear, cold waters of mountain streams and lakes that flow to the Arctic Ocean, beginning at the Summit Lake divide 43 km north of Prince George.

Cousins to salmonid species, grayling are easily identified by one distinctive

Stunning colours and graceful beauty—an Arctic grayling from the Missinka River north of Prince George. *Photo Danie Erasmus.*

feature—a long dorsal fin of more than seventeen rays. Grayling are beautifully coloured: backs range from blue-black to blue-grey, sides of pinkish-coloured iridescence and diamond-shaped spots. They are small: average length of 30–35 cm, weight of 0.5–1 kg. The world record weight for grayling is about 2.5 kg. They live from ten to twelve years, similar to bull and rainbow trout. I believe the longevity of these species is due to their cold-water habitat; nature has provided them a long life because their growing cycle is short, their winter dormancy period long.

A migratory species, grayling may travel up to 200 km to reach tributary spawning grounds of major river systems. They begin their generation cycle at spring breakup, heading for the creeks and streams of their birth. Eggs hatch three weeks after fertilization; fry remain in the small feeder creeks for the summer, migrating in the fall to overwinter in the major river system.

Grayling are outstanding dry fly adversaries, rising freely to midge, caddis and mayfly just like their rainbow cousins. If they have a fault, it's that they are too easy to catch, making them prone to overharvesting. Like rainbow, grayling leap and run when hooked, making them a quality sporting fish for the fly fisher.

Brook Trout

Brook trout, another member of the char species, is native to eastern Canada and North America, but not to BC. The inventory of brook trout for BC hatchery programs is cultivated by the Kootenay Trout Hatchery.

Brook trout have several features distinguishing them from other trout species: red spotting with blue halos, wormlike markings on the dorsal fin and pinkish belly fins edged in white. They live an average of only five years, having a common length of 20–30 cm and maximum length of 50 cm.

Known to take on a deep-bellied football shape as they mature, brookies are not surface feeders, preferring weedy habitat in the bottom zones of lakes and streams. With their pale pink and mild-tasting flesh, brook trout are favourite table fare for the ice-fishing crowd, a treat for the skillet when caught.

Brook trout are stocked in several hike-in lakes in Eskers Park near Prince George, and are commonly found mixed with rainbow inventory in some Interior Plateau lakes. This practice of mixing stock is under review, however, as brook trout are carnivorous to all fry species including their own, and can decimate a rainbow stocking program when introduced in the same water.

The brook trout's ability to spawn in a lake or stream environment makes it a difficult fish to eradicate once started in a system. They spawn in autumn, eggs hatching six to twelve weeks after fertilization.

As fish for the fly rod, brook trout are not highly sought after. Their fight quality is a head-down and dog-it-out scenario, but I enjoy catching them for their fine eating and never hesitate to bring them home for dinner.

West-Slope Cutthroat Trout

Cutthroat trout, both sea-run and inland varieties, are a native species to the west coast of North America. The cutthroat of Yellowstone Park, the east and west slopes of the Rocky Mountains and the coastal anadromous strains have adapted to the environment and habitat they were given when glaciers receded to form the natural boundaries and perimeters in which they had to survive. Some adapted to ocean life, returning to coastal river systems to spawn; others modified their genetics to live inland in lakes or streams.

The cutthroat is a truly beautiful fish; the inland species is characterized by distinct markings of an orange or yellow-orange slash on the underside of each side of the jaw and a yellowish-green body with hints of pink and red on the body and belly. They are heavily spotted, more distinct on the posterior portion. The mouth extends well past the eye of the trout; teeth are present on both upper and lower jaws as well as in the back of the throat.

An aggressive fish, the cutthroat takes dry flies with reckless abandon. We don't have this species on the Interior Plateau, but I have a fondness for them that I have to write about. The coastal cutthroat was the sport fish passion of my youth. Growing up on the coast over sixty years ago, I can still recall the first cutty I ever saw caught—a fine two-pounder taken on a dew worm in the Nikomekl River—bright silver, olive back, spots from head to tail. I was nine-years-old and the memory still sticks with me even though I didn't catch it. The cutthroat became my pursuit for many years, the fly rod my weapon, until I was introduced to the rainbow trout in the early seventies, and the rest is history.

They are wonderful sporting fish, and have recently found another place in my heart—they bring my boys and me together in the Rockies for a week each fall to fish the east-slope streams of the Forestry Trunk Road and the Kootenays.

Lake Trout

The lake trout is a native species to North America, found mainly in the deepest and largest lake systems of northern Canada. I have never caught one because I don't fish the lakes they inhabit. Shame on me for having to make that statement—the lakes are usually too big for my float tube and pontoon boat.

They can be found in many different colourations depending upon the environment and depth they occupy—backs of pale grey, dark or light green, brown and black, accentuated with contrasting light spotting and wormlike markings on their back and dorsal fin.

Lake trout are long-lived, attaining colossal weights of up to 50 kg in larger lake systems. They spawn in late autumn in their home lake, the female laying only up to a thousand eggs, a minimal amount for fish of this size. The eggs have a long incubation period of sixteen to twenty weeks, fry emerging near ice-out time to meet the oncoming spring.

Lake trout are middle- and bottom-depth feeders, targeted by trolling at depths of 15–50 m with weighted rigs and heavy line. Because lake trout are predaceous, they can also be caught near the surface with flies—trolled minnow, leeches and frog patterns have some success.

There are numerous large lake systems within a two-hour drive of Prince George that hold wild lake trout populations, including Cluculz, Stuart, Nation, Ootsa, Natalkuz and Bowron lakes. There are special restrictions on their retention, well-deserved for a native fish that can live for forty plus years and survive the onslaught of fishing pressure in a fragile environment.

Kevin Smith works a glide on the Blackwater River during spring high-water season. *Photo Brian Smith.*

Kokanee

Kokanee is a freshwater species of sockeye salmon that is not anadromous, meaning it does not migrate to ocean life as does the sea-going sockeye. Genetically they are the same fish; their migration habits are another unexplained marvel of the wonderful world of nature. Kokanee occur naturally in lake systems throughout the northern hemisphere, especially Russia, Japan, Yukon Territory, Alaska and British Columbia.

Differentiated from other salmonid species by its brilliant silver body, the kokanee has a forked tail, lack of black spotting and the presence of teeth on its upper and lower jaws. A sockeye's red flesh is prized for its flavour and appearance, a favourite target for the fisher who enjoys fish from the smoker.

Living an average of four years, kokanee mature at the small size of 25 cm. Spawning occurs in late fall in gravel beds of the home lake, or in small creek systems entering the lake. Male and female both turn a brilliant red, the female producing an average of five hundred eggs for fertilization. Several days after spawning, both genders die, typical of all salmon species. When the young alevin emerge from spawning gravel in early spring, they become a favourite target of native rainbow trout, which abandon all sense of security to chase down and gorge on the helpless fry. This is especially true in shallow rivers and creek systems tributary to the home lake. As alevin migrate into the lake system, big trout are lined up at the creek mouths to gather the protein of salmon progeny.

Kokanee feed in the upper zone of their lake, only a few feet below the surface. They are genetically programmed to feed on plankton—microscopic floating organisms—and can be caught by trolling methods using brightly coloured flies or lures of silver and red. They are decent fighters, but they don't get to a respectable size for the power category—usually 25–30 cm in length and an average weight of 0.5 kg. But kokanee do make up for their size in taste—in the fry pan or on the barbeque.

Lake Whitefish

This coarse fish is found everywhere in Canada that natural fish species can reproduce, to the point of being considered a pest to seasoned fly fishers. We were happy to catch them in our youth—not so happy to hook them as our level of experience increases.

Lake whitefish are large-scaled and silver-coloured, with a dark back, forked tail and no teeth. They are bottom-feeders, aggressively competing with trout for food. This situation is not healthy for trout when the balance of fish population and insect life in a lake is not sustainable.

This species can get to a size over 5 kg, but averages 1 kg in weight and 40 cm in length. Because they bottom feed, fly fishers will catch them by trolling a deep sinking line and nymph patterns. This fish, however, is not a target for sport fishermen.

Mountain Whitefish

Also called Rocky Mountain whitefish, this widespread species is native to lakes and streams of western North America. British Columbia boasts a natural abundance of mountain whitefish throughout its major coastal river systems: Fraser, Skeena, Bella Coola and Columbia.

The mountain whitefish has common similarities to the whitefish that reside in lake habitats: large-scaled, silver colouration, forked tail, lack of teeth and round mouth. The major difference is size—the mountain whitefish averages 20–30 cm in length and 0.5 kg in weight. They are long-lived, up to twenty years, and spawn in late fall.

Mountain whitefish are competitive with trout species for food sources, mainly bottom feeding on nymphs, larvae and leeches. In the Blackwater River system, they are as plentiful as trout, and I find the best way to target trout is to fish a dry fly or an emerger just under the surface, keeping my patterns off the bottom where the Rockies lie in waiting. There are days, however, when trout don't rise; I'm happy to drag the bottom to get into a mess of whitefish—which will bite anything—and stubborn, fickle trout.

Northern Pike Minnow

Every freshwater system has its scavengers and least welcome fish species. The northern pike minnow takes the prize in Central BC because it is found everywhere, hanging in the slow current and backwater eddies of streams, reminding one of catching an old boot or log when hooked.

The pike minnow reaches an average length of 30–40 cm and weighs 0.5–2 kg. They are identified by several characteristics: deeply forked tail, back lacking an adipose fin and a large, wide toothless mouth that extends past the eye.

Thank the fish god they are mostly bottom-feeders; if they were all I had to fish for, my life would be a sorry affair.

Times, Tackle, Safety

Memories of outings last fishing season—a rainbow trout rising freely to your dry fly, or the wrist-jarring pull of a heavy rainbow as it seizes your deep offering of a nymph pattern—these are reminiscences that fly fishers recall during long winter seasons in the Interior.

Fly fishers are dreamers. We fantasize about home waters we love, or continually seek to discover new rivers and lakes to find out if we can love them.

Photo Brian Smith.

During open-water season, we find a myriad of excuses to get onto the water, even more to get out of work around the house. When winter storms grip the off-season, we retreat to the fly tying bench, scheming to reinvent and tweak patterns we fished with perfect satisfaction last season. The fly rod collection we thought was perfect for every situation beckons to be augmented with something new, or perhaps our plans for next year include learning to spey cast, a traditional European method well-suited to fly fishing for steelhead and salmon on western rivers.

Some British Columbians are fortunate to have access

to fly fishing year-round. In the Central Interior, we don't. Our friends on the North Coast enjoy brief respites from winter when warm southwest winds blow in for a few days, and they can target cutthroat, Dolly Varden and steelhead. We get opportunities to see open water on the Plateau during winter, but during quick thaws there is always ice flowing in the rivers and covering the banks, making wading dangerous and difficult. And yes, there are ice-fishing flies available, but one can hardly imagine drilling a 6-inch hole in a frozen lake and dangling a hand-tied fly in it. Oddly enough, it happens; shrimp are a staple item for winter trout, and a scud pattern works well through the ice.

Effect of Light on Stillwater Success

Light—bright or dull—affects fish attitude much the same way it influences us, whether good or bad. We like the radiance and glory of a sunny day; fish don't. A bright sunny day will send them packing from shoals into the depths, searching for a zone with lower light conditions. Or, when they do search the shoals on a bright day, large trout will zip in for a quick look and a bite and then retreat quickly into the drop-off zone. A knowledgeable fly fisher will learn to adjust tackle and thinking to comply with ever-changing light penetration into the water. As the sun progresses to overhead at noon, follow the fish to six-metre depths to improve your chances. During late afternoon and evening as the sun's rays weaken, observe fish appearing on shoals again, and track them back to shallow water! Many insects such as mayflies hatch sporadically on sunny days, holding off major activity until a warm cloudy system moves in. Caddis hatches reach their peak during evenings. They are also lovers of low light conditions.

Early spring fishing typically presents low light situations: the ice has just come off the lake, water temperature hovers around 5°C and the sun is low in the sky. Fishing is rated fair to good for up to a week after ice-out, depending on wind velocity, temperature and the beginning of spring turnover. Trout are concentrated in the upper high-oxygen layer of the deepest part of the lake, on shallow shoals and in schools, and once a preferred trout-holding area is located the fishing can be very hot for a while.

Spring turnover, the mixing of oxygen-starved water with more dense oxygen-rich surface water, will soon occur. If the ice comes off the lake in a good windstorm, this turnover can happen immediately, which is recognized by murky water and dead, decaying bottom vegetation floating on the surface; the result is poor fishing for at least a week to ten days while oxygen levels stabilize and water clarity returns. For success during turnover, concentrate on fishing the edges of the lake and, if you know the location of underground springs or creeks entering the lake, work these places over; oxygen-starved trout will be lying in schools near the source of clean, rich water.

As spring advances into early summer, increased light from the sun warms the lake, which stimulates bottom plants to begin the process of photosynthesis, converting light energy into carbohydrates, thus invigorating floral growth and releasing new oxygen. As the sun climbs progressively higher in the sky, light penetrates deeply into the lake, causing trout to seek deep, cooler water and lower light. Trout are most active on shoals during early morning, evening, and when significant hatch activity takes place. There is nothing like a damsel or dragonfly migration, caddis hatch, or heavy mayfly spinner fall to arouse trout to venture onto exposed shoals for a quick meal.

When hatches are in progress and feeding activity on the surface is limited, pupa, nymph and emerger patterns are the order of the day. Trout often take

Staffan Lindgren casts into the peace and tranquilty of Hart Lake.
Photo Dezene Huber.

an offering at bottom or mid-depth of the lake while the fly fisher imitates the ascent of a rising insect. The largest trout are most often found in the bottom zone, concentrating on the millions of insects in larva and pupa stages scuttling about in droves, staging for their migration to the surface. This restless pre-hatch insect activity is often overlooked, because insects emerging on the surface have captivated the fly fisher's thoughts and actions. Pre-emergence activity can last for days, the insect making many false starts before it begins to migrate to the surface. In the midst of a heavy hatch there are many times more insects on the bottom in the staging cycle than those emerging on the surface. This is the time for a slow-sinking wet fly line, or the floating line and long 6-m leader, and the patience to let your fly sink for several minutes before beginning the retrieval.

During spring insect migration periods, train yourself to anchor well onto the inside edge of a shoal. Cast your full range of fly line off the edge into the drop-off zone. Let the line sink several minutes, and then retrieve the pattern using a slow hand-twist crawl from deep water to shallow shoal—you will often be surprised at the result. In spring, insects migrate to the shoal *from* deep water rather than shoal *to* deep water, which is a small detail but important when imitating the natural progression of insect movement. If this action fails to produce results, raise anchor and move further toward the drop-off zone, resuming the same procedure.

Of course, fish may be up on the shoal awaiting migrating insects as well. This is prime time for a dry line with strike indicator set at a constant depth, which keeps the imitation in the same target zone at all times. Or, if you are like me and prefer to not use an indicator, fish with a dry line and leader that is 25 percent longer than the depth of water you are fishing.

Fall presents the same fishing conditions as spring, but in reverse order: waning light angles, cooling water, plant life entering a dormant state of growth. Trout activity on shoals increases in the fading light as fish seek food to store reserves of fat for survival during oncoming winter months. Late summer and early fall is prime time for water boatman and backswimmer surface activity— trout are always in superb condition in fall season, and aggressively greet the flight of this insect with reckless abandon. Alas, their nuptial flights last only about a week, but are savoured in a fisher's memory for years. Leech, scud, bloodworm and midge dominate feeding action for the trout, with most fish being taken in less than 4 m of water.

During the fall period, insect migration is the opposite of spring—they travel from shoals into deep water. Fall is the time to anchor in deep water, cast to shore, and bring the imitation across or from the shoal into the drop-off zone. This is also a time for small imitations—a size 10 scud that resembles a mature insect in the spring should now be changed to a size 14 or 16 hook, which better represent the young of the year. A good rule of fly fishing is to drop two sizes of pattern for late-season fishing. But, beware of too many rules! I have done really well using Jack Shaw's "red apple" theory at any time of year, but especially in the fall. Offer trout the largest leech in your bag, and they will most often take it.

Fall turnover occurs in all shallow lakes, but usually not to the extent of spring turn. In our North country, fall turn usually takes place in the first few weeks of September, preceded by a late-August warm spell. For me, it is always disheartening to run into fall turnover on my favourite lakes—winter is coming fast, and I hate to waste even one opportunity for a fishing day in the fall.

Wind action is another factor that can have a dramatic effect on light. Strong winds create movement and turbulence on the lake's surface, affecting the penetration of light rays. I am not a huge fan of fishing during heavy wind. If I can't keep my craft anchored, I find it is not worthwhile trying my luck with the fish. Often during a strong wind, a fisher can find points of land that will harbour pockets of flat water on the lee side. Try these spots—if a hatch is in progress, the edge of the wind line can be a great spot for picking up the odd fish.

Barometric Pressure and Weather

The most important definable measure of fishing success, or the lack thereof, that I have encountered in my forty years of fly fishing is rising or falling barometric pressure. I'm not saying that a good day is not possible when the barometer is falling but in my experience, the best fishing days are enjoyed when the barometer is rising, when skies are clearing after a barometer fall, or during spells of consistent high-pressure weather patterns. To paraphrase my friend Brian Chan: "To have a successful day on the water, you must find *happy* fish." Whether it's lake or stream, moving and rising fish are happy fish—they are searching for food and are blissful about it.

Fish will often feed furiously the few hours before a barometric change, and for short bursts during the peak of a change. The reason for this is the quick release of pressure after a barometric fall. When the storm finally hits and spills its wrath, there is a sudden rise in pressure and fish react with an eager feeding spree. An example of this occurred when I was fishing Dragon Lake two days after ice-out and during spring turnover. I picked up three nice trout during a ten-minute hailstorm, but the fishing was unproductive in the preceding hour as I watched the storm approach, and for several hours afterward.

During northern summer seasons, the barometer can rise and fall several times during the course of a day's fishing. On a hot day, pressure often builds into a storm by late afternoon, preceded by lightning and thunder. A warm soft rain aids fishing success on most occasions; lightning and thunder are good reasons to head for the safety of shore.

The prevalent weather patterns on the Interior Plateau come from a south-westerly direction off the Pacific Ocean. This means wet or dry weather, depending on the ocean climate systems. Most really wet schemes wring themselves out on the long ride to the Plateau before they hit our fishing country, but when cold weather patterns decide to roar in from the Yukon or Peace River country, your best bet is to stay in camp and wait it out. The falling barometer will surely be uncooperative for fishing luck. We rarely receive a weather system from the east, but if it happens it is always a poor weather sign because the Rockies are within a hundred kilometres of the Plateau. A weather system coming from due south will often precede a fair weather spell, stimulated by systems coming from the dry Okanagan and Thompson desert areas.

Temperatures in Central BC during July and August average a daytime high of 21°C and a low of 8°C. May and June can be unpredictable, with tempera-tures averaging a high of 18°C and a low of 5°C. Rainfall during summer is moderate, averaging 52 mm in May and 62 mm during the months of June, July and August. Our sunshine hours are high during summer, averaging 270 per month from May through August. For a month in late June and early July, during summer solstice, you can fish in decent light until after 10:00 p.m.; this is the prime damsel and caddis hatching period—lucky us!

Interior Plateau lakes, because of their low elevation, are ice-free and have completed spring turnover by mid-May. They fish best during May to July, but weather can be unpredictable. Prepare to withstand a climate that can offer a 20°C variance during the course of 24 hours—from freezing at night to short-sleeved suntanning conditions at noon. So, take warm clothes and blankets but don't forget the shorts!

As a general rule, creeks and rivers in Region 7 Zone A are closed to fishing from April 1 to June 30. A few of our best open early—the Stellako on June 1 and the Blackwater on June 15; both are Classified Water fisheries, requiring a special CW licence. The Crooked, Willow, Bowron and Nechako rivers are exempt from spring closure, open to fishing year-round with no CW licence requirement, but a bait ban and single barbless hook regulations are in effect all year. Our rivers and tributaries fish best from July to September; many fish migrate from river to lake systems for overwintering and then back to the river for summer feeding after runoff in spring.

Lunar Thoughts

A full moon is a wonderful experience to behold while camping, but seldom the best time of month to plan a fishing trip to Interior lakes. Solunar tables and fishing calendars indicate that the best time of month for fishing is several days before, during and after dark of the moon. Moon phases affect insect hatches to a great degree, with the heaviest emergence activity occurring during the last quarter of the moon.

In spite of doom and gloom predictions found in lunar tables, I still think the best time to go fishing is whenever you can. I have never been sorry for going fishing, but admit I often look up the Solunar forecast *after* a fishing trip, just to check the tables and confirm the times I found fish were on the feed. They are amazingly accurate predictions, so much so that I do believe in them, but not enough that a poor forecast will stop me from going fishing.

Creeks and Rivers

In my experience, rivers and creeks are not affected as strongly as still water by barometric or weather conditions. They are certainly affected by changing light conditions, the quarry always preferring structure—the shade of a bank, or shadow of a rock or log—to open water. Warm, cloudy days are preferred weather conditions for mayfly hatches, whether in lake or river.

In river systems, fish are opportunists; the largest fish take the best feeding lies. It is always best to approach a likely hole or run with one thought in mind: "Where would I lie if I were a big fish?" The best answer is to look for structure—the deepest part of the run, side current or back eddy, ledge, the slack water behind a rock—any place that restricts or alters water flow and allows food items to drift naturally to a resting spot. Work your way to that spot a few feet at a time with your casts; if unsuccessful, only then work the rest of the run. When you're river fishing, take your best shot for the lunkers first.

Lakes are cleansed and renewed by spring turnover; creeks and rivers by spring runoff. Beginning with snowmelt and ice-out during April and May, river flows peak during June, settling into prime condition from July through October. Salmon carcasses, winter wildlife casualties and decayed plant life are flushed out of the system during runoff; corners and gravel beds are rearranged; new pockets and runs are formed. Aquatic organisms and fish adjust to a new season, often much different than the last. This is the way of moving water; it is constantly eroding and rehabilitating its structure, changing from one year to the next.

I am beginning to understand what Roderick Haig-Brown meant in 1946 when he wrote *A River Never Sleeps*. On page 352, he states quite simply: "A river is never quite silent; it can never, of its very nature, be quite still; it is never quite the same from one day to the next. It has its own life and its own beauty, and the creatures it nourishes are alive and beautiful also. Perhaps fishing is, for me, only an excuse to be near rivers. If so, I'm glad I thought of it."

Like Haig-Brown, I also love rivers, above all other fishing places. The constant motion and seemingly unruly behaviour of a river has a way of straightening my mind, sharpening my mental reflexes and settling my attitude. Rivers are relentlessly challenging, whether you are contemplating the next step or how best to ford across stream to get the best poke at the next run. Each seam, every rock and all obstacles test your skills. Where are they? What will they take? Which fly—how best to present it?

There is also something precious about catching wild fish, regardless of size, that a hatchery trout cannot reproduce. Wild fish are exceptionally strong and beautiful, each strain endowed with its own markings, characteristics and habits engrained through generations of survival against odds that are totally out of their control. These indigenous species are prized—I hope we will always be graced with their presence.

Fly Rods, Reels, Lines and Leaders

Fly Rods

What is the perfect fly rod for all occasions? Each style and action—slow, moderate, moderate-fast and fast—have their own merits depending on the water being fished. Fishing in the North varies from big, fast rivers to small streams and creeks, from small pothole lakes to medium and huge lakes. Wind is not a big factor on small lakes and rivers, but it is a considerable issue when fishing large water. A fly fisher requires a minimum of two fly rods to get the most out of the sport; most of us can't stop there, needing four or five to get by.

Still-water fishing challenges include the need for distance casts, a long rod for playing a fish from a boat or float tube and the power to buck wind if required. If I had to choose one rod for lake fishing, my preference is a 9-foot 5-weight with a moderate-fast action. I fish a 10-foot 5-weight rod on occasion, handy when working water that has exceptionally large fish or if I expect to be fishing in heavy wind, but casting the extra length of a 10-foot all day can be tiring, so I prefer to work with the 9-foot rod for 90 percent of my lake fishing. I fished a 9-foot 4-weight in still water for many years, and love the rod immensely, but because I release many fish, a 5-weight plays them out quicker, resulting in less stress to the trout.

For stream fishing, rod choices depend on the size of the river and its fish. Large and mid-sized streams like the Stellako, holding an abundance of 50-cm or larger trout with oversized shoulders, beg for a 9-foot 4-weight or 5-weight rod. Smaller rivers and creeks, like the McLeod, Blackwater and Nazko demand a shorter rod—a 7-foot 6-weight or 8-foot 3-weight rod will fit the bill nicely. Rivers and creeks are demanding, requiring both short and long casts, constant mending of fly line and pinpoint accuracy to rising trout. When fishing rivers, it isn't necessary to use a strong rod because the river takes a lot of power away from the fish, making it necessary to manage trout through currents and obstructions rather than bully them into shore. A light-action rod offers softness on the strike, resulting in more positive hook-ups, less breakage on the take and runs of a strong fish, and allows the use of very fine 6-X or 7-X tippet demanded by finicky trout in ultra clear water.

Many fly fishers prefer fast-action rods; they load quickly, are very responsive, generate tight loops and cast a long line in all conditions. I have built many fast-action rods for friends and my sons over the years, but still prefer the moderate action of IM 6 graphite material for my style of fishing. I sacrifice extra distance and power, but enjoy the soft strike response and the big rod bend when playing fish that only a moderate or slow-action fly rod can offer.

Butt action—stiff, soft or moderate—determines the action of a fly rod. Other variables like "feel" and "power" are subjective. A stiff-butted or fast-action rod allows the tip section to load and deliver the fly line, whereas a moderate or soft-butted rod will flex right to the grip, allowing a progressive transition of power. To determine the action of a fly rod, first join all sections together, then hold the rod against a floor or ceiling and put a bend into it—action will be revealed by the amount of bend from tip to grip.

A fly rod, if you wish it to become your close friend, should reflect the personality of the user. Type A individuals tend to prefer a fast rod, one that responds to the way they like to fish—hastily, covering a lot of water. On the other hand, a more laid-back individual might prefer the slower pace of a softer rod, needing to feel the rhythm and finesse of the instrument more than the power of a long cast. Cane rods, which I have used but never owned, are the ultimate in softness and tempo. Then again, I have many friends whom I consider to be easy-going individuals who prefer to use fast-action rods—it's all a matter of preference, and what makes you confident in your pursuit of trout.

Fly Reels

Expensive fly reels are pretty to look at, but a fly fisher working within a budget is better off putting money into top-quality fly lines than breaking the bank on a costly reel. For most encounters with lake and river fish on the fly, a moderately priced reel will suffice. I spent as a general rule three hundred dollars on two fly reels of the same model with three extra spools over twenty years ago, and still use them for fifty or more fishing days per year. They have never required repair—only a minimum of yearly maintenance—and I see no reason why they won't last another twenty years. However, this statement on pricing policy goes out the window when purchasing fly reels for steelhead, salmon and large prey over five kilograms. This is demanding sport and only the best equipment will survive the power and abuse that these fish can muster.

The primary purpose of a fly reel is to store fly line. The reel, to be functional, must have smooth action, a minimum of moving parts, and a precise fit from spool to frame. Nothing is more frustrating than hooking the best fish of your day, only to have the reel jam, tangle the fly line and make a fool of you. Most of us started fly fishing with cheap equipment, or hand-me-downs from a fishing father like me. You know the game—I purchase new gear; the kids get the partly worn-out stuff.

In today's money, I consider two hundred dollars for a fly reel a fair and reasonable price—one that should come with a lifetime warranty and function well for at least twenty years. A top-quality reel, however, can set you back as much as five hundred dollars or more. Spare spools for the reel are a must—you need at least five extra spools holding different sink rates of fly lines to accommodate the variety of conditions encountered in a season on the water. In my opinion, if cost is a consideration, your money is better spent on extra spools and high-quality lines than expensive reels.

Fly Lines

A top-quality set of fly lines at eighty dollars each is well worth the investment, and can offer a fly fisher many seasons of enjoyment and performance; some of the lines I use today have served me well for twenty years. To fish effectively in still water, you need at least five different weight-forward lines: floating, #1 slow full-sink, #2 sink-tip, #2 medium full-sink and #3 fast full-sink. The list of available lines continues to a #6 full-sink, and there are many variations and lengths of sinking tips to choose from as well. Each of these lines is offered in a series of line weights designed to match the weight of the rod; for example, a 5-weight fly rod will perform at its best using a 5-weight fly line. Most fast-action graphite fly rods will cast lines that are one weight heavier than the rod; for example, shooting 5-weight lines with a 4-weight rod, or 6-weight lines with a 5-weight rod.

Floating lines are used for dry fly fishing on the surface, and for nymph fishing water depths of less than 6 m. I find the use of two dry lines most effective—one set up with standard nylon leader of 4 m for dry fly fishing, and another set up with a fluorocarbon super-sink leader of 6 m for chironomid, scud or emerging insects coming onto the shoal. Weight-forward tapered dry lines are most effective in still-water fishing, as they are designed to offer the fisher better casting distance than double tapered lines.

Full-sinking lines are effective for fishing lakes with deep drop-offs, or trolling the edge of shoals in water deeper than 5 m. They are designated by numbers 1 through 6, rated by sinking speed in inches per second (US measurements). For example, a #1 slow-sink line is designed to sink at 1 inch per second, a #3 fast-sink at 3 inches per second, and so on.

Slow full-sink #1 line is effective for fishing water depths of 2–5 m, and of the full-sinking lines, they are the easiest to cast because of their lightness. These lines are extremely efficient when allowed to sink several minutes before starting the retrieve; a 30° angle of ascent from the bottom allows the fly fisher to work the pattern longer than other full-sink lines, and mimics an insect in slow migration to the surface. I prefer these lines to all other full-sinking alternatives; the key to using them is having the patience to allow them to get into the zone. Some days, during a high barometric period, it's like watching paint dry to let it sink properly. They are similar to dry lines for effectiveness during an intense hatch; work them slowly and you will be rewarded.

Sink-tip lines are efficient for depths to 6 m, depending on the sink rate chosen. They are designed with a long floating running section, and a multitude of wet-tip assortments from 2–10 m. Tips range from #2 to #6 sink rate. For lake fishing, I like the #2 line, 4 m clear tip, which fishes well in depths up to 5 m. Because their floating belly and running line holds the tip on an angle similar to an intermediate line, sink-tip lines are also effective at imitating emerging insects. I find the only disadvantage with sink-tip lines is the "hinge" effect when casting, especially true with long heavy #3–6 weights.

Full-sink lines in sinking ranges #2–6 will fish water from 6–10 m deep. They are most effective when trolled deeply along a sharp drop-off, or on midsummer days when fish are huddled in the bottom layer of the lake. These lines get to the fish in a hurry, and can save the day when all other methods to raise fish prove fruitless. On a bright, sunny day when insects are not emerging and fish aren't moving or showing, #3–6 full-sink lines worked deeply along a drop-off can often produce results.

Because of the expense of setting up a fly rod properly, the most affordable method is to decide on a rod weight you enjoy using and then spend a few years gathering the necessary lines and spools together. If you wish to have a multitude of weights, a good budget is required to outfit them all. However, by purchasing two reels of the same model plus three extra spools, you can set up two rods with identical reels and interchange all the spools on both rods.

River and stream fishing presents further variations in setups for the fly fisher. To get the most out of the experience, small streams are best fished with short, light rods, most commonly 3- and 4-weights, which are best handled with an ultra-light reel and double-taper floating line.

A double-taper floating line is designed with a tapered tip section of 3 m on each end, fitted with a level belly section through the middle 20 m. They are intended to complete roll casts and short casts efficiently, and to present the dry fly more softly on the water than a weight-forward fly line, which is more proficient at distance casts.

For nymph fishing situations on streams, a 2-m sink-tip has saved the day for me on many occasions, getting the fly down to a good depth better than the dry line. These are the only lines I use on trout streams.

If budget is the biggest consideration, or a novice is just getting started, and the fly fisher has one rod choice, an 8-foot-6 or 9-foot 5-weight outfit will handle rivers, creeks and all manner of small lakes encountered in Central BC.

Leaders

Fly lines deliver the offering, and leaders present it. Often overlooked in importance, leader and tippet choice are critical decisions when related to fishing success. Advancements in material technology have benefited the fly fisher greatly. Higher breaking strengths are being produced with much smaller diameters, which equates to less visibility in the water, enabling the fisher to fool larger fish with finer tippets. Because leader and tippet are the first (on the strike) and last (if it fails) contact with fish, it pays not to compromise. Purchase the best quality material.

Fluorocarbon tapered leader and tippet material is the only substance I use for all sinking-line situations because it has many advantages over nylon as a choice for subsurface fishing: lower visibility, higher knot strength, superior abrasion resistance and a sink rate that is several times faster. Fluorocarbon is twice the price of nylon material, but I feel the advantages easily outweigh cost because of its better performance underwater.

Fluorocarbon is not useful as floating leader or tippet, however, because of its inherent sink rate. Nylon copolymer blend is used as all-purpose material, and is an excellent choice for floating-line fishing situations. This blend has some excellent characteristics: low memory that resists coiling and allows the leader to lie straight on the water, high abrasion resistance and good floating properties when lubricated.

Leader manufacturers have standardized on an -X series of measurement (US) for determining the breaking point on leaders and tippet. The scale begins at 7-X (2.4 lb), ending at 0-X (14.1 lb). If you are from the old school (over 50) like me, you will understand pounds better than the -X scale. For Scientific Angler regular tippet the general scale cross-references as follows: 6-X is 3.1 lb; 5-X is 4.4 lb; 4-X is 6.0 lb; 3-X is 8.1 lb; 2-X is 9.5 lb; 1-X is 12.1 lb. Fluorocarbon tippet is different to scale, as will be other manufacturers.

Many fly fishers build their own leaders. Personally, I don't like the series of knots needed for correct tapers, which allows maximum turnover of the fly. I think the more connections and knots you build into a leader, the more weak points you will surely have. I prefer to purchase 3-m leaders tapered to 3-X or 4-X, and add between 1 m and 2 m of 5-X to 7-X tippet for a total length of 4–5 m.

Map Books and Road Safety

The Interior Plateau is prime country for the logging industry. Operations have escalated recently because of pine beetle infestation throughout the Chilcotin, Cariboo and Central Interior. This fact alone is reason to carry a map book and compass, and to be observant and cognizant of road and fire safety rules while travelling the back roads of all regions. New spurs have been added to many main roads to access and log dead pine trees, and map distributors simply cannot keep up with the required mapping to keep their books current. It is the responsibility of adventure seekers to be aware of where they are going, leaving with loved ones a detailed itinerary of their destination and expected return.

The Angler's Atlas is published in Prince George by Sean Simmons. Sean has developed a series of atlases that include all fishing regions of BC and the east slopes of the Alberta Rockies. They contain bathometric charts of popular lakes, stocking records of each, and directions on how to get there. Free maps are available to download from the website at www.anglersatlas.com.

Mussio Ventures Ltd. of New Westminster publishes an excellent series of map books that cover all regions of BC. The *Backroad Mapbook* volumes cover all aspects of wilderness travel needs in each region: freshwater fishing, wilderness camping, multi-use trail access, paddling routes and winter recreation opportunities. They are well laid out, a must for any adventure seeker and available at fly shops and bookstores in each region of the province. For more information, visit the website at www.backroadmapbooks.com.

Bear Safety

The BC Interior is first-rate bear habitat: low human population density, superior berry-growing climate, and home to major sources of protein for bears including salmon, small rodents and game. There are few times I venture into the bush with a fishing rod that I don't see several black bears; though, gladly, I have had few encounters with grizzly bears in this neck of the woods. Grizzlies are present within 30 km of Prince George, but black bears are regular visitors to city streets on garbage days during their fall feeding frenzies. Each year, many bears are put down by conservation officers in our city, the fault of ignorant homeowners who leave garbage out overnight or do not pick their fruit trees. Rural homes throughout the North are even more susceptible to bear problems, but rural people expect and welcome animal visits, taking more precautions with their property than most city folks.

Safety from wild animals while travelling and camping in bush country comes down to vigilance—recognizing signs such as fresh scat or tree markings, being extra cautious with cooking and cleanup, and having a general respect that we are the visitor to the animals' territory.

A lot of research has gone into bear safety, but there are many common opinions that are false. For example, wearing bear bells to signal your presence. Bear bells are pretty much useless; one is far better to talk loudly, whistle, sing, yell and make lots of noise instead—hallelujah for taking the kids camping. But do put bear bells on small children in bush country, which makes them easier to locate and keep track of. I carry a whistle as part of my tackle vest—handy for bear warnings along hiking trails, and also to signal my fishing buddy if needed.

Be careful: if tenting, don't sleep in clothes you've cooked in; if cleaning fish, don't bury entrails—better to pierce the bladder and dispose of them deep in a lake or river, where the nutrients will add to the water value. Store food properly in sealed containers, not in the tent or sleeping quarters. Garbage should be burned completely, or hung high up in a tree away from the campsite.

If you have a surprise encounter with a grizzly bear, experts recommend that you give ground, back away without direct eye contact and vacate the area. If attacked, you will seldom win; drop to the ground, assume the fetal position, protect your head with your arms, keep your face to the ground and pray.

Black bears are less predictable than grizzlies. If a black bear is stalking or attacking, the aggressive approach is recommended—yell, make lots of noise, enlarge yourself and be prepared to fight back with a weapon, and they will usually back off. If a sow bear is with cubs, do not place yourself between cub and mother, if this happens by accident exit quickly in the opposite direction.

If you spend a lot of time in the bush, knowledge of animals and their traits is important; entire books have been devoted to the subject. For more complete information, I recommend a visit to one expert's website: www.mountainnature.com.

River Classifications

With the advent of modern pontoon boats, the opportunity to fish wilderness water has been immensely enriched. Along with this accessibility, and afford-ability of good equipment, more people are venturing into backcountry, getting into areas that are more pristine, less pressured and largely overlooked by the main fishing populous.

Canadian rivers are classified by risk assessment—the larger the number, the more dangerous the river. Pontoon boats priced at around a thousand dollars are capable of navigating Class 3 waters. Better, more expensive pontoon boats over that dollar figure, in the hands of an expert, manage Class 4 waters in relative safety. You need to learn how to handle a pontoon boat safely because things can go wrong, and running through a whitewater drift is not the place to first learn how to avoid a sweeper or rock pile. Class 4 is not fishing water, but it may be necessary to navigate through to better water. If in doubt, portage difficult sections of the river. Most importantly, even with the best equipment, practise your skills on lower-class waters before attempting to navigate difficult water, or take a course in watercraft safety.

Canadian River Classifications, in brief summary, are as follows:

Class 1—flat water with mild waves; few obstructions that are easy to avoid; some manoeuvring required; slight risk to swimmers; self-rescue is easy.
Class 2—straightforward rapids with wide, clear channels; occasional manoeu-vring required; rocks and medium-sized waves are avoided with training; swimmers seldom injured; group rescue seldom necessary.
Class 3—moderate waves; narrow channels due to obstructions such as rocks or gravel bars; quick, accurate river reading required with instinctive manoeuvres; recommend to paddle with a partner.
Class 4—for experts in whitewater strategy; difficult, with narrow channels obstructed by rocks; steep and narrow drops.

(Source: www.canadiantraveladventures.com)

The North Cariboo

Quesnel–Nazko–Blackwater Country

Marked by glistening emerald lakes, virgin pine and spruce forests, lush grass-lands, meadows and pristine headwaters, the North Cariboo offers everything the fly fisher dreams of—solitude, romance (if you love water) and larger than average trout.

Lakes in this region are more alkaline than the northern Central Interior, where nutrient and fauna growth is more abundant in the high pH water; insects flourish and fish grow more rapidly. Spring is a few weeks earlier and summer a few weeks longer, adding much-needed warmth and stability to the fish-producing summer season.

Rivers of the North Cariboo begin in high mountain ranges—small creeks that tumble from alpine meadows, then meander through swampland gathering others, forming the headwaters of renowned fly fishing rivers such as the Black-water, Chilcotin and Nechako. Where rivers and creeks flow into a basin, lakes form, offering the wandering angler still-water opportunities and the hope for trophy trout that come generously to the fly.

This is the North Cariboo, land that is relatively similar to the way it was over one hundred years ago: sparsely settled cattle country, abundant with free-range Crown land and dense wilderness—where Man is still an intruder simply because of the country's rugged character.

Quesnel

Dragon Lake
Elevation: 595 m
Surface area: 225 ha
Maximum depth: 8 m
Mean depth: 7 m
Annual stocking records: 2007: 25,000 Blackwater Dragon/Blackwater wild fry and yearlings. Average previous five years: 45,000 yearlings per year.

Dragon Lake is situated on the outskirts of the city of Quesnel, a fishery that offers the best opportunity on the Interior Plateau to tempt above-average-sized trout with a fly. Blackwater strain rainbow trout weighing up to 7 kg can be found in Dragon—most of the time travelling the shoals in schools; when you find one, the opportunity for several exists.

Interior anglers, suffering from cabin fever after being cooped up through our long winters, are joined by others from all over western North America to challenge the lake at ice-out and before spring turnover. Dragon is normally ice-free early in April. The spring of 2008, however, gave us a late cold snap and Dragon didn't open until early May, resulting in delayed hatches and a poor early-fishing season through May and most of June. There were many truck and camper units with BC and Washington state plates sitting at Robert's Roost in late April, waiting in vain for the ice to come off, hoping their vacation time wouldn't expire before they could wet a line. If you had time to wait, the late summer and fall fishing made up for the spring—it was exceptional, with over 80 percent of the catch exceeding 50 cm.

Dragon Lake has an egg collection facility that gathers Blackwater River strain progeny from mature fish. They are then transported and reared at the Clearwater Hatchery, and later trucked to the region as juvenile fry to contribute to the stocking programs of many of the area's lakes. The Blackwater River rainbow strain has been most successful for the facility at Dragon. The fish are strong, sturdy and grow rapidly. These trout, because of their river heritage, are genetically adapted to feeding on coarse fish, which helps keep the lake clean of species like chub and shiners that are capable of rapidly reproducing in still-water environments.

Dragon is a low-elevation lake with shallow mean depth, allowing the water to warm early in the season, and not freeze until late November. If the ice comes off at its normal time in early April, and the month of May offers high temperatures near 20°C for two or three weeks, prolific hatches of chironomid, mayfly, damselfly and caddis will happen simultaneously during the day, sometimes spelling the end to good fishing mid-June through August. But for the month of May, fishing can be phenomenal and the condition and fighting quality of the trout will be superb—I'll want to be there as often as possible.

I caught the overlapping hatch scenario for three days in mid-May 2004. One warm spring day I released seventeen rainbows from two to three kilograms each: four on a black/silver chironomid early in the morning, six on an olive/yellow damsel nymph in mid-morning, four more on a dry mayfly spinner in the afternoon and three on the cinnamon caddis dry in the evening. That was a fishing day that I will always remember—especially for connecting with so many large trout on the dry fly, and with multiple patterns.

The entire lake is an extensive weedbed and it fishes well everywhere, but for fishing consistency, access and solitude, I like the south end of Dragon the best. There is a good transition zone stepping from shoreline into 6 m of water along the south shelf, which extends in a horseshoe-shaped fashion to both east and west shores. Fish tend to move around a lot in the lake. If you want to chase them, bring a powerboat and look for moving trout, as they will usually show on the surface with regularity when the bite is on. If you're not finding moving fish, keep a watchful eye toward the middle of the lake and be prepared to follow them.

Productive patterns for spring fishing Dragon and all North Cariboo lakes are: bloodworms, red and maroon, size 10–14; chironomids, black, brown and olive with various rib combinations, 12–16; micro leeches, black, maroon and red, 10–14; mayfly nymphs, olive and brown, 12–14; mayfly duns and spinners, 14; damselfly nymphs, olive, 10–12; and cinnamon caddis, 12–14. The recipes for these imitations are offered in detail in the section on insects and fly tying. Chironomid and bloodworm fishing holds up through the months of April, May and June and overlaps with mayfly, damselfly and small cinnamon caddis fly hatches from late April through early June during a normal year.

Fall fishing at Dragon Lake from late September until freeze-up can be superlative for trophy rainbow: best patterns include bloodworms, micro leeches, and yellow shrimp in size 10-14.

The accommodation at Robert's Roost on Dragon Lake is the finest among the region's campgrounds (see website at www.robertsroostcampsite.ca). Motel and hotel service is available in nearby Quesnel, and the lake is a five-minute drive from city centre on paved roads.

Ten Mile Lake

Elevation: 707 m
Surface area: 243 ha
Maximum depth: 21 m
Mean depth: 11 m
Annual stocking records: 2008–2004: average 45,000 Pennask 2N. 2007–2004: average 25,000 Kokanee.

Ten Mile Lake, 15 km north of Quesnel, is about the same size as Dragon. The north end has the deepest hole, with a transition drop-off zone running from the shoreline that progressively steps off into the cavity—along this inside shoal is the best area on the lake to locate schools of feeding fish.

Ten Mile is 100 m higher in elevation than Dragon, and opens the week following, which is especially useful to know because if Dragon is into turnover, Ten Mile will still be fishing and the trip need not be wasted. Ten Mile has been stocked with several different strains of hatchery rainbow trout—all leapers. The size expectation of large rainbow trout is not as good as Dragon (up to 3 kg) but there is consistent opportunity to expect a brace of fish in the 1–2-kg range, and kokanee can always be caught trolling attractor patterns on top of the water column.

The same patterns and conditions that applied to Dragon Lake will apply to Ten Mile: strong emphasis on chironomid and bloodworm impressions early in the year, overlapping with mayfly, damsel and small caddis imitations as warmer weather progresses into late May and June.

Ten Mile Lake has a BC Parks campsite with public boat launch, beach and showers and all other amenities only ten minutes away in Quesnel. The campsite opens the May long weekend and it is a fine place for the family to get in some fishing, spend time at the beach—weather permitting—and walk or bicycle the excellent trail system around the lake when the fish aren't biting. From Ten Mile Campsite Dragon Lake can be fished within a fifteen-minute drive or Nazko country can be reached in an hour and a half.

Bellos Lake
Elevation: 954 m
Bathometric charts: not charted
Annual stocking records: 2008–2003: average 4,000 Pennask and Premier strain fall fry.

A little gem of a lake, Bellos lies on top of the mountains on the east side of Hwy. 97 heading north to Prince George from Quesnel. To get there, turn right about 20 km north of Quesnel onto the Umiti Pit (1700) Road, follow it about 4 km to the top of the hill and take the first left to Bellos, which you'll come to on the left side of the road. The last section of road to the lake is suitable for pickup truck only, or four-wheel drives if the weather has been wet for a few days. One year I carefully dragged my 18-foot trailer in there, so it is accessible for camping facilities. There is a rough campsite situated in the meadow at the north end. There are no facilities, but there is safe access for car-top boat launching, float tubes or pontoon boats.

Bellos will normally be ice-free with spring turnover finished by the first week of May. The lake will fish well until the end of June, and again in September/October until freeze-up. Expectations for fish larger than 2 kg are unrealistic.

During the several days I have spent on the lake, however, I've released a number of prime, well-conditioned trout in the 45-cm range.

The lake lies in an L-shaped configuration north to west. Shallow at the north end, the deepest hole is located off the corner leading to the west end with good drop-off shoals extending along each side of the hole. This is not a deep lake as it sits in a cradle on top of the surrounding mountains, having no features that suggest a depth greater than 6 m.

Pattern recommendations for spring fishing include the ever-reliable blood-red micro leech, mayfly nymph, bloodworm and black chironomid with various rib combinations of gold, silver and copper.

Nazko–Blackwater Country

Reached by pavement 100 km west of Quesnel or by logging and secondary roads 150 km south from Prince George, the Nazko–Blackwater basin is bountiful, offering the fly fisher some of the prettiest country and finest wild rainbow trout fishing in the North Cariboo.

The basin is cradled in hills and valleys north of the Itcha and Ilgachuz Mountain ranges and drains roughly eight thousand square kilometres of lakes, creeks, swamps and rivers as they meander north and east to the Fraser River.

The Blackwater strain of native wild rainbow in this area has developed naturally over thousands of years to compete in a coarse-fish environment. BC Fisheries use this valuable genetic strain of trout as brood stock for many northern lakes, practised wherever coarse fish such as pike minnow, whitefish and shiners challenge introduced hatchery trout for aquatic food organisms. Study results have proven there is a significant decrease of coarse fish population where the Blackwater strain has been brought in.

Nazko River and Tributaries

Nazko in the Carrier language means "river flowing from the south." Bands of Carrier First Nations have resided in the valley for thousands of years, establishing settlements or summer camps at many of the area's best fishing spots.

The first European homesteaders laid down roots in the valley during the early 1900s. Because electricity didn't arrive until 1984, isolation was a way of life until only recently, but today there is internet service available through dial-up, proving that progress is inevitable in this fast-paced world, even to a homesteader.

The Nazko River begins its northward journey at the outlet of Nazko Lake, meandering peacefully for 100 km through the valley collecting tributary creeks and rivers along its path. All of these streams contain rainbow trout; it would take a few weeks of summer vacation to fish them all, but I would love to do it some day. Notable tributaries worth exploring include Wentworth Creek, Snaking River and the Clisbako River. They look fishy because they are—chock full of small to medium-sized (20–30 cm) rainbow, whitefish and pike minnow that respond readily to a fly.

Typical of slow-moving streams passing through meadows, the Nazko silts up easily on the corners—one false step can be a wet and oozy one. Willows line the banks on the valley floor, but many spots that see few fishermen through the entire season can be accessed if one has a flair for bushwhacking. The Nazko below Honolulu Bridge has water rated Class 1–2 (safe water) for difficulty, but for better fishing results plan a drift by canoe or pontoon boat.

Heading southeast on Honolulu Forestry Road a few minutes' drive south from Nazko townsite, Nazko River is easily accessed from the road for 35 km, where the Honolulu Road ends at the bridge crossing. The Nazko Lake Road begins at km 35, heads south and eventually peters out to a rough trail that accesses Nazko and Gem falls and the headwaters of the Nazko River at the northern tip of Nazko Lake Provincial Park. The wilderness chain of lakes in the park—Tchusiniltil, Tzazati, Nastachi, Tanilkul and Nazko—all contain wild rainbow trout, and boasts a remote canoe route for the adventurous souls among us. Access to the south end of the park and the canoe route can only be gained by the Alexis Lakes Road that heads north off Hwy. 20 west of Alexis Creek and Williams Lake.

At the 35-km crossing, Martin Meadow Trail continues along the east bank of the river for about 20 km, offering seclusion and remote access for hikers or well-equipped fly fishers who have vehicles suitable for narrow paths. Down this path the Nazko runs into and out of Tzazati Lake, another body of water that is fishable to the wandering angler.

Spring runoff in river systems of the North Cariboo usually peaks in mid-June and the rivers open July 1, making for a short fishing season of July, August and September. Runoff can vary from heavy to medium, depending upon snow-pack in the mountains and rainfall during April and May. The Blackwater River opens June 15, but its tributaries are subject to spring closure until July 1. I enjoy getting at these small rivers near opening day and during high water because prolific stonefly hatches invariably happen during this time, causing every fish in the river to look up for a good meal. The river systems are usually clear but the water is high into the banks, making for tough wading around hanging willows, alders and small logjams. Again, drifting the streams to corners, holes and gravel bars is the best method to search the water thoroughly.

Below Nazko townsite the Nazko River becomes pastoral and slow moving, snaking its way through meadows and ranches along the valley floor to its confluence with the Blackwater River 30 km down the gravel road.

The Nazko and its tributaries hold wild rainbow trout, whitefish, pike minnow and the odd huge Dolly Varden trout. If you choose to fish nymph and bottom patterns such as stoneflies, Hare's Ear Nymphs, mayfly nymphs, Prince Nymphs and black Woolly Buggers in sizes 8–14, you can expect to catch a fifty-fifty combination of coarse fish and rainbow trout.

I like to begin my days on the water fishing a dry fly exclusively, because it is trout that I seek and trout to a dry fly are unmatched by any other method. Reliable dry fly patterns for all river systems of the North Cariboo are Elk Hair Caddis, sizes 12–18, colours cinnamon and tan; stimulators, 10–14, orange and yellow; adult stoneflies, 6–10; Mikaluk Caddis, tan, 10–14; and Adams traditional and parachute, 14–18. The fish in these waters are not fussy or sophisticated; bushy patterns that float are fair game and usually don't get far without being inhaled.

Size expectations in this river system are 20–40 cm for rainbow trout, averaging 30 cm, with the odd lunker that will reach 45 cm. They are beautifully marked: heavily spotted, strong red stripes and dark green backs—typical of the Blackwater strain living in the tannin-coloured waters of the basin.

As with most rivers, the farther you walk or drive the larger the prey. The largest bull trout I have seen taken was 60 cm, about 3 kg. These big boys are found off the beaten path, hanging out in the deep pools of remote canyon water and sweeping corners where fishing pressure is light; they eat everything thrown at them.

The community of Nazko has a store, hot showers and gasoline along with food supplies and camping amenities. Across the street from the store, the community manages Marmot Lake Campground, which offers a public boat launch, good swimming, clean campsites, wood and a baseball diamond. Not a bad spot for a fishing reunion.

Bishop (Brown) Lake
Elevation: 1,143 m
Surface area: 232 ha
Maximum depth: 16 m
Mean depth: 7 m
Annual stocking records: none: wild rainbow trout, some coarse fish.

When Honolulu Road ends at km 35 and crosses the Nazko River, Nazko Falls Road begins, leading to Bishop Lake, also called Brown Lake. To access Bishop, follow Nazko Falls Road for about 8 km to the junction of the Brown Creek

Forest Service Road. Turn right and follow this road for 5 km, taking the second left down to the lake.

Bishop is a medium-sized lake, lying north and south. The deepest hole is found toward the south shore, in the middle of the lake. A gradual series of shelves leads outward from the hole in all directions, allowing outstanding insect migration paths to extensive shoals on the east and west shores.

In the mid-'90s, Bishop was one of those go-to lakes that were discovered to contain large wild rainbow trout. It gave up 4-kg rainbows for a few years, but as often happens with "new" lakes, quickly became overfished and abused. When BC Fisheries regulated a two-trout restriction and closed the lake to ice fishing, pressure and catch limits eased, the lake recovered nicely, and it is once again a good lake to spend time at. The expectation of connecting with rainbow in the 3-kg range is very good.

Bishop is a clean, dark-bottomed lake—tannin-stained waters such as these are incredible chironomid and leech fisheries because of their mud and sand foundations, and they have the ability to generate many kilograms of fish per hectare. Patterns that work well in dark waters are chironomids, sizes 12–16, black and brown with silver, gold or red ribbing; Chironomid Bombers, 10–12, grey and black; Blood Bugger Leeches, 8–14; and dragonfly nymphs, 6–10.

Marmot Lake
Elevation: 850 m
Surface area: 54 ha
Maximum depth: 16 m
Mean depth: 9 m
Annual stocking records: 2008–2003: 10,000 Blackwater/Dragon strain fry.

Marmot is one of those small still-water lakes that can best be termed a "sleeper." It is common for fly fishers to routinely bypass it on the way to more remote lakes, without taking time to learn the secrets of the little lake on the side of the paved road. Perhaps it is the moodiness of Marmot—it will rarely give up a limit of trout—or perhaps it is not far enough into the bush to be termed a wilderness experience, but either way Marmot is a very high-quality fishery. The lake has several beautiful shoals—offering superb caddis, chironomid and mayfly hatches—and the trout are always in marvellous condition.

The deepest hole is directly off the boat launch, which can be the most productive spot when fishing is slow or during summer heat waves. The lake has abundant shoals at the north and south ends, and into the small bay at the southwest end; all contain gorgeous silver-bright fish.

Lakes in the Nazko valley are normally ice-free in late April, have turned over and are fishing well by the May long weekend. Fishing will hold up well into July and August if the weather remains normal during spring opening. If you're lucky enough to fish this area's lakes in late September, as has happened to me on several outings to Marmot over the years, you will have a good chance of being alone because many locals are hunting moose and deer for their winter larder.

Marmot gives up fish in the 3-kg range, but they are tough to catch. The best bet for picking off the big Blackwater strains is to go deep with leech and shrimp patterns along the shelf of the deep hole, with at least a #3 full-sink line. Working the shoals at north and south ends during caddis and chironomid hatches is also productive when the bite is on. Do not expect to have twenty-fish days on Marmot—though I am sure they are possible—expectations for several per day in the 40–60-cm range are more realistic.

The facilities at Marmot include the above-mentioned campsite run by Nazko community with all amenities, and there is a rough unserviced forestry campsite at the north end. The campsites are excellent spots to set up headquarters for day trips to the Blackwater and Nazko rivers and tributaries, plus various lakes in the valley; most fishing water is within thirty minutes' drive by good gravel road. When I'm camping in this area, I'll often set up at Marmot, fish nearby river systems by day, and return to have dinner and fish Marmot in late afternoon, hoping to catch the evening rise.

Fishpot Lake
Elevation: 1,021 m
Surface area: 87 ha
Maximum depth: 12 m
Mean depth: 4 m
Annual stocking records: 2007–2003: 5,000 Blackwater/Dragon strain fall fry.

Another of the small but productive lakes in the area, Fishpot lies at a higher elevation than Marmot and will fish well during the heat of summer. Little lakes like Fishpot and Marmot are ideal for float tube or pontoon craft and seem to fit into a day just perfectly; you can either explore the entire lake or just poke around a few shoals without expending a lot of effort.

Fishpot Lake Recreation Site can be reached by taking the Coglistiko (4000) Forest Service Road, the first left past the Marmot Lake Campground, for about 15 km. This campsite is suitable for campers or smaller rigs, but preferably four-wheel drives because the steep hill access to the site can be tricky when wet.

Fishpot Lake Resort is situated on the east side of the lake, complete with cabins, campsites, showers and RV spots if one prefers the rustic amenities of civilization. Visit the website at www.fishpotlakeresort.com.

The lake has extensive shoal areas and one deep hole of 12 m in the middle across from the resort. The shoal at the south end is a beauty—weedy, with gradual slope and a great deal of water 4 m deep; perfect bottom conditions for prolific insect populations such as shrimp, caddis, damsels and mayfly. The same shoal conditions exist at the north end of the lake as you come through the deep hole: graduated slope from 10 m in the hole, stepping up to 2 m near the shoreline.

Fishpot will reward the angler with trout in the 3-kg range, but the average is 0.5–1 kg—strong, scrappy Blackwater strains that enjoy cruising the shoals during daylight hours.

Blackwater River and Tributaries

I can't think of the Blackwater River without daydreaming of the glorious days I have spent fishing this fantastic wilderness river, enjoying its pristine pleasures and fine dry fly fishing in quiet seclusion at least 90 percent of the time.

The Blackwater is located in a divide separating the Ilgachuz and Itcha mountain ranges, where the headwaters of the Dean River begins its journey seaward and the Nechako and Blackwater rivers begin their passage to the Fraser. The Blackwater basin drains roughly five thousand square kilometres of wilderness through its lakes and tributaries, beginning with the Eliguk, Tsacha, Kluskus, Euchiniko and Kluskoil lakes and tributaries flowing from the west. The Batnuni lakes and branches of the Euchiniko River enter from the northwest, joined by the Nazko and Baezaeko rivers and their lakes and tributaries from the south. Blackwater empties all of her riches into the Fraser River just north of Quesnel.

The Blackwater is a lonely river that receives only limited fishing pressure. As the fish swims, there are just three bridge-crossing access points to the entire 320-km length of the system, and a few rough trail accesses suitable for a short-wheel-based 4x4, all-terrain vehicle, or horse. These bridge crossings are about 30 km apart but due to canyon water, good-sized boulders, and risk of sweepers and logjams through the chutes of some of these stretches, I don't recommend floating sections below the Euchiniko River takeout at Gillies Crossing without the services of a knowledgeable guide. In spite of its difficult access, there are lots of places where a short hike into a canyon along the road can lead to a full day of fishing enjoyment.

There are a few off-road access points worthy of mention that I have uncovered over the past fifteen years of wandering her banks, fording her shallow spots and learning her secrets.

From the Nazko Road, about 1 km above Nazko Bridge at the West Road River Recreation Site and twenty-five minutes north of Nazko townsite, Teepee Lake Trail skirts the Blackwater as far as Chine Falls (Chinee Falls) at Kluskoil Lake, hooking into the Alexander Mackenzie Heritage Trail after about 30 km of bushwhacking. This unmarked trail is slow going, narrow and rough. The 10 km I have travelled by 4x4 are not difficult or wet, but wide enough to travel if you are in the mood for some good fishing and exploring, and you're driving a short-box vehicle or riding a good horse. Try the meadow run about ten minutes by vehicle along the trail, and the good water near the mouth of the Baezaeko River about 10 km upriver.

At the Nazko Bridge campsite a walking trail follows the south side of the Blackwater all the way to Kluskoil Lake, a distance of about 30 km. Maps show the path as going through, although I know it isn't well-used or maintained, and I reckon it becomes more of a game trail the farther you venture. I have walked forty-five minutes up, finding several good runs, deep corners and boulder sections. There is also good fly fishing water accessed by a river-wading hike downstream from Nazko Bridge, working your way to the mouth of the Nazko River about 1 km away.

Three popular and easy day drifts are accessed from the campsite: one going north halfway to Gillies Crossing, another continuing to Gillies Crossing through the mouth of the Euchiniko, and the last from the Baezaeko River put-in to the Blackwater and back to the campsite. Two vehicles are needed for the drifts—Gillies Crossing is about twenty minutes' driving time; the Baezaeko about ten minutes—both are rated Class 1–2 water.

To access the Baezaeko put-in, take the first logging road about 1 km south from the campsite, follow the road about 5 km to the river crossing, put in and follow the Baezaeko for a short 1 km float to the Blackwater. On this drift, concentrate your fishing efforts on the upper, middle and lower sections after you enter the river, as there is a long float of unproductive shallow water between the middle and lower sections.

There is excellent canyon water that can be accessed about 2 km before Batnuni Bridge, the second crossing of the river driving east on the Batnuni Road. Park your vehicle at the road pullout or at little West Lake across the road from the canyon and follow any of the trails to the river. This area has wonderful pocket water, a swift canyon stretch and a few productive corner runs, rewarding me with many memorable outings during low-water periods of August and early September.

Another horse trail that can be travelled by 4x4 is reached from the Blackwater Road at the third crossing. Heading north up the hill from the Blackwater Canyon campsite take the first left turn, then left again and you are on the Alexander Mackenzie Heritage Trail, which follows the river in a westerly direction along some long stretches of canyon water eventually leading you back to the Batnuni Bridge area. There will be lots of scrambling to get at the river, but the results are worth the effort.

The average size of wild Blackwater River rainbows is 30–40 cm in easily accessed sections of the river. Rumour has it the farther upriver one goes, the larger the trout. The typical Blackwater rainbow is feisty, well-fed, and a line ripper, true to its wild and aggressive nature.

The nutrient-rich river produces prolific hatches of midge, mayfly, stonefly and caddis from opening day in mid-June through late September. The rocky sections and corner pools often hold fish by the dozens, and it is not unusual to catch and release fifty to sixty trout in an afternoon when stoneflies and caddis are coming off, using size 8–12 bushy flies such as adult stoneflies, stimulators and Mikaluk Sedge.

Besides the Nazko River, two other major tributary rivers entering the Blackwater from the south are the Coglistiko and Baezaeko rivers. The Coglistiko is a tributary to the Baezaeko, entering from the west just north of Fishpot Lake. Both rivers offer excellent wilderness fly fishing for wild Blackwater strain rainbow trout, and are accessible from the Coglistiko (4000 Road) that heads west from the Marmot Lake Campground. Like the Blackwater, there are few access crossing points to these rivers, but rough camping spots are available at the bridges. The Baezaeko has a marked trail along its entire length that begins near the Coglistiko (4000) and Michelle (4300) Road junction, which follows the river through the valley floor to its headwaters in the Itcha Mountain Range, a distance of over 100 km. Continuing north at this junction on the Coglistiko–Michelle Road leads you to the upper sections of the Coglistiko River and trailhead access to the Euchiniko Lakes by way of the 25-km Kluskus Trail.

The Euchiniko River, which empties a progression of lakes from the west—Klunchatistil, Comstock, Batnuni, Snag, Hanham, Boat and Titetown—enters the Blackwater below Gillies Crossing. The Batnuni Road, which follows the Euchiniko for about 50 km west from the Nazko Road, accesses all of these lakes. They are decent fishing but more suitable for trolling tackle than fly fishing, offering kokanee as well as wild rainbow, Dolly Varden and a host of coarse fish. The Euchiniko has good to excellent fishing in its upper reaches, using the same flies applicable to the Blackwater and Nazko.

There are three Forest Service campsites on the Blackwater, located at each of the crossings—rustic free-of-charge campsites with lots of firewood, all with river settings and pit toilets. For large camping units, the Blackwater Canyon Forest Service and Marmot Lake community campsites are best, and small rigs, campers and tents fit nicely into the smaller sites at the Batnuni and Nazko Bridges. There are no services in the area other than the store in Nazko or the fishing resorts, so I recommend you carry an extra container of gasoline if you plan to do a lot of exploring. This part of British Columbia begs to be discovered, but the nearest gas station is Nazko, which could be a two or three hour drive and 100 km from where your adventure tour may end.

The Blackwater River is rated from Class 1 to 4 for difficulty, the middle section below Chine Falls and the Nazko Bridge rated Class 1–2. There are some sections below the Gillies Crossing put-in on the Nazko Road that are rated Class 4, requiring a short portage. All canyon water below the Batnuni and Blackwater bridges should be scouted before attempting a run as the river compresses into narrow channels with rock obstructions, deep pools and swift corners that could trap sweepers during runoffs.

Yimpakluk Lake
Elevation: 869 m
Surface area: 65 ha
Maximum depth: 14 m
Mean depth: 6.4 m
Annual stocking records: 2008–2003: average 7,500 Blackwater/Dragon strain fall fry.

If you don't mind fording a river and bouncing along a wagon road for the opportunity to fish a lake that sees little pressure and the trout average 45 cm, Yimpakluk could be your lake. Reached from Batnuni Road, take the first left turn at the Alexander Mackenzie Trail marker a few kilometres past the junction with Pelican Lake Forest Service Road. You must ford the Euchiniko River at this point; the bottom is gravel and should only be attempted after spring runoff with a high clearance 4x4. Travel the rough trail west for about 6 km and take the short left fork at this point, then the right fork to the crude lake access. I haven't challenged the Euchiniko ford during early spring runoff, but I suspect it may be tough to get through because my wife's Jeep (oops) was pushing water with the bumper in late August.

In front of the campsite off a visible shoal is a hole that reaches the maximum depth of the lake. Yimpakluk is a clear, algae-laden lake with a weed bottom and shoals that are close to the shoreline, accentuated with sharp drop-offs extending to deeper water. Across from the campsite off the south shore there is an island with good-looking shoals and shelves surrounding it; prime habitat for insect migration.

Pattern selection is standard offering for this part of the country: chironomid, leech, scud, mayfly, dragonfly nymph and caddis. I've had my best days during late August and September using the Blood Bugger Leech in size 12.

I rank Yimpakluk as a high-quality remote fishery that will produce consistent results because of its access restrictions, and the fact that few people know where it is, or how to get to it.

Upper Blackwater River Waters

The mind-boggling array of creeks, lakes, rivers and swamps that form the upper Blackwater River system is a fly fisher's paradise. A myriad of wild native species—Dolly Varden, bull trout, rainbow, whitefish and introduced kokanee—are present in abundance. The lakes have enchanting names: Eliguk, Tsetzi, Tsacha, Kuyakuz, Kluskoil, Euchiniko and Kluskus. They conjure visions of wilderness, dotted and interrupted by ancient Carrier villages occupied for centuries before the coming of Alexander Mackenzie in 1792. The area contains some of the last remote, active Carrier Indian reserves and villages, which carry on with life and customs much as they were two hundred years ago.

The upper Blackwater River enters and exits the chain of lakes, and is mostly Class 1–2 water navigable by canoe or pontoon boat, with some portages around marked falls with Class 3–4 rapid sections. There are many rough campsites along the route, with the journey from Eliguk Lake to the Nazko Bridge taking a good week or two to complete, even longer if you plan to fish the route properly. The *Backroad Mapbook: Cariboo Chilcotin Coast BC* available at most fly fishing and outdoor stores, covers the paddling, camping and trail routes of this area in detail.

The best time to fish this part of the country is mid-July through September, well after spring runoff. The Blackwater pushes a lot of water, and can be high and difficult to fish through the early summer season if rainfall exceeds normal. I have always found the water level more predictable in late August, when the seemingly endless swarms of mosquitoes, blackflies, and no-see-ums have subsided and the slippery river can be forded and criss-crossed without risk.

Nechako River Country

Three great northern rivers begin on the slopes of the Itcha and Ilgachuz ranges in the North Cariboo–Chilcotin: the Nechako, Blackwater and Dean. Each takes a different route to its final destination: the Dean travels west to the Pacific Ocean, the Blackwater east to the Fraser and the Nechako north to the fertile Nechako River Valley, then east to meet the Fraser River at Prince George.

The Nechako is a proud river. In spite of its course being altered in the early 1950s by construction of the Kenney Dam, which supplies power to the Alcan aluminum smelter at Kitimat through the Kemano Powerhouse, the Nechako continues to be a solid contributor to fisheries of the Central Interior. The damming of the river produced several huge reservoirs: Ootsa, Whitesail, Natalkuz, Eutsuk and Knewstubb lakes, and together they created over two hundred kilometres of waterways on the Nechako Plateau.

The turbulent Nechako River forms a narrow canyon below Knewstubb Lake at Kenney Dam, picks up the Cheslatta River about 8 km downstream, and then flattens as it enters the Nechako Valley, succumbing to a Class 1–2 difficulty stream for the rest of the 320-km passage to the Fraser.

Flowing northward 150 km to Vanderhoof, the Nechako collects dozens of tributary creeks and unnamed lakes; many are accessible only by trail, and most contain wild indigenous trout. Some lakes, like Hobson and Chief Gray, are trophy class; most are just darn good fishing, such as Tatuk, Finger, Cicuta and Lavoie.

The Nechako supports the world-class trout fishery of the Stellako River, flowing from the west into Fraser Lake, and also the Nautely River as it exits out of Fraser Lake. Gathered from the north are the Stuart River and its numerous tributaries draining into Stuart Lake, including the Necoslie and Tachie rivers. The Chilako River, another major branch, enters from the south about 80 km east of Vanderhoof. Then all of the Nechako system empties into the Fraser at Prince George.

Kluskus Forest Service Road Access

The Kluskus Road, which provides access to a multitude of lakes and rivers in the Blackwater–Nechako divide, is reached by turning south onto the Kenney Dam Road at Vanderhoof. Travel west about 25 km and turn south onto the Kluskus Road about 6 km past Nulki Lake. From this junction, the road runs hundreds of kilometres south into the North Cariboo, ending at the Blackwater divide. At the 73-km mark, the Kluskus Road loops west on the 500 Road to Kenney Dam, and back to Vanderhoof via the Kenney Dam Road.

Several quality fishing lakes and rivers can be accessed within thirty minutes of each other, which tempts a fly fisher to set up camp at Hobson or Cicuta for a week and prepare day trips to fish all of the area's best water. If resort accommodation is what you seek, there are several good lodges within an hour's drive of all the fishing spots: Finger Lake Resort (www.fingerlakeresort.com), Nechako Lodge on Knewstubb Lake (www.nechakolodge.com) and Tatuk Lake Wilderness Resort (www.tatuklake.com), which offer first-class facilities and float plane trips into remote wilderness lakes and streams. Tatuk and Finger lakes, as well as nearby Lavoie, are good fly fishing lakes on their own merits.

This area is a little more wet and bushy that the North Cariboo, but fly patterns remain the same with the ever-reliable leeches, olive shrimp, dragonfly nymphs, bloodworms, chironomids and damselflies catching most of the trout.

Hobson Lake
Elevation: 906 m
Surface area: 72 ha
Maximum depth: 7 m
Annual stocking records: 2007: 2,500 Blackwater AF3N triploid fry. 2005–2001: 2,500 Dragon/Badger/Tunkwa strains every other year.

Named after renowned pioneer cowboy and author, Rich Hobson, the lake is accessed by turning north near the 9-km mark on the 500 Road. The narrow 1–2-km path to Hobson is rough and slow but not slick or difficult, which allows pickups, campers or small motor homes admission to the lake. Hobson has a three- or four-vehicle Forestry Service campsite with pit toilet, tables and a dock.

Hobson is one of those rare small lakes that can sustain a large trout fishery. It is endowed with extensive shoals and generous weed habitat for food production, but also has enough depth and aeration to overwinter fish as long as the population is controlled. It is managed as a high-quality fishery, with catch-and-release restrictions to ensure that the large fish percentage is sustained. During several outings to Hobson in the last few years, we have caught trout ranging from 30–65 cm, which is a good indication that the fishery plan is working, as trout in a number of age groups were represented.

All of Hobson is a fishery. Much of the water is shallow weedy bottom with a gradual merge into the middle of the lake, which contains a medium-depth hole of 7 m. Hobson is small enough to cover fully by float tube or pontoon boat in a day's fishing, working a pattern from shore into the middle, searching weedbeds for foraging trout or deeply trolling a large offering through the hole.

The best times to catch a hatch for big trout are early May for chironomid fishing, anytime in June for damselfly, late June to mid-July for caddis, and again in early September through late October for water boatman, leech and shrimp action. If you fish Hobson, you'll encounter windy days when you might try the hike into Chief Gray, and calm days when you'll swear it's the best little lake you've ever fished.

Chief Gray (Bitch) Lake
Elevation: 914 m
Surface area: 33 ha
Maximum depth: 16 m
Mean depth: 8 m
Annual stocking records: 2007 and 2005: 1,700 Blackwater AF3N triploid fry. 2003: 2,500 Dragon diploid fry. 2001: 2,500 Badger/Tunkwa fry.

Chief Gray is recognized as the premier hike-in lake of the Vanderhoof region. Access is by a good 4-km trail that runs northwest from Hobson Lake campsite and is suitable for packing a float tube, with closed admission to motorized vehicles. The lake receives little pressure and is a catch-and-release fishery, ensuring that Chief Gray will remain a quality experience.

The north half of the lake is the most productive area to fish, working through the weedbeds and drop-offs along the east shoal, then probing the 15-m hole in the middle to coax a lunker to your fly. Trout are a nice average size of 40–50 cm, but there are many available in the 70-cm range. Expectations during the prime season of mid-May through July are from fifteen to thirty fish per day, and the action is non-stop if weather conditions are right and the fish are cooperative.

Chief Gray is one of my favourites; it has a wilderness feeling about it, and the hike is well worth the effort because of the unspoiled country and prime, well-conditioned rainbows that this jewel of a lake offers.

Cicuta (Rum Cache) Lake

Elevation: 891 m

Surface area: 174 ha

Maximum depth: 12 m

Annual stocking records: 1995: 2,500 Genier strain yearlings. 1993: 2,500 Tunkwa yearlings. 1990: 2,500 Badger yearlings.

Cicuta was a must-do lake back in the early 1990s. It was originally stocked in 1986 with thirty thousand Tunkwa fry, and soon began giving up rainbows in the 4-kg class. However, the trophy fishery was not well policed; poaching and overfishing depleted the large trout, resulting in the lake being closed down in the late '90s so the fishery could be rebuilt. Cicuta recovered nicely and was reopened in 2004, but I hear there is an overabundance of small trout—it's good lake for the family right now.

Reached from the Holy Cross Road either south from Hwy. 16 West at Fraser Lake sawmill, or from the Kenney Dam and 500 roads, the access road is suitable for pickup truck, camper or small RV. The well-treed Forest Service site has seven campsites, pit toilets and a boat launch.

I fished it back in its heyday, and had some memorable outings releasing numerous beautiful, silver-chrome trout. Cicuta has a dark bottom with tannin-stained water, and the bathometric contours set up like a dogleg left golf hole. It's difficult to read the shoals because of the dark bottom, but the lake is a consistent depth of 4–6 m with a 10-m hole that extends west for several hundred metres on the dogleg. Fore!

Cicuta reminds me of Bishop Lake in the North Cariboo, and is as good a leech and chironomid lake as you can find because the tannin water, mud bottom and salad-type vegetation is prime habitat for these insects and supports large trout. It's good to see Cicuta coming back to life.

Cheslatta and Nechako Rivers

Continuing north on the Holy Cross Road 6 km north of the Cicuta Lake turn-off, the road crosses the Cheslatta River, which carries on to meet the Nechako in its canyon section. There is a Forest Service recreation site, with trail access down both sides of the Cheslatta to the Nechako. It's a turbulent piece of river, blasting its way down a short run from Murray Lake to the Nechako, but holds some really nice wild rainbows in the backwaters and eddies below the bridge.

Eighteen-metre high Cheslatta Falls, where the waterway dumps into the Grand Canyon of the Nechako, is the picturesque end of the journey for this river. Along the path near the falls an observant hiker can glimpse remnants of ancient Carrier First Nations campsites, pit diggings and dwelling sites.

The Nechako of today is not a renowned trout fishery, but certainly could be if the reservoir discharge was better regulated with cold-water input. Sadly, before the dam was built it was a more prolific salmon spawning river than the world-famous Adams. Today, low flows coupled with summer heat raise the river temperature to the point where historic sockeye salmon survival is unsustainable; however, it continues to support the summer sockeye runs of the Stuart, Nautely and Stellako rivers.

The Chinook fishery of the Nechako is alive and well, supporting an average of seven thousand fish for the past five years. The peak of the Chinook run reaches the Nechako in mid-September after summer low-water conditions have subsided, permitting the weary salmon to complete their 1,100-km journey, spawn and then die.

The Cutoff Creek FS Recreation Site on the Kenney Dam Road, about 18 km below the dam, marks the first put-in for water craft on the Nechako. From there, it's a 15-km drift through Class 1–2 water to the next take-out at Greer Creek FS Recreation Site. The next drift, from Greer Creek to the Hwy. 16 West bridge at Fort Fraser, is a long one of about 50 km through Class 1–2 water, with trout fishing in all sectors rated as fair to good for rainbow up to 2 kg.

The stonefly hatch will invariably come off during high water in early June, which is the most likely time to coax larger trout of 50 cm to the surface. The peak window for this hatch is a short period of only a week or two, but the reward can be stimulating as a large trout grabs your dry fly and heads for fast water with your reel screaming—try my Salmonfly Adult.

June through August, small caddis are always a good bet when river fishing. The Soft Hackle Emerger works as a searching or emerger pattern, and a tan-coloured Mikaluk Sedge size 14 will produce good fish numbers when caddis flies are hatching.

Redfern River (Rapids)

A book on fly fishing wouldn't be very interesting without talking about some crazy places to search out. The Redfern River (called Rapids in the *Backroad Mapbook: Cariboo Chilcotin Caost BC*) is one of those dream destinations—I haven't been there, but I will someday. The problem is this untamed North country has many "Redferns"; getting to them, however, without roads and planes, takes time and money, which usually keeps most of us from crazy wonderful places.

The Redfern River is only about 4 km in length, draining from the east end of Eutsuk Lake into Tetachuk Lake, both parts of the Nechako Reservoir. For the adventurous, you can get to the Redfern by vehicle and boat portages from south of Burns Lake, but the best way is to hire a float plane to drop you there and then a pontoon boat for several days. This involves an organized venture, packing bare essentials; some people are up for this, but if not, the Redfern River Lodge on Eutsuk Lake awaits you. For information and accommodations, contact the lodge (www.redfernriverlodge.ca) and I'm sure you'll be rewarded with the trip of a lifetime.

From what I've read about the Redfern, it compares to the trout fishing of my beloved Blackwater River—anything that floats high and dry is a target, which calls for adult stoneflies, bushy caddis imitations and stimulators. But don't get too technical—these trout don't see a lot of people and aren't afraid to put on a show for their guests. Rainbows will average 40 cm in the Redfern; the problem is you will likely release up to fifty of them every day, and lose some very large ones in the 60-cm range because Eutsuk Lake contains wild bows in the 10-kg class! The best time of year to fish this part of the country will be after high water in June, and prime time will be late June and the month of July, slowing but still good through sporadic hatch activity in August and September.

Nechako Valley West—The Stellako River

The Stellako is a world-class fishery, but only 11 km in length. If you go there, you will meet people from all over the world who make the journey to fish for its trophy-class wild rainbows. Some US visitors I have met on the river have been making the pilgrimage for over thirty years.

To access the Stellako, drive west on Hwy. 16 from Prince George for 160 km, turn left onto paved Francois Lake Road 4 km west of the Village of Fraser Lake, and continue on this road 11 km to the east end of Francois Lake. The river exits the east end of Francois, where there is a pull-off at the Glenannan Bridge for day parking and river trail access. You can also visit the Stellako Lodge across the river, where you can park an RV or stay in comfort with Irwin and Trudy in their rustic cabins. The lodge offers first-class dining several nights a week (Irwin is a chef by trade), and you can google the fly fishers in the "bridge run" while you dine, and wish you weren't eating.

Resident rainbows of the Stellako are wild indigenous stock, as is the entire system of lakes, rivers, and creeks that feed the river. The Nithi River, which enters Francois Lake in the southeast corner about 4 km from the Stellako's mouth, is the spawning ground for Stellako rainbows, and has been for thousands of years.

Size expectations for trout on the Stellako range from 20 cm for juvenile fish to 60 cm for the five- and six-year-old mature adults. According to BC

Fisheries, the fifteen-year average inventory of the river is three thousand trout, with about five hundred fish at the mature adult stage. The native fish mature at about 45 cm and are heavily spotted and wide-shouldered, displaying a deep red band—truly beautiful trout. They are extremely strong, able to pop 4-X tippet on the strike and first run if you tighten too quickly or get surprised by the take.

The Stellako, because of its short length, can only support a minimum of mature fish and nursery stock. The health and abundance of trout in the river is directly tied to the fall cycle of returning sockeye salmon, which peaks every four years. In September the returning Stellako sockeye, which began their migration in the Fraser River estuary over one thousand kilometres away, return to the creeks and rivers of their birth in the Francois system. The amount of waste matter, salmon eggs and fish carcasses that flush through in late fall is often the difference between life and death for native Stellako trout, as they prepare for six months of harsh winter conditions and reduced water flows.

A popular pontoon boat drift-river, the Stellako offers Class 1–4 water including a Class 4 set of falls just past the power lines near the 7-km sign. The pullout is well-marked, involving a short 20-m portage. The 5 km of water below the falls is placid, easygoing water all the way down to the Hwy. 16 West bridge take-out, but some of the upper sections require tricky manoeuvring and quick decisions as you race through the swift, rocky runs. For novice river runners, you must float the Stellako with a buddy who has been down previously, or at least consider drifting the river with a companion. Once you are in the river, there is no public road access until the bridge take-out. The areas that I prefer to concentrate on are all in km 1–6: the rock gardens in the upper section, the fast boulder portions of water in the middle, and the area around and below Millionaire's Pool to the Big Eddy. There is a detailed map of these various sections at the bridge put-in.

Technically, a fly fisher can love or hate the Stellako. When a hatch is on during daylight hours, even small nursery stock can be difficult to catch unless your drift is perfect and your imitation is the precise size and colour of the emergence. The bridge run receives a lot of pressure, but is laden with trout, both mature and juvenile. During a hatch there can be hundreds of trout in all size ranges rising, blatantly refusing every floating offering unless it's a perfect artificial fished without drag. But, if you wait until the last hour of daylight (10 p.m. in July), an Adams size 18 will take all ranges of fish that were zipper-mouthed on the surface all day. At times, with no hatch in progress, you'll swear there isn't a fish in the run; this is when wet fly emerger and stonefly nymph patterns work the best. And don't overlook fishing the soft section of river mouth above the bridge.

As you move downriver, fishing pressure decreases and the Stellako becomes a little more forgiving to the fly fisher but, because of the gin-clear water and solitude, the fish are wary of all intruders and your presentation must be just right to coax them to your fly.

The Stellako is amazingly fertile, comparable to middle sections of the Skagit River of Manning Park in water clarity and size. Because its headwater exits from a large lake and the river has no major tributaries, it can run high but never blows out. There are prolific hatches of insect life throughout the open season, many overlapping, but the most consistent producing dry patterns for me are adult stoneflies, mayflies, midges, stimulators and—my favourite—the caddis in tan or cinnamon. Nymph and emerger patterns fished floating-line or sink-tip are effective during the day in hot weather spells of July and August. During mid-September through October, a single-egg pattern fished dry or sink-tip line will outshine all other patterns as trout key in on spawning sockeye salmon.

Opening day on the Stellako is June 1, a Classified Water licence is required and the river is a catch-and-release fishery. Prime times are the months of June, July, August and October: June for the stonefly hatch, late June through August for everything and late September and October for targeting trout on egg patterns.

From the end of July onward, fishing pressure on the river decreases—this is a good time to come if you prefer more seclusion. August is a quiet time for fishers—warm days, cool evenings, sporadic hatches of cinnamon caddis, midge and mayflies—a reflective time for the river and its trout, and my favourite time to visit for a few days.

Prince George West

Travelling east between Vanderhoof and Prince George on Hwy. 16, the Nechako Valley gives way to hilly terrain, lodgepole pine and spruce forests. To the south along Blackwater Road are lakes and rivers drained by the Chilako River, and on the north side of the highway the Nechako winds its way through the hills and valleys to Prince George. On the south side, creeks of Cluculz, Bednesti, Norman and Graveyard lakes drain to the Nechako; the Chilako River empties Tatuk, Finger and Lavoie lakes, then assembles creeks from Bobtail and a multitude of other small lakes and streams and also heads for the Nechako. All of the big lakes contain good numbers of wild trout, some augmented by stock from the fisheries program.

Within 160 km of Prince George, there are over 1,600 lakes; only 700 have been assessed for inventory of fish. This means there are a lot of unnamed lakes, beaver ponds and creeks that must contain fish, as the water is all connected to fish-bearing maiden rivers. I go nuts just thinking about what some of this water must hold.

Cobb Lake

Elevation: 777 m

Surface area: 210 ha

Maximum depth: 10 m

Mean depth: 5 m

Annual stocking records: Rainbow trout: 2008: 10,000 Blackwater/Dragon strain yearlings. 2007–2001: 15,000 Tunkwa/Badger/Genier mixed diploid stocks, yearlings. Eastern brook trout: 2008–2001: 20,000 Aylmer AF3N triploid fingerlings.

Cobb Lake receives as many fish per year from the stocking program as any lake in the Prince George area and, combined with easy access and an open area for camping, it is an excellent choice for a day or weekend outing with the family. The lake is managed as an average-quality high-use fishery for both winter and summer recreation. Amenities offered are a boat launch (4x4 recommended), pit toilets and numerous picnic and camping spots.

Accessed from Finmoore Road on Hwy. 16 West across from the rest stop at Cluculz Lake, the Cobb Lake turnoff is about 6 km north. Turn east at the sign, cross a small spawning creek and turn right onto a well-maintained short gravel road that is suitable for all vehicles including autos.

Cobb usually opens the third week of April, and fishes well at ice-off and after the spring turnover. One of the best areas in the lake to work a fly is the large weedbed and shelf at the west end directly off the boat launch and camping area. During early May, this area attracts a lot of spawning rainbows as there is a creek that exits through the west end. The southeast end, where a small creek enters the lake, is another good area to fish if you target the abundant eastern brook trout population.

I like to fish Cobb in late April and May with mayfly, shrimp and damselfly nymph patterns, and again in October and November just before freeze-up with leeches and scuds. Eastern brook trout, difficult to catch most times, are easiest to attract in the fall by fishing deep with shrimp and using attractor colours and bodies such as patterns with yellow, red and tinsel makeup.

Prince George South—the Blackwater Road

Another 80 km of fishing country can be accessed by turning south off Hwy. 16

West within Prince George city limits onto the Blackwater Road, which is paved for about 30 km and then turns into a good gravel secondary road leading to the Blackwater River Canyon, and the first access point to the river from the north. This main road gives access to several fair fishing lakes, including Mackenzie East, Mackenzie West and Punchaw.

About 20 km south of Prince George on the Blackwater Road, the Pelican Forest Service Road angles off to the right, moving in a southwest direction for 70 km to the Batnuni Lake Forest Service Road. Along the way a number of lakes offer decent fishing—Barton, Lintz, Tagai, Pelican and Kevin—but my personal favourites are Tory and Meadow. This is Chilako River drainage, which eventually empties into the Nechako.

Tory Lake

Elevation: 730 m
Surface area: 19 ha
Maximum depth: 10 m
Mean depth: 3 m
Annual stocking records: 2,000 Tunkwa strain yearlings every other year.

Tory Lake is accessed at km 43 of the Pelican FS Road, and comes complete with Forest Service campsite, rough boat launch and a pit toilet. Generally regarded as a drive-by lake, it sits in a small bowl-shaped trough along the road and doesn't get much traffic. Perhaps it's the difficult hill to drag a boat up or down? Or maybe the access is too close to the road? Whatever the reason, Tory gets a lot of lookers and little pressure.

A diminutive lake at only 19 ha, Tory has one deep hole; the rest of the lake is shoal, but it produces enough large trout to be classed as a high-quality fishing experience by the latest fisheries assessment survey of 2004. In this study, 32 percent of the trout netted exceeded 40 cm in length. I can attest to those results, having caught few trout less than 30 cm in my sixteen years of fishing Tory.

An ideal float tube lake because of its steep hill access to the shore and its small size, Tory can be worked thoroughly twice over in a day's fishing; or a fly fisher can reach the opposite shoal where fish are seen rising within minutes. Most trout are concentrated in the 10-m-deep hole, coming onto the visible shoals to feed, which makes the lake an excellent choice for searching rising fish with a floating line and dry fly.

Every year in mid-June, I enjoy several wonderful days on Tory using a Mikaluk Sedge pattern, releasing up to twenty nice trout averaging 35–40 cm.

Most are taken in 2 m of water as they dash to the shoal to intercept a skittered caddis. Other productive patterns are leeches, shrimp, bloodworms and chironomids. The damsel migration of early June and water boatmen fall of early September also attract a lot of attention from the willing trout, which are only too happy to clobber anything that imitates the insects.

The next time you drive by Tory, take a good look—you will usually see moving trout, and most will be keepers. They are excellent table fish, but catch-and-release or limited kill should be practised because the lake is too small to support a large quantity of trout plus maintain a high-quality fishery if regulation limits are taken.

Meadow Lake
Elevation: 881 m
Surface area: 34 ha
Maximum depth: 7 m
Mean depth: 3 m
Annual stocking records: none: wild rainbow, coarse fish.

Meadow Lake is accessed from the Pelican FS Road just before the 56-km mark by turning southeast on the gravel road that heads uphill, and following the path a few kilometres to the marked FS Recreation Site turnoff. A quiet, forested recreation site awaits, with car-top boat launch, pit toilet, several campsites and picnic tables.

You can probably tell by now that I prefer little lakes, those quiet spots that offer remote camping, bare essentials and an opportunity to catch better than average-sized trout. For me, the quantity of fish caught is not as important as the quality. I also favour wild fish over hatchery stock, even though our hatchery program in BC concentrates on wild progeny for collection. Wild trout in their home environment seem to fight better, jump higher and run harder than counterparts raised in hatcheries.

There are some good-sized fish in Meadow—up to 3 kg. A variety of sizes is caught during a day on the water; you can expect 25–35-cm trout as an average, with anticipation of some in the 40–50-cm range.

The lake is tannin-coloured and shallow, lying on top of the Plateau among beaver lodges, creeks and meadows. The best fishing is anywhere from the graduated shoreline into the middle of the lake, where a deep hole of 7 m offers the fish an area of refuge and cooler water temperatures.

What you will catch at Meadow is a good dose of northern solitude, excellent outdoor camping and superb wildlife viewing. It's not always about the fish!

Grizzly Lake (West)

Elevation: 982 m

Surface area: 137 ha

Maximum depth: 7 m

Mean depth: 3 m

Annual stocking records: 2008–2001: 5,000 Blackwater/Dragon strain yearlings.

A little over an hour's drive from Prince George, Grizzly Lake is accessed by turning off Hwy. 16 West past Bednesti Lake south onto the Bobtail Forest Service Road. Continue to km 59, and take the marked road west about 4 km to the FS Recreation Site, where you'll find a 10-unit campsite, pit toilets and boat launch.

Grizzly Lake is managed as a high-yield fishery, producing above-average catch results per fishing hour. Expectation for trout over 40 cm is about one in five, the normal catch length about 30 cm. Healthy populations of lake chub reside with the trout, which is why the Blackwater rainbow strain has been introduced—these guys enjoy a piscivorous diet when they can get one.

I have fished Grizzly—a weedy, shallow lake of consistent depth—on several occasions, doing well on olive shrimp and ever-reliable leech patterns. It doesn't seem to matter where you fish, the trout are well dispersed throughout the lake. When I am faced with unknown bottom contours and heavy weedbed growth, a good starting place is a point of land, creek mouth or small bay—all are found at Grizzly.

From the Grizzly Lake campsite, other decent fishing lakes are within a short drive: Woodcock, Naltesby (Bobtail), Little Bobtail and Eulatazella (Graveyard).

Chilako (Mud) River

The Chilako River drains Tatuk Lake, one of the largest natural lakes on the Nechako Plateau at 1,894 ha. Tatuk is good fishing for native rainbow trout, so it only makes sense that the Chilako is also decent. Like the Blackwater River, the upper Chilako is clear but dark, meandering over gravel beds as it winds its way to the Nechako. The lower river, as it flattens to farmland, is silted and muddy; hence the local name for the lower Chilako: the Mud River.

The upper Chilako receives very little fishing pressure, and is accessed from the Pelican Chilako Forest Service Road (100 Road) by turning west at the 50-km point of the Pelican Lake FSR, 7 km past Tory Lake. This well-maintained gravel road takes you near the outlet at Tatuk Lake, where you will find Tatuk Lake FS Campsite; the Upper Chilako Forest Service Campsite is on the river. If you look at the *Backroad Mapbook* of this area, you'll see a myriad of small unnamed pothole lakes, water just begging to be explored by an adventurous fly fisher—I've heard they are interesting. The Lower Chilako sections are accessed from Upper and Lower Mud River Road, turning south or north off Hwy. 16 West about 20 km west of Prince George.

Drift the river with care, always alert for logjams and sweepers. Though the water is Class 1–2, it is a forested river with narrow corners and limited road access; once in the river, bushwhacking is the only way out. In this waterway, a canoe is more practical and manoeuvrable than a pontoon boat.

Fish the remote upper reaches of this river, concentrating on quick rocky runs and corner pools with undercut banks. When you come across a favourable piece of water there will likely be enough trout to keep you busy for a few hours, because they stack up like cordwood in these prime spots. There are no marked drifts on map books, but the 100 Road is not far from the river during the 50-km drive to Tatuk Lake, so a little bushwhacking or hiking is in order to reach these upper sections.

All river patterns work on the Chilako: Adams, midges, caddis, stoneflies and muddler imitations. Size expectations are an average of 30 cm for rainbow, larger for the occasional Dolly that you might catch in deep pools.

You will often see moving trout on Tory Lake. In mid-June I use a Mikaluk Sedge pattern. *Photo Brian Smith.*

Prince George North

The North country is vast, untamed, misunderstood and under-fished, with the southern beginnings of the Arctic watershed just 43 km from the northern capital—and my home—Prince George. In the 1960s and '70s, Prince George was like today's oil patch of the Peace River country and Alberta—a place to make good money for a short stint. In the forest industry sector, three pulp and paper mills were built, and sawmills abounded. Skilled tradesmen, professionals and entrepreneurs arrived, service businesses sprang up from the growing economy, and the city grew and flourished.

These days the city is evolving into a hub for transportation and a learning centre. In less than fifteen years the new university, UNBC, has become the top-ranked small university in Western Canada and third-ranked in Canada, lagging only behind long-established universities in Atlantic Canada. People want to retire here now—it's no longer a hick mill-town without an identity.

Our forest industry is diminishing; the Interior Plateau has over fifteen million hectares of beetle-infested mature pine forest to dispose of and renew, and the new forest can't be harvested for fifty years after planting, and longer after natural generation. We need to diversify our economy, have the vision to recognize new opportunities and evolve within our region's given strengths: land, water, wildlife and natural resources in abundance.

Outdoor recreation is one of those strengths, a golden target for clean future resource development. I discussed the Nechako River opportunity in Chapter 4; others exist within the areas both north and east of Prince George—areas of sparse population but with high densities of wildlife sustained by mountains, lakes and rivers. Tourist recreation prospects are plentiful: fishing, hunting, skiing, snowmobiling, hiking—all in an area of forty thousand square kilometres with fewer than one hundred thousand inhabitants.

It's the fly fishing that we are interested in, arguably the best the Central Interior has to offer. Driving north from Prince George up Hart Hwy. 97, in five minutes the elevation abruptly increases from 575 m at city centre to 700 m, and the highway remains roughly at that height for the 250-km drive to the Pine Pass in the northern Rockies.

It's hilly terrain; every valley has a creek or river forming lakes where it spreads. All watersheds have some form of fish, the majority are native strains and species left to their own resources, unaffected by provincial fish-stocking programs.

The country north of Summit Lake abounds with water, the landscape fed from small lakes, creeks, streams and big rivers that run north to Williston Lake Reservoir. The rivers and lakes are remote, not classed as "destination" waters by the fly fishing elite because of their distance and limited access, but are chock full of native wild fish. The waterways are steeped in early BC history; the fur-trading post at Fort McLeod, situated in the middle of our northern section, was the first European settlement west of the Rockies.

The rivers of the Carrier First Nation's voyageurs and trappers are still here: the Crooked, Parsnip, Nation, Fraser, McLeod and Peace; those that led the adventurers and their bounties of fur back to the North West Company's western headquarters at Fort Chipewyan in Northern Alberta. They produce a variety of native sport fish: rainbow, arctic grayling, Dolly Varden, bull trout, rocky mountain whitefish, burbot and northern pike minnow. All can be caught on the fly, with rainbow and grayling the choice for the dry fly, and the big and aggressive but elusive bulls greedily taking subsurface minnow patterns or anything that appears to be food, including small rodents that stumble into the water systems.

A good reference book for this area is the Angler's Atlas *Omineca Lakes Region 7A*; the best detailed maps are found in the Mussio Ventures *Backroad Mapbook: Northern BC*. Both are readily available from fishing supply stores in Prince George.

Eena Lake
Elevation: 762 m
Surface area: 45 ha
Maximum depth: 23 m
Mean depth: 6 m
Annual stocking records: 2005–1993: 5,000 Pennask, all female triploids, AF3N. 2008–2006: 5,000 Blackwater AF3N.

Eena Lake is the closest lake to Prince George that produces a quality trout fishery. It's accessed by turning west off the Hart Hwy. onto Chief Lake Road, about 15 km north of the Hart Bridge. Continue for about 12 km, and then follow

Chief Lake Road as it takes a right turn north. After 5 km, turn west on Eena Lake Road for 2 km, left on Woods Road, and then right on Quinn Road, which leads you to the boat launch. There are no campsites or facilities, the boat launch is only suitable for car toppers, and the one restriction is electric motors only.

Eena opens early in the year, normally late April, although I have fished it as early as Easter weekend in mid-April. It's a small lake with two deep holes, one of 23 m at the north end, another of 14 m at the south end, which give the fish holding areas with cool water during hot weather. Eena has a lot of structure, from an island in the southwest to widespread weedbeds, shoals, points and inlets throughout the lake. The lake was rehabilitated in the late '80s, restocked with non-spawning Pennask Lake triploid females, and reopened in the early '90s to really good fishing. Over the past several years Eena has begun to produce chunky trout in the 50-cm range in spite of pressure from ice fishing and easy access throughout all seasons.

Mayflies, caddis, damselflies, chironomids, dragonflies and freshwater shrimp—all are in abundance at Eena. When conditions are right in late May and throughout June the mayfly hatch is phenomenal, and can produce spectacular dry fly fishing, especially during warm, cloudy afternoons. Chironomids, shrimp and leeches are staple patterns at all times. One of the best areas to work a fly is the west side of the small island, where you'll find an extensive weedbed that runs northeast to southwest from the deep hole in the north end. This area is 2–6 m deep, contains a wealth of structure, and can be worked thoroughly with floating, intermediate full-sinking or sink-tip lines. During warm summer days, put on your # 3–6 full-sinking line and work the shelves surrounding the deep holes, but always anticipate dry fly action during evenings, while enjoying the long summer nights and red sunset skies of Prince George North.

Vivian Lake
Elevation: 779 m
Surface area: 45.1 ha
Maximum depth: 8 m
Mean depth: 4 m
Annual stocking records: 2008–2001: 5,000 Pennask/Tunkwa rainbows; 10–20,000 eastern brook trout, Aylmer AF3N.

Vivian is another little lake in close proximity to Prince George that offers the local angler an opportunity to get in a few hours of fishing during the evening and still be home in time to tuck in the kids or to get a good night's sleep. To access Vivian, travel west on Chief Lake Road, which continues as Ness Lake

Road past the 12-km mark. Vivian is found beyond the pavement, a few kilometres along the gravel section, by turning north on Exer Road, which follows the lakeshore and takes you to a rough but solid boat launch road at the northwest end of the lake. It is possible to access Vivian with a boat-mounted trailer and 4x4 vehicle, however, this involves backing down a long, rough hill. I suggest that paying the five-dollar launch fee at Vivian Lake Resort is a better option if you trailer a boat.

The resort is an excellent option for family fun. New owners, Arlene and Brian Ellison and their partners Dave and Carol Ellison, purchased the property in 2007, and are steadily building up a local clientele of weekend visitors and campers who have rediscovered this little gem of a lake, which is only forty minutes from downtown Prince George. They offer cabin rentals (some wheelchair accessible), camping, boat launching, group functions and year-round recreation.

Fishing prospects at Vivian have made a comeback in the past few years, likely from having minimal pressure and a consistent stocking program for many years. Bolstered by the extensive stocking program, there is a substantial inventory of eastern brook trout in the lake; many are reportedly in the 2–3-kg range, but they are tough to catch. Most fly anglers target rainbows, and manage to take the odd brookie if they are fishing deeply-sunk scud or muddler patterns. I haven't solved the puzzle, but I know that some lucky fly fisher will unlock the mystery of catching eastern brook trout regularly at Vivian, and will have some fine fishing as a reward for the effort.

Substantial weedbeds at the north and south ends of Vivian cultivate immense populations of scud, damsels, midges, mayflies and leeches that grow good-sized chunky trout. It is not a deep lake, maximum 8 m, which makes the entire lake fishable with a #3 sink line, or even intermediate in most situations. Pennask rainbows like to feed in mid-depths, and are well-suited to this water. I like to fish the shelves at the north and south ends, venturing from shallow to deeper water until I find the feeding zone. The lake vegetation at Vivian is a dominant green; most of your fly patterns should also be shades of pale olive green.

Lakes of Eskers Provincial Park

The eskers formed ten thousand years ago when glaciers receded, leaving gravel and sand ridges that shaped the unique land formations dominating the park. The collapsing ice also left behind small lakes, which were recently stocked with eastern brook trout along with rainbow in an attempt to create a sustainable and diversified fishery. The brookies also propagated a number of neighbouring lakes through connecting streams, enabling the char to become the dominant species over rainbows. Unlike our native rainbows, brook trout are able to spawn in lake systems that have decent gravel beds; connecting streams are just a bonus to them. Lately, the focus of our provincial fisheries management team in the North has been on rebuilding the rainbow fishery in Eskers Park, and using sterile triploid stocks of brook trout when stock is needed.

The lakes of Eskers Park are a float tuber's paradise! Turning north off Ness Lake Road (which accesses Vivian Lake) at the very end of Ness Lake, the south end of Eskers Park is accessed by a well-signed paved and short gravel road suitable for all vehicle travel. A good trail heads north from the parking lot; the first stop at 3 km is Camp Lake, then Kathie Lake at 6 km. As always with fishing, the longer the hike, the better the prospects. This is true with Kathie, especially during the fall season, when it can be very good. If you're up for a little more hiking, rumour has it that Byers Lake, located by a short trail from the west end of Kathie, is well heeled with brookies too. Check out the other lakes that connect with creeks and streams in this area—bets are on that they're propagated with brookies and you just may find a "secret" fishing spot for yourself.

Crooked River

Summit Lake is the southern boundary of the Arctic watershed, and little Crooked River flows from the north end of the lake. Because the elevation of the plateau changes very little past the Hart Highlands of Prince George, the Crooked runs quietly for much of its journey to McLeod Lake. The swamps and ever-present willow thickets, plus the leisurely pace of Class 1–2 water make it an ideal canoeing river for wildlife enthusiasts of all ages and physical abilities. Be prepared, however, for obstacles, short portages over and around beaver dams, blockages, and some long stretches of slack water that require paddling. When canoeing or kayaking the Crooked, I recommend wearing waders and good footwear because many obstacles cannot be navigated through thick willows on the shoreline and the soft and dangerous river bottom around numerous beaver dams. Sometimes, the only passage is over or through the barrier on foot.

The Crooked is another local river that is always fishable because it empties a lake and, having only a few small tributary creeks, never blows out. The Class 1–2 water is better by canoe or kayak than by pontoon or motorboat because it's narrow and shallow in many spots, posing navigation problems. The river is open year-round, restricted to 10-hp motors, and catch-and-release for rainbow trout April 1 to June 30.

The Crooked River system is a wilderness experience seldom offered to fly fishers who live in close proximity to a major city like Prince George. The rainbow and coarse fish are likely propagated from original Carp Lake species, creating what I believe are genetically common strains of fishes. The many connecting lakes along the Crooked and the McLeod rivers through to Carp Lake and the Williston Reservoir offer both winter refuge and ideal spring breeding opportunities for all species of wild fish that inhabit the waterways.

The complete 80–100-km snaking length of the Crooked River to McLeod Lake can be drifted. The best time is early summer around the June solstice, when the river is still high enough from runoff to be navigable, mayfly and caddis hatches are in full swing, and days are long. By midsummer, it's shallow and requires a lot of lining, bushwhacking, and navigation of beaver dams to get through the difficult sections. The Crooked is accessed by a number of logging roads north of Summit Lake, and hosts several spots for overnight camping and river runs.

Crooked River Run
#1—Summit Lake to Railroad Track at Hwy. 97 North
The Tallus Road, a few kilometres past the first visible sighting of Summit Lake on your left, will take you to the top end put-in. There is a Forest Service campsite and boat launch for large boats at Summit Lake, which is an ideal spot for headquarters as it is only a few kilometres from the upper bridge crossing and your drift launch area.

This first journey is about 10 km and will take you close to Hwy. 97 North, where there is a take-out on the east side over the railroad track. Along all of the Crooked River routes, the best trout fishing is found at creek entrances, in gravel-lined quick sections, corners and tail-out seams. Once you recognize these spots and stop to fish them, you will find fish stacked in these areas—action can be non-stop. Unless you find trout rising to a hatch, scoot through all of the slow-moving water to find gravel bottom and quick runs, where trout will be waiting.

Crooked River Run
#2—Railroad Track at Hwy. 97 North to 100 Road Bridge
This section is accessed from the Hwy. 97 North take-out from Crooked River Run #1, marked by a creek going under the highway and a concrete barrier, about 8 km north of Tallus Road at Summit Lake. There is a short dirt road leading to the river, which has a couple of rough campsites available for a tent or truck-and-camper unit.

There are a few nice runs that hold trout right at this section. The put-in for the drift to the 100 Road Bridge is best accessed by going over the track a few hundred yards downstream of the campsite. The float to the bridge is about 5 km, the first section slow moving and unproductive, but once the river narrows and gets into the bush the current picks up, gravel sections are noticeable and fishing can be excellent.

Crooked River Run
#3—100 Road to 200 Road

The 100 Road is also accessed from Hwy. 97 North, about 65 km north of Prince George. The access spot is at the Forest Service campsite at the 100 Road Bridge take-out, which is only a few kilometres from the highway. The lower section of this run is probably the best water on the Crooked, boasting Livingstone Springs, warm, spring water that keeps this section open year-round, and excellent fish-holding water at the 200 Bridge run. Some fly fishers enjoy the challenge of fighting snowbanks and deep drifts along the river to get in a little winter fishing recreation; others pull their canoes or pontoon boats from storage, put in at the 200 Bridge, and paddle upriver to the springs to try

Danie Erasmus tangles with a wild rainbow on the Crooked River.
Photo Nathan Shaw.

their luck. During late winter, small midge hatches will begin, the trout will turn on in this section and the fly shops will be abuzz about the great winter fishing on the Crooked.

It's about a 10-km drift from the 100 Road Bridge to the Crooked River Canyon FS Recreation Site at the 200 Road Bridge. Unfortunately, the first 6 km are mostly slack water. When I floated the run with Danie Erasmus in June 2007, we paddled our pontoon boats about two hours before we found fishy-looking water. We had to navigate several bush jams and beaver dams; none of the obstacles were insurmountable, but the lack of productive fishing water made for a short day of "fishing time."

Fishing here is the same as in the upper section; concentrate your efforts on the fast water and transition areas with structure, and move through the slow sections. For a drift alone without a partner (I don't recommend this, but some people do it), you can launch a pontoon boat at the 200 Road Bridge, paddle upstream with little effort and challenges, then fish back to the bridge. Livingstone Springs is about a twenty minute paddle upstream from the 200 Bridge. It's difficult to describe how to recognize this fertile area of the Crooked as there is no visible spring; only a swampy area of stubby willow growth and an increase of weed cover in the river. The spring meanders in many directions as it quietly perks out of the ground, lending life and much-needed open water to overwintering white swans, and offering a refuge to hungry fish during all seasons.

Crooked River Run
#4—200 Bridge to Davie Lake

The fourth drift of the upper section is from the 200 Road Bridge downstream to Davie Lake, about a 4-km float that begins with a short canyon section of Class 2-rated rapids at the bridge, the journey ending at the lake take-out.

The rest of the Crooked River runs quietly through a series of small lakes: Davie, Redrocky, Kerry, and ending at beautiful McLeod Lake, another one of our Northern jewels. All of these lakes contain native trout and coarse fish, some better fishing than others. These sections are not marked canoe routes, but access to the river is available at each of the lakes, and the river is a leisurely paddle through all segments. These slow sections change every year. New beaver dams are built and old ones vacated, and as the river changes its course an adventurer must be able to recognize and navigate through obstacles that don't appear on the maps. Be prepared for and expect some rigorous exercise whenever you run a river.

Fly fishing on the Crooked can be very good, but also difficult if you don't find fish where they are supposed to be, so you have to be prepared to do some prospecting and river-wading to access remote reaches and the better stretches that are away from the busy bridge runs. Fly patterns are not tricky—the standard river selection will take fish.

I recall a warm mid-June evening on the Crooked 100 Road Bridge run several years ago. Mayfly and caddis hatches were overlapping and there were countless bugs in the air, so plentiful I was concerned about opening my mouth and taking an unwanted meal. There were so many trout and whitefish surfacing for the morsels it was difficult to concentrate on the drift of the fly; if one missed it, the next fish would take it. My buddy and I fished well into dark, releasing dozens of trout in the 30–35-cm size range—conditions were right, and the trout thought so too!

Mature native rainbow trout of the Crooked are a truly beautiful strain: heavily spotted, sleek, and banded by a red stripe and gills. Some fly fishers insist (and I agree) they are the prettiest trout in the North.

Crooked River Provincial Park

Whether it's hiking, fishing, suntanning or just sitting around, this regional park offers something for everyone. Trophy trout fishing is a short ten-minute walk from the campground to Hart Lake, and about twenty minutes away there is fishing by belly boat in seclusion at Squaw (Square) Lake or hiking and river fishing at Livingston Springs on the Crooked River. Wildlife can be viewed everywhere in the park, and the provincial campground and day-use picnic sites on Bear Lake boast sandy beaches and the warmest water in the Prince George area.

The park encompasses 873 ha, heavily forested with local species of trees: birch, lodgepole pine, spruce and alder. During berry season in July and August, huckleberries, saskatoon and low-bush mountain blueberries are plentiful, along with gooseberries, black currants, raspberries, strawberries and salmonberries. Wild cranberries mature later in the summer. The park really is a wonderful area; with the logging community of Bear Lake a few kilometres up the road, supplies can be replenished for your day trips around the area. Centring your activities at the campground, various journeys from a short hike to an hour's drive can lead you into some of the North's best fishing in small lakes and medium-sized rivers, the bonus being very little pressure from other anglers because of the vastness of the area. Most lakes and rivers have small Forest Service campsites, where you can camp for free and get the wilderness feeling to boot.

For full detailed information on the park, the website can be found at www.britishcolumbia.com/parks.

Hart Lake

Elevation: 715 m

Surface area: 56 ha

Maximum depth: 9 m

Mean depth: 5 m

Annual stocking records: 2007–2005: 10,000 Blackwater AF3N and diploid (2N). 2004–1996: 10,000 Blackwater/Dragon. 1995–1993: 30,000 Premier/Dragon.

Hart Lake has been the trophy rainbow trout fishery of Prince George for fifteen years, consistently producing trout in the 50–60-cm class, the average size 35–45 cm. The lake lies within the boundaries of ooked River Provincial Park, a ten-minute trail-walk from the campsite on Bear Lake.

When I moved north in 1992, Hart Lake quickly became my go-to fishing water, my recreation expanding to other waters soon after. Having previously concentrated my fly fishing in the southern half of the province, I was amazed at the average size and quantity of these northern trout in comparison to the Kamloops area; twenty-fish days became common, forty not unrealistic and under ten a "quiet" day on the water. Hart Lake is one of the reasons I stay in this part of the country.

Hart is accessed by pavement, a right turn into the parking lot 0.5 km before the Crooked River Park turn-in. There is no direct boat launch; however, I have seen all makes and models of small boats dragged over the tracks and down to the water to get in a day's fishing. The best and easiest method to fish Hart is by float tube, pontoon boat or canoe. The lake is small and round, allowing for a leisurely circle tour in about six hours, a perfect day-tour on a lake.

Fishing is productive all over Hart Lake, including the middle at times, but the four corners and long shelves leading up to them usually produce the best results. In early spring through late June chironomids hatch daily, overlapped by some of the heaviest hatches of mayflies that I have witnessed on any lake. Mayflies will hatch best on cloudy days, often during a nasty thunderstorm, and will continue emerging into August if conditions are right and evenings stay cool. Several years ago, I enjoyed one of my most memorable fishing days ever on Hart during a late-June mayfly hatch—over twenty trout to the Callibaetis spinner one afternoon during a gentle rain, half of them over 50 cm.

During spring, best patterns to fish at Hart are chironomids, bloodworms, small leeches and olive or grey mayfly nymphs. Summer months offer opportunities to fish shrimp, bloodworm and leech patterns. Caddis is not a big diet item at Hart, nor are dragonfly nymphs, but a damsel nymph pattern is deadly during early June right through July.

Fall is gobble-up time at Hart and surrounding lakes as multiple hatches are over. From mid-September to early October, fish feed on the dominant insects that are always available to them: leeches, scud, backswimmers, bloodworm, chaoborus larvae and midge. Interspersed with bottom feeding and the odd midge hatch, trout enjoy the frantic and heroic episode of the mating flight of water boatman, which can last a few weeks and provide fabulous entertainment for the fly fisher.

You have to remember that you are fly fishing in the North country—everything in spring takes place a few weeks later, and lasts a few weeks longer than in the south or the Cariboo. Reverse that scenario in fall—winter comes sooner, and often suddenly. Fishing is about time, temperature, barometer and opportunity!

Wicheeda Lake

Elevation: 898 m
Surface area: 53 ha
Maximum depth: 7 m
Mean depth: 3 m

Annual stocking records: none; wild rainbow trout.
Wicheeda has everything a wilderness fly fisher will ever wish for: breathtaking scenery, wild trout of large average size, remote hike-in access, gin-clear water and white marl shoals. It is the treasure of the North country, and one of my favourite places to fish.

The lake is accessed by the Chuchinka (700) Road bearing east from the community of Bear Lake. Turn right off Hwy. 97 North at the Petro-Can, travel to the end of the paved road and turn right again. Turn left at the stop sign; bear right on the 700 Road, turn left at the 704-km junction, and right at 714 km. The road is good gravel but rough, bumpy and not easy on vehicles and tires; pickup truck or 4x4 recommended. The access road to the trailhead is at about km 56 of the 700 Road where you'll turn right onto the Wichcika FS Road. Shortly you will cross the Wichcika Creek Bridge; access to Wicheeda is about 4 km up the road, where you will take the first left into a clearing and travel a short 4x4 path, which leads to the trailhead access to the lake.

You could possibly drag a canoe or pontoon boat into Wicheeda through the trail, but it would be a lot of work. I recommend a float tube for fishing this lake, which is the easiest to pack for this ten- to fifteen-minute hike. Wicheeda is swampy at the first entry point; the best access is gained by a further five-minute hike through the swamp (I hope you're wearing your waders and boots) and bush to the left along the shoreline, putting in near an old cabin site.

There is access to the north end of the lake via a rough track that is only suited for high clearance, short wheel-base 4x4 or ATV. I haven't been on this road as I don't have a vehicle that I want to risk; however, I have heard of the odd truck-and-camper unit making it in (with a great deal of trouble).

When fishing Wicheeda, I pack only floating and intermediate sink lines as the lake has a glorious number of white marl flats, interspersed with small weed patches in which the trout seek cover. Because the water is crystal clear and the bottom white, you can see the lake's floor in 6 m of depth, and spot trout travelling the rushes and weed patches that surround the lake. Sight fishing is the most rewarding method at Wicheeda; kick your way along the shoreline, marvel at the scenery and watch for cruising fish. With the average trout size of 40–50 cm, coupled with their eager response to dry flies and visual targets, this little lake is a phenomenal experience for the fly fisher. And the trout are silver bullets!

There are two main sections to fish at Wicheeda Lake. The first is the small bay that you enter when you hike in; the second is accessed through a narrow channel at the north end of this bay. The fishing can be so intense and rewarding that it is not uncommon to spend the entire day in the small bay and never venture into the main lake, as has happened to me on most occasions.

The elevation of Wicheeda is almost 900 m, one of the highest trout lakes on the northern Plateau; ice-off and insect hatch activity take place one to two weeks later than most other waters north of Prince George. But because of this elevation, it is a good choice for fishing right through hot summer spells when other waters have turned off. The best times to fish Wicheeda are late May through June after spring turnover using chironomids and damsels, late June through summer using caddis, scud and dragonfly nymphs, and anytime for leech patterns. Northern lakes with cool water like Wicheeda will offer minor midge and chironomid hatches during open water at all times of year—always be prepared to seek feeding trout activity with a size 16–18 midge or chironomid dry and pupae patterns.

It's strange how memories about fishing exploits haunt your soul. I recall vividly a Labour Day weekend several years ago, when I trekked into this little lake for the umpteenth time. As is often the norm at Wicheeda, my partner and I were the only ones on the lake; the water had cooled, and fish were on the prowl for anything that resembled food because winter was only a month or two away. It was cold the night before, the trail and brushes were covered in melting hoarfrost and fall was in full colour. Fishing was slow to begin with; the sun needed to warm the lake surface for activity to begin. Around noon, trout started to move in the little bay. There was no hatch activity, but I had that intuitive feeling that this was going to be a banner day. Well, I put on a #10 Caddis Tan dry fly, hunted the shoals and weed patches for rises, and all hell broke loose for four hours; a spectacular afternoon of ten-plus trout coming to the net. The largest was 60 cm, average 45–50 cm; as memorable a day as I can recall anytime or anywhere for rainbows of this size and quality.

Wicheeda is a fragile fishery. The regulations are: daily limit quota of three trout, bait ban and single barbless hook. If you fish this lake, please respect the resource and the thousands of years it took to generate the lineage. These are wild native trout, and deserve to be released with care and reverence.

Firth Lake System—Firth, Hourston, Junkers and Unnamed Lakes

The Firth Lake system is another unique area of Prince George North that supports a wild rainbow trout fishery, offering both superb angling for voracious natural trout and a remote wilderness experience equal to anywhere in the province. To witness the rise or pull of a wild trout to a fly, and to admire the strength of its battle is both a humbling and rewarding moment in a fly fisher's life; these times don't come often enough for most of us. These lakes are connected by a common creek system, intertwined in a twenty-square-kilometre net of water ending in the Parsnip River. The trout are likely a common strain, which I believe is related to the Crooked River species. Like mature Crooked River trout, the fish are heavily marked with stripes and spots, beautiful creatures to behold.

Main logging roads to the lakes of this area are best accessed by 4x4 pickup truck or high-clearance RV. The access routes from the main to Firth and Junkers lakes are 4x4 only, as they are steep little tracks that are slick when wet and rough all of the time. More than one truck and camper has stalled on the Firth Lake campsite exit and been marooned for a few days, waiting for a pull from another 4x4. Junkers has only one camping spot that is suitable for a tent only, and not accessible by truck and camper because of turnaround restrictions. Hourston is accessed by paddling through the northeast channel of Firth, and the two unnamed lakes are reached by continuing past Junkers a few kilometres and taking a short hike through the bush.

I get the chance to fish the Firth system only about three or four times per year; after all, there is a huge amount of fishing pleasure to accomplish in a short four months of prime angling time. If I were to choose the perfect time to camp and fish Firth, Junkers and their nearby waters, I would opt for the best lunar periods (dark moons/last quarters) somewhere in the four weeks of late June to mid-July. Chironomid, midge and mayflies are still active, damsels, caddis and dragonflies are beginning to appear, and scuds and leeches will always work when nothing else is happening. If the lakes are off, within twenty minutes' to an hour's drive you can be fishing the Crooked, Pack or McLeod rivers for their wild trout.

Firth Lake
Elevation: 814 m
Surface area: 377 ha
Maximum depth: 36 m
Mean depth: 16 m
Stocking records: none; wild rainbow trout.

Firth Lake is accessed from the 42 Mile Main Road, which splits east from Hwy. 97 North just past Whiskers Bay Resort. Travel this main road for about 5 km, and take a left at the BC Hydro communication building just past the substation; continue down this short path and steep hill to Firth, where there are five FS campsites and a car-top boat launch.

Firth is a large lake, containing six times the acreage of Hart and scattered with numerous sunken islands, which always makes for exciting fly fishing. Ideally, a boat and motor is the best method to cover the lake's hot spots and drop-off zones. When I see the bathometric record of a lake with sunken islands, I want to salivate—my thoughts return to similar lakes of the Kamloops area where I learned to trout-fish in the 1970s: Peterhope, Plateau, Roche, Hihium, Lac le Jeune and Knouff.

Lakes that have irregular bottom depths create an underwater terrain much like a mountain range; fish follow the valleys of a lake like automobiles travel an alpine road, weaving through the contours in packs, cleverly seeking the protection of deeper shelves, but hanging close to the weed line where food opportunity and sustenance are nearby. Seasoned trout fishers know this, and learn to fish drop-offs and islands in such a way that these feeding zones and travel paths are covered completely. It simply becomes a matter of *when* the trout will appear in these zones, not *if* they will materialize. I like to anchor on top of these islands, or work the circular edges, casting to deep water or along the ledges, working the fly slowly through the corridor of cruising fish.

Firth, because of its hilly topography, presents wonderful challenges for fly fishers to create their own luck. The south corner has a raised island and a sunken island 3 m deep, located 10–20 m off the inside depression on the south side. This corner has a graduated series of shelves starting at the shore, slowly dropping from 3 m to 27 m deep past the raised island.

The northwest corner also contains generous trout habitat terrain. There is a graduated shelf, and a small inlet bay that is prime caddis, dragonfly and damsel environment. These insects love flats and shelves that contain lush weed growth and less than 4 m of water.

At the north end, you have a variety of good fishing potential: a raised island with shoals around it, a sunken island on the northeast side buried in 3 m of water, and a channel leading to Hourston Lake with a progression of gradients from 12 to 3 m deep. Off the north tip of the raised island is the deepest hole in the lake at 36 m. The north end is potentially the spot where the largest fish will hang out—lots of structure, deep holding water and feeding flats to encourage insect life.

Hourston Lake

Firth and Hourston lakes are joined by a short channel located at the north end of Firth. Unfortunately, there is no bathometric or history record for the lake, but details pertaining to fish inventory at Firth apply to Hourston because of the connecting channel.

Hourston is a narrow lake at the canal access, opening into a wider bay, with a creek outlet running east to the Parsnip River. The total acreage is about one-fifth the size of Firth, enough water to hold fish, but isolated from Firth in a more wilderness setting—a nice environment to play in.

Junkers Lake

Oh, Junkers—it's another of my favourite lakes in the North, where you won't catch many limits, but you will be rewarded by wild trout of large average-size, beautiful scenery and an almost hallowed experience.

Junkers is accessed by turning onto Firth Lake Forest Service Road, about 30 km north of Bear Lake. This road does not carry on to Firth Lake, but accesses Junkers and the two unnamed lakes in the Firth Lake system. At the decommissioned spot, hang a right over the creek culvert and then a quick left; travel east about fifteen minutes, staying on this main road, which will turn north at a junction. From a high point in the road, Junkers will shortly come into view on the left. The path down is steep and a bit rough, but not a problem for 4x4 vehicles; if you can't chance it, park up top and walk your gear down. One of my local fishing buddies, Danie Erasmus, won't take his new Toyota down this access path yet—we take my more experienced Chevy when we go to Junkers. The lake is pickup boat launch only, best fished with float tube, pontoon boat, canoe or small craft.

Junkers, like Hourston, has no historical records. The trout are wild, propagated through the interconnecting creek system from Firth Lake. The lake is about 1.5-km long, and 0.5-km wide, with a shallow and narrow neck in the middle that splits the lake and opens into the north bay. Junkers offers prime fish habitat, owing to generous weedbeds, marl shoals, and deep holes offering cover and protection.

If I were a trout, I think I could enjoy life at Junkers because there are few visitors. Last October, during hunting season, I spent two hours on the lake flirting and taking photos of a feeding bull moose before he decided that I had floated too close to him, and he rumbled off into the bush. A party of hunters was camped up top off the main road, but they had already killed and hung three moose; the area has lots of big game.

Because of its small size, Junkers can be thoroughly fished in a day. I like to concentrate on the shelf areas: one in front of and around the small island, another at the inlet and outlet necks of the shallow channel, and the last in the far north end near the inlet creek. The trout are strong and frisky, ranging in size from 30–60 cm, averaging about 45 cm. They dance all over the lake when hooked, and don't give up easily. Junkers is another nugget in the North.

McLeod River

If you are from the Lower Mainland and have done some exploring with your fly rod, you'll understand what I mean when I compare the McLeod River drainage to the Skagit River. They have similarities: fertile water with trail access, wild and explosive rainbows, untouched scenery and a small-river feeling. The comparisons stop when you consider fishing pressure, because the McLeod receives no more than a few handfuls of fly fishers in a *season*. During my twice-yearly fishing excursions to the McLeod over the past ten years, I have never encountered another party of fly fishers on the stream. Those are pretty good odds! The McLeod is artificial fly fishing only, and is home to several indigenous strains of fish: rainbow and Dolly Varden trout, whitefish and northern pike minnow.

McLeod River is part of the Carp Lake drainage, containing an area of about two thousand square kilometres west of the community of Fort McLeod. The river begins in the drainage about 20 km west of Carp Lake, picks up small tributary creeks and a few unnamed lakes and swamps, flows into the west corner of Carp Lake, and finally exits from the north end. Access to the river at the outflows from Carp and War lakes can be travelled safely by automobile. At the community of Fort McLeod, turn west onto Carp Lake Road at the Carp Lake Provincial Park sign; the McLeod River, though never visible, roughly parallels this narrow road on the right side for the 32 km into Carp Lake. The first road access point is the bridge crossing at km 22, where the McLeod descends into a spectacular series of cascades and drops, the War Falls. As you travel farther to

Carp Lake, the river is now on your left. Access to the McLeod River Trail can be gained at various points: War, Rainbow and Minnow lakes campgrounds, at several parking pullouts, and finally at the Carp Lake Campground headwaters.

To access the less civilized west section that runs into Carp Lake, turn west onto the 100 Road off Hwy. 97 North about 6 km south of Bear Lake community, then northwest onto the Davie Muskeg (200) FS Road at km 213. Stay on this FSR to about km 300 where the McLeod crosses the road just past the 8800 Road. I have not fished this area of the McLeod, and have no history on the inventory, but I'm sure it contains fish. Like much of this wilderness north of Prince George, the fishing remains relatively unchallenged except for local knowledge.

In addition to the Davie Muskeg (200) Road, access to the headwaters of the McLeod can also be gained from the Carp Lake Campground by 4x4 vehicles. Continue past the campsite to km 34, travel west on the McLeod Tsilcoh FS Road to about km 52, then south on the Davie Muskeg (200) Road about 10 km to the bridge.

Trout fishing the McLeod can be exhilarating; forty-trout days are common during the peak caddis and mayfly hatch activity season in July and August, tapering off in September as river flows diminish. A few years back, I released sixty-five rainbows one afternoon in early August, all on a #16 caddis. The best dry fly patterns, and probably all you'll ever need on the McLeod, are of the caddis and mayfly variety. An adult stonefly or stimulator pattern will also take fish; however, the stonefly hatch is usually waning by the time the river opens to fishing on July 1. These wild trout don't seem to care about finesse and don't see many fly patterns; if it floats high and looks like an insect, it'll be attacked after a short drift.

McLeod River is a walk-and-wade adventure. The total length is 58 km; some of the areas in the section above War Lake could perhaps be fished by canoe, but it's too narrow in many spots for a pontoon boat or other craft, and not worth the effort of dragging a vessel through the trails. I recommend you carry bear spray, fish with a buddy and make lots of noise when walking rivers in this part of the country because bears seem to enjoy a walk along a river trail as much as we do, and this is grizzly habitat.

One of my favourite sections of the McLeod is along the interpretive trail to War Falls, which follows the river from the parking lot and park entrance sign above the bridge at km 22. There are four substantial cascades totaling 500 m of river that make up the falls, the last about 15 m high. Below the last waterfall and the trail's end, the river dumps into a deep pool, then gently flows into numerous runs and glides along the route to McLeod Lake, 30-odd river kilometres away.

I have caught only small trout between the cascades; but the section below produces rainbows up to 40 cm, average 25–30 cm, and a few bull trout over 60 cm. I have fished only about three corners downriver from the lower falls because my time has usually been spent playing and releasing trout most of the day. The farther you descend the river, the more tangled it is with deadfalls, sweepers and logjams that need to be traversed. I haven't been down more than a half-kilometre, but the tributary McDougall River enters about 7 km downstream from the bridge run. So much more to explore…

Carp Lake

Elevation: 846 m
Surface Area: 5,676 ha
Maximum depth: 39 m
Mean depth: 17 m
Stocking records: none; wild rainbow trout, many species of coarse fish, and burbot.

Carp Lake was an important fishery for Carrier Native Indians for hundreds of years before Simon Fraser established Trout Lake Fort at Fort McLeod in 1805. Fraser stated in his journal that the Carrier Indians came to the lake "to catch immense numbers of fish of the *carp* kind," and so named the lake. I think these fish would be burbot, a species of freshwater cod for which Carp is recognized and targeted by local fishers.

Carp is accessed by continuing along Carp Lake Road past the McLeod River access points to km 32. The lake is classed as a family destination for many reasons: It is within a provincial park offering over one hundred campsites, playground, horseshoe pits and picnic shelter. There is also a boat launch suitable for large craft, hiking trails and a variety of fishing challenges. The north shore has extensive sandy beaches, though the water is pretty cold for swimming through most of the summer season. There are wilderness campsites on several of the many islands that dot the lake, offering tenters a backwoods experience seldom afforded through the Provincial Parks program.

Carp is a monstrous lake by Northern terms—one would think it lends itself to trolling flies and lures with motorized vessels, but it has enough structure with islands, shelves and channels to be an effective fly fisher's paradise. Most of the shoreline is gradual sandy beach, tapering to 6 m deep for several hundred metres, slowly dropping to 36 m. Carp's deep zone of 18–36 m covers about 50 percent of the total surface area of the lake, benefiting the fishery and allowing a high-quality fishery through the season.

Against the Cariboo and Rocky Mountains

Heading east from Prince George on Hwy. 16, your first impression of the Interior Plateau leading to the Rockies is about the landscape you are entering: low mountains forested with an abundance of spruce; clear virgin streams draining to the Fraser; pristine lakes; and, mostly, a noticeable lack of settlement. Seldom do you venture 10 km east of the city without encountering moose or bear, even grizzlies, and scads of lesser game.

About 80 km east of Prince George, you'll pass through an ancient stand of old-growth cedar that follows the Rocky Mountain Trench and stretches south past Blue River. This interior rainforest, nurtured by heavy rainfall during summer and high snowpacks of long harsh winters, sustains cedars in a region that only a few hundred kilometres south is too dry to support them.

North and east of Prince George, the Rocky Mountain Trench separates into the Arctic and Pacific watersheds. When you look at the maps of this area you'll notice an absence of large lakes, but a maze of small and medium-sized lakes and creeks, and a number of good-sized rivers that flow into the Fraser: the Salmon, Willow, McGregor, Torpy, Bowron, Morkill, Goat, Dore and Holmes. These rivers drain the thirty thousand square kilometres that comprise the quadrant in this chapter, the creeks and small lakes containing the fishing secrets of an area that is relatively unexplored by most sports fishers, and remains a mystery to most of us who venture into it. It's quite untapped and, for the adventurer, takes many years of searching and wandering to get to know and understand its bountiful fishery resource. I am unfolding only a smidgeon of local knowledge; I'm sure there are many more chapters to be written about this part of the region in future years.

All of the rivers and creeks contain fish, but most of the native trout in streams of this quadrant are small, except for the gregarious bull trout; rarely will you catch trout over 40 cm, the average size being 20–30 cm in creeks and rivers. There are, however, many small named and nameless lakes that hold trout in the 50–60-cm range but are rarely fished—these treasures are waiting to be discovered by adventurous souls, perhaps through reading these pages.

Willow Forest Service Road Access

The Willow FSR is a good all-season road that takes the fly fisher over 100 km southeast of Prince George into the logging grids and waters of the Stony, Narrow and Bowron lakes drainage. To access it, drive about 20 km south of Prince George on Hwy. 97, and turn east on Willow FSR, which slices across the south end of the Buckhorn area of rural Prince George, then cuts into the bush and heads into hilly and mountainous terrain that stretches to the Cariboo Mountains.

The area has many roadside lakes that are good camping spots, Francis and Ste Marie lakes for example, but they are not known for their fishing. There are, however, some pretty good waters along the route, with a balance of creek and river fishing for wild rainbow and Dolly Varden, lake fishing for rainbows that are both the wild and stocked variety, and deep lake fishing for native lake trout.

Frost Lake
Elevation: 908 m
Surface area: 27 ha
Maximum depth: 5 m
Mean depth: 3 m
Stocking records: none; wild rainbow trout, coarse fish (suckers).

At about km 28 of the Willow FSR, the unmarked Frost Lake Road cuts north. Take this road, make an early right at the first logging road, and you'll jostle and bounce along this rough little route for 10 km to Frost Lake. The road is bumpy but firm with rock and gravel base and there is no danger of being stuck, but pickup or 4x4 is recommended for clearance and slower speed control options.

Frost is a neat little lake. The trout are wild and scrappy and, when chironomids are popping, will take small midge dry flies off the surface all day long. There are some larger brood fish of 50–60 cm, but the average trout is about 30 cm, normal for a small non-stocked lake.

Frost doesn't get much attention from the crowds, averaging only a few fishing days per month. It is a place of solitude with a meadow campsite, good parking and car-top boat launch. The bay to the left of the campsite is weedy and only 2–3 m deep, but can be fast fishing, holding mostly small nursery trout of 20–30 cm. The 4–5 m deep hole in Frost is oblong in shape, the middle of it running east to west directly in front of the campsite. My best luck for larger fish has been along the shoreline to the east end, mooching among the cover of snags and sunken timber.

Frost is excellent chironomid water: larva, pupa and adult. Leech patterns are also effective because of the dark, tannin-coloured water.

Opatcho Lake

Elevation: 833 m

Surface area: 40 ha

Maximum depth: 24 m

Mean depth: 7 m

Annual socking records: 2008–2004: 2,500–3,000 Blackwater/Dragon AF3N yearlings; Tunkwa/Premier stock in earlier years.

Opatcho has been managed as a trophy fishery for the sixteen years I have resided in Prince George, and I wish I could say it has been good to me because it's a nice little lake: gin-clear water, abundant shoals, a deep hole of 25 m, and a good campsite with easy access. Trouble is, the fish can be moody as hell, and can produce more zero days than any lake I know in this region. It's got that nasty reputation, however, of seducing fly fishers by throwing the odd 60-cm, 3-kg trout in your direction. What self-respecting fly fisher will not put up with a few fishless days to grapple with one of those lunkers? If you can hit it when it's on, you're in for a heck of a show.

Opatcho is easy to get to by taking a left turn north at about km 41 of the Willow FSR. There are six campsites, a car-top boat launch that is one of the best around and one year-round residence on the lake, which was a fishing lodge many years ago.

Opatcho Lake has a long shelf of 1–2 m deep water off the boat launch, and one also off the west end, which graduates in a circular fashion from 3 m to the 25-m hole in the middle. Ringed with weedbeds, especially the west end, the lake supports prolific hatches of chironomids, mayflies, damsels and dragonflies. Leech patterns dragged deeply over the ledges are excellent producers of large trout when hatches are not available, but I think the best opportunities of the season to catch the lunkers of Opatcho could be during the first mayfly hatches of spring, or when damselflies begin their shoreward migration, around the end of May or early June.

Lakes like Opatcho with circular ledges can be a challenge to the fly fisher. Often I see trollers working them in a straight line, which only allows you to fish one depth of water. I like to fish them in a zigzag fashion, shallow to deep and back to shallow, until I find the correct zone where trout are lying or I notice hatching activity that will bring trout onto a shoal. In lakes like Opatcho, fish often will travel in a circular direction when feeding, mooching their way along at a preferred depth, sometimes slipping back into deeper water for relief, and then reappearing on the same line twenty minutes later. Experienced fly fishers recognize this habitual activity, and adjust their method to take advantage of the feeding lanes.

Opatcho can be a humbling lake—I usually give it a go once or twice a year, generally when I'm in the mood for a possible skunk, or have had my fill of banner fishing days elsewhere. It's one of those lakes that you can fish all day waiting for a strike, and more often than not bust a big bugger off because you've been surprised when it does happen, which is why I keep going back for more.

Willow River

Hardly anyone fishes the Willow River, especially with a fly rod. I've seen spin casters and worm droppers working the deep corner runs on occasion, but have never witnessed a fly fisher or pontoon boat on the water. I think it's another well-kept secret of the Prince George area, just waiting for fly fishers to explore. Like the Bowron, the Willow has wild trout that average 25–35 cm, and is protected by allowing retention of nothing less than 30 cm, which keeps the easy-to-catch nursery stock in abundant supply.

Willow, a medium-sized river similar to Blackwater and Salmon rivers, begins in the valleys near the historic town of Wells northeast of Quesnel, and flows northwest to enter the Fraser about 30 km north of Prince George. It collects the drainage area south of the Bowron River watershed and north of the Cottonwood River from hundreds of creeks and lakes to form a major tributary to the Fraser, entering it above the settlement of Shelley.

Upstream of the Willow North Recreation Site, which is 2 km above the Hwy. 16 East rest stop, the Willow is Class 1–2 water, navigable by canoe or pontoon boat. Downstream of the recreation site, the Class 3–5 white water, and especially Willow Canyon below Hwy. 16 should not be attempted even by experienced canoeists, drifters or kayakers.

To access the upper river, continue east past the Opatcho turnoff on the Willow FSR where, at the 41-km bridge, the road splits into Willow (Buck) North FSR and Willow FSR South (500 Road). From this point, the upper river is reached by bearing southeast on the Willow FSR South, the lower river from Willow FSR North. You can also work your way upriver from Hwy. 16 East by turning south onto the Willow North FSR at the rest stop on Hwy. 16 about 30 km east of Prince George, where it's about 20 km to the 41-km bridge and junction.

It's a long way to Hwy. 16 East from Wells where the Willow begins its journey northwest to the Fraser, about 100 km as the crow flies. There are spots where road access is easily gained, but the best way to fish the remote sections and find those secret spots where trout stack up is to drift the river by canoe or pontoon boat. The upper and lower sections have a number of 4–15-km day trips that are worth the effort for the fly fisher; if the fishing isn't up to your speed, the scenery and wildlife will surely entertain you.

Fly fish the Willow as you would all streams in the north: floating line, long leader and dry flies. Our standard dry fly patterns will work well for you: midges, caddis, stoneflies and emergers; for nymph fishing, try mayflies, stoneflies and caddis pupae.

Grizzly Lake East
Elevation: 962 m
Surface area: 72 ha
Maximum depth: 6 m
Mean depth: 2 m
Annual stocking records: 2008–2003: 3,000 Pennask/Premier yearlings.

Sitting on top of the hills surrounding the Willow River drainage, Grizzly Lake is one of those fast-fishing spots that kids and parents can enjoy together. It's an old sawmill site converted into a Forest Service campsite, boasting an open grassy area with room for kids to play, pit toilets, a good car-top boat launch and room for multiple recreational vehicles.

Grizzly East is accessed by turning northeast over the bridge at km 41 of the Willow FSR and continuing to km 47 on the 300 (Coalmine Road), where you bear east on the Grizzly Road for about 5 km to the lake. The access roads are well-travelled and in good condition for all-vehicle travel.

Pennask fish prefer to feed in open water and Grizzly is a perfect lake for this species of rainbow, having a consistent depth of 2–3 m. When you enter the campsite at Grizzly, you think you are facing north up the lake, but you are actually looking southwest. The middle of the far south end is where the deep hole of 6 m is located. It is a good spot to fish during hot weather or to find the largest concentration of fish during a hatch or insect migration.

I've had good success at Grizzly with dry flies, both Mikaluk Traveller and midge, usually right in the middle of the lake. Being one of the highest elevation lakes in this area, hatches develop a week or two later, and will remain consistently good through summer months when other lakes have gone off the cycle.

Leech patterns are always reliable producers, and because of Grizzly's consistent depths type 1 intermediate full-sink or floating lines teamed with fluorocarbon leaders are usually what is required, which is a nice change from dragging fast full-sink lines around a lake.

Fourteenmile Lake
Elevation: 1,033 m
Surface area: 62 ha
Maximum depth: 7 m
Mean depth: 2 m
Stocking records: none; wild rainbow trout.

One of the prettier little spots around Prince George that supports wild trout, Fourteenmile Lake is a long way off the paved road, and drains to the Bowron River. Spotted with islands and shoals, it's another piece of water that receives little attention from the fly fishing crowd, but offers terrific action for wild trout in the 30–40-cm range.

The lake is accessed by continuing along the Willow (500) FSR South in a southeast direction past Stony and Slender lakes to an unmarked logging road about 5 km past Slender. Turn right, cross a creek and Fourteenmile Lake is 5–6 km down the road.

Fourteenmile Creek, which exits the lake at the rough Forest Service campsite at the east end, has year-round flow. Along the south shore, two small creeks enter the lake, providing spawning habitat for the native trout.

As you enter the mostly shallow lake from the campsite, there is a series of circular shelves leading into a 4-m hole in the small bay where the creek outflows and, as you work your way down the lake, less than a metre of water for half the distance to the northwest end. In the far west end, two small islands, one sunken at 1–2-m depth and the other exposed, offer shelves and shoals on the north and south sides leading up to 6-m depth—these are the best fishing spots in the lake.

In the early 1990s, I fished Fourteenmile for the first time with my then (and still considered, though long gone from PG) fishing partner Don Clarke, who said he was taking me to a spot where there are so many fish concentrated in a small area and the competition is so fierce, that you can watch several of them coming for your fly every cast. Truer words were never spoken—the numbers of trout that were bundled into the small areas between those islands in the northwest corner was mind-boggling.

The trout are a smaller variety, wild and streamlined like river and creek trout, and aggressive to the fly. For some reason (perhaps it's the 60 km of gravel to get there), I haven't fished Fourteenmile for over ten years. I plan to get there again this year to see if the trout still gang up on the fly fisher, and maybe introduce a few buddies to some fast fishing.

Bowron River Forest Service Road Access

Running north and south from Hwy. 16 East about 30 km past the Willow River Rest Area and 60 km east of Prince George, the Bowron Forest Service Road cuts into a vast wilderness that takes the traveller southeast about 60 km into the Bowron Lakes area, or north of the highway 20 km to its terminus at the community of Hansard and the Fraser River.

Our fishing paradise lies along the southern journey, where logging roads slice east toward the Cariboo and Rocky Mountains, driving headlong into steep terrain and bountiful scenery. Along the way, there is a smattering of small lakes and creeks draining to the Bowron River valley—these are our playgrounds. Never forget you are venturing into grizzly country; you must keep a clean campsite, and if tenting, keep your food in sealed containers in your vehicle and away from your sleeping quarters!

Bowron River

Flowing northwest and entering the Fraser River before the big river makes its turn south at Giscome Canyon, the Bowron drains the Bowron Lakes Provincial Park chain of lakes and streams, world-famous for its canoe circle route. It's another low-pressure northern river that sports rainbow trout, Dolly Varden, coarse fish and even a small Chinook salmon run.

If you are travelling east from Prince George, the quickest route to the river is to turn southeast onto the Beaver Bowron FS Road just east of the Bowron River Bridge on Hwy. 16. This cutoff route will meet the Bowron FSR about 18 km east of the highway, which follows within close reach of the river all the way to Haggen Creek about 50 km from Hwy. 16 East, and further into the Cariboo Range. Pull off and fish anywhere that looks tempting.

The Bowron is a clear, free-flowing river of moderate size, about 100 km long (as the crow flies), and yet another of the untapped river resources available to the fly fisher within an hour's drive of Prince George. Even though the trout are small, averaging 25–35 cm, they are wild and have lots of spunk and energy when hooked. The rainbow trout take dry flies readily, and all species of fish will jump all over a deeply drifted stonefly or Hare's Ear Nymph.

South of Hwy. 16 East, the Bowron is an ideal river to drift by canoe or pontoon boat, offering Class 1–2 water that is easily navigated by fly fishers of average boating ability. The drifts are unmarked on the *Backroad Mapbook*, but you are never too far from the river and can judge your day trip distance in segments. I like day trips of 5–7 km of river because I enjoy stopping to fish the good-looking runs slowly, and taking the time to see the country and wildlife, avoiding the tendency to rush to the next hole—there is no pressure to get there before the next fly fisher, because there isn't one.

Spruce 1 and 2, Pinkerton, Tumuch, Slim and Papoose Lakes

The Bowron FSR takes the fly fisher to all of these lakes, some a little rougher to get into than others and some accessible only by short trails. They have inventory of all species of native trout and are not famous for their fishing, but like most unknown and seldom-fished bodies of water left to their own resources, they can be full of surprises and are wonderful quiet spots to set up camp and enjoy the northern wilderness.

Dolly Varden trout is a species that has found a good home in this eastern section of the region because it requires pristine unpolluted habitat. They hang out in the deep pools of their home streams, but you will rarely find a stream that is heavily populated with the species because it establishes its presence in harsh, cold environments where the winters are long and the summers short. Their home streams can provide food prospects for only a limited number of their cannibalistic lot.

The Spruce Lakes are accessed by turning east off the Bowron FSR about 2 km past the Tumuch FSR turnoff, which is about 11 km past the Beaver Bowron junction on the Bowron FSR. I have not fished these lakes, but by the looks of the road (trail) on the map, I recommend four-wheel drive to gain access to them.

Spruce Lake 1 is 19 ha with a mean depth of 5 m. The west end is mostly marsh, and has a deep hole graduating to 10 m in the centre of the east end, which would be the logical place to find the best trout.

Spruce Lake 2 is the larger of the two at 35 ha, has a mean depth of 8 m, and two deep 16-m holes located in the east and west ends. The middle portion is shallow, with a narrow channel connecting the two ends. This lake has an interesting profile, and should produce the best fishing of the two Spruce lakes.

Pinkerton Lake is reached by turning east on the Tumuch Road, about 11 km past the Beaver Bowron and Bowron FSR junction. At about km 20, the Tumuch FSR splits and turns north and south; take the south route and the Pinkerton turnoff is about 7 km down, on the west side of the road. You can see the lake from the road; vehicle access is easy and there is a good car-top boat launch and rough FS campsite on this east side. Pinkerton is a small lake of 23 ha, but a deep one, with an average depth of 14 m; the deepest hole at 36 m is in the centre. Bob Melrose, a friend and fellow fisher, tells me it used to be excellent fishing, and I think it still is.

Tumuch, Slim and Papoose lakes are also accessed from the Tumuch Road, but from the north branch at the 20-km road split. Both branches are called the Tumuch Road, which carries along in a circular loop of about 80 km, returning to the split.

Tumuch Lake is about 6 km up the road. It's a good-sized lake of 141 ha, and deep, averaging 7 m. Lakes of this depth in the North country are prime habitat for lake trout and kokanee, fished by trolling deep with plug gear for lakers or, for the fly fisher and kokanee, working the deep edges of shoals with a sink-tip type 2 line and minnow patterns. We don't target lake trout or kokanee with flies in this part of the province, which I think is another area of fly fishing that could be interesting if a fisher wants to put some effort into giving flies a try.

Slim Lake is accessed by a rough logging road or trail about 4 km past Tumuch, and is really nothing more than a long, narrow channel and widening of Slim Creek, which begins south of Tumuch Lake, exits the east end and continues its run to the Fraser, crossing Hwy. 16 East 175 km from Prince George. The lake is weedy and less than a metre deep for the most part, having a small hole of 3 m near the middle section and another 3-m spot near the west end.

Papoose Lake drains to Slim Creek and is reached by a short 0.5-km trail from a small campsite, which can be found by taking a north turn onto a short logging road 6 km past Tumuch Lake on the Tumuch Road. This is another small, shallow lake of 21 ha that at times produces decent fishing and pleasant surprises.

West Everett Lake

Elevation: 1,155 m
Surface area: 11 ha
Maximum depth: 12 m
Mean depth: 5 m
Stocking records: none; wild rainbow trout.

Not well known, but relished by those who venture to it, West Everett is another prize of the North country that deserves to be explored by the fly fisher and appreciated for its quiet beauty and wild rainbows. Everett is a hike-in lake with a float tube, but it's only about a twenty-minute effort from your parked vehicle.

There are no camping facilities near the water, but you could pitch a tent or set up a truck and camper in the parking lot area.

To reach Everett, continue past the Pinkerton Lake turnoff on the Tumuch Road about 5 km, turn east and stay on the Tumuch Road for about 20 more km, where a short logging road cuts to the right and back to a parking lot near Everett Creek. After twelve years, I can still remember the route to Everett by noticing the rugged face of a solitary outstanding mountain peak on my east side as we neared the lake. I think you'll know what I mean if you take the journey—the peak will be in your face as you fish the day away.

From the parking lot, step over the deactivation log in your path, cross the creek and continue walking southwest along the old logging cut road until you see the lake through the forest on your right. The trail into Everett is not well marked because the lake is seldom fished; you have to enter the lake through a clear-cut (probably overgrown by now) and bushwhack on a rough trail into a marshy bay on the southeast side.

Everett is a crystal clear lake, with a gradual series of shoal water that drops into a 12-m hole in the west end. As you continue along the south side of the lake, there is a small island; fishing is good around the island and into the middle of the lake as the depth quickly drops to 6 m, then 8, 10 and 12 m. The island area is a good spot to work a damsel or dragonfly nymph during summer months, and leech patterns or scud imitations anytime.

My friend Dave Ziril introduced me to Everett back in the late 1990s, and I am ashamed for not making the trip there lately. It's about a two-hour jaunt from Prince George; a full day to hike in, fish for four or five hours, and get back out in time for dinner. I think the best bet is to skip the dinner, or pack two meals, and enjoy a full day when you venture into these remote spots. Everett reminds me of the days that I fish Wicheeda—full days, magnificent scenery and solitude, and I pout when I have to pack up and leave.

Slim Creek, Dore and Goat Rivers

The endless list of fly fishing opportunities in creeks and rivers of this remote section of the Central Interior is astonishing. The further east you go and the more distance off the highway you travel on the logging roads, the more isolated the water and the better the chance of finding a creek or stream that will satisfy your hunger for a wilderness experience in a way that only a dedicated fly fisher can understand. We yearn for those days of unexpected pleasure: discovering secluded places where trout come eagerly to the dry fly; tangling with wild rainbows that challenge your 3-weight creek rod; grappling helplessly with a 3–4-kg bull trout that suddenly chomps your minnow pattern—or more commonly, the bull trout decides the rainbow you are playing is his property, not yours, and decides to tackle both of you. These are some of the streams of the North that will tickle your dry fly fancy, or jolt you into reality.

Slim Creek drains the Tumuch, Slim and Papoose lakes. You'll find small rainbow trout, Dollies big and small, and whitefish in this clear, pretty little stream that crosses Hwy. 16 east of Prince George. There is limited road access above and below the highway, but a trail follows the creek upstream for about 5 km and meets the Everett Road. I haven't wet a line in this water yet, but it's on the list—the little stream beckons, and each time I go by, I gaze longingly at it.

The Goat River is one that by sight will perk up any fly fisher—crystal clear water, good flow, nice-looking pools and boulder pockets that fish can hide behind. The Goat River Forest Service Road cuts south about 2 km east of the rest stop on Hwy. 16, and catches the river when the road swings west. From this point the road follows the river for about 13 km to the junction of the Milk and Goat rivers, where you'll find the Goat River Trailhead, which follows the river and takes you on a long 60-km-plus hike into Bowron Provincial Park, ending at Isaac Lake. If you continue on the Goat River FSR past the trailhead, it carries on along the Milk River for another 50 km or so. The Milk very likely has the same fishing lore and inventory as the Goat, and is yet another stream that beckons exploration by the fly fisher.

The Goat has pretty good fishing for the entire length, targeting Dollies, rainbow and whitefish in a beautiful setting. I have fished around the rest area with good success, but am yearning for a trip by hiking that trailhead into some real wilderness country. There is just so much ambition and so much water, but so little time when you're a fly fisher!

Thoughts on Fly Tying: Materials, Terms and Instruction

Show me a box of one thousand flies with ten of mine in it, and I can pick mine out in minutes, because I think every fly tier, after many years of trial and error, experimentation and thought, eventually develops a personal style of tying.

The handicraft is hundreds of years old, which means there is very little original thought that can be gleaned from researching insects that have not changed in appearance for thousands or millions of years. There is, however, a generation of new fly tying products on the market that permits the modern fly tier to give new "looks" to old patterns; in this way many patterns have been reinvented from traditional dressings.

I still use many natural materials and consider my style traditional, but I often tweak other fly tiers' ideas and even my own whenever I can. It's in this realm that I believe (and it may be considered controversial) you can call your-self an "originator" of a fly pattern. That's the beauty of fly tying—you can be creative with your thoughts as well as those of others. My children have been collecting and fishing with my so-called rejects for many years—they have made excellent Christmas presents.

Before this book ventures into the world of insects the way I see them, and how my experience and research interprets their makeup, I offer some thoughts on fly tying materials, terms and instructions that I hope will help the novice fly tier understand some of my jargon, and perhaps provide some new ideas to expert tiers that will help them become even more proficient at their hobby.

Brands

Brands I refer to are for reference only and are what I have chosen to use for my flies during forty years at the vise, which is by no means a slight to other makes on the market that I'm sure are equally as good. The models I refer to work well for me because of their styles, availability in specific colours I am looking for, or in most cases, old habits that I am accustomed to.

Tying Thread

I refer to UTC thread in dressings of my fly patterns. I have a preference for UTC brand because it is strong, lies flat (as opposed to round) on the hook, and is available in a host of colours. It's nylon, similar to floss but much finer, less expensive than Kevlar, and is sold in a 70 denier (fine) for hook sizes 6 to the very smallest dry flies and 140 denier (heavy) for steelhead and salmon hooks.

Uni-Mono or Danville's mono in "fine, clear" designation is my preference for tying trout patterns smaller than size 6 that require the use of deer or elk hair, because you need a fine thread that you can tug on without fear of breakage. If I need to tie deer or elk hair on steelhead and salmon hooks, I'll use Danville or Uni 3/0 monocord.

Hooks

The styles of hooks you tie your flies onto are considered important because the length of the fly's body is determined by the shank length of the hook, and the insect's appearance can be greatly affected or altered by the curve of the hook. With the advancement of laser technology for hook production, all top-quality fish hooks are sticky sharp. The most popular brands for tying trout flies are Mustad, Tiemco and Diachi.

Nymphs, traveller sedge pupae and large dry flies like stoneflies or traveller sedges are nicely represented by choosing a hook with a 3-X long shank and sweeping, rounded and curved body style like Tiemco 200R. A size 16 in this style of hook has the length to tie an impressive little mayfly nymph that would otherwise require a standard hook in size 10. I also use them for chironomid bomber patterns.

Small caddis pupae and chironomids are suited to the short, curved style of hook, like Tiemco 2457; these models are 2-X strong and 2-X short, made of heavy wire and sink well without adding additional weight. When you tie with these hooks, wrap the abdomen well past the bend of the hook, tails (if any) pointing downward past the gap.

Emergers are also tied on curved hooks with short shanks, but I prefer to use fine wire styles like Tiemco 2487, which are 1-X fine and 1-X short, which permits my emergers to ride the surface with their wings, but dip their tails (shuck) and abdomens under water.

Small dry flies over size 10 are always tied with 1-X fine wire hooks, such as Tiemco 5210, Mustad 94840 or Diachi 1180, which aids in floatation of the patterns.

I purchase barbless hooks when available, or crush the barbs of my hooks with vise jaws when I tie flies. If you release fish and use a dry fly, a long release (one that gets off after the take) is considered easier on the trout than playing one to exhaustion, and if you do lose one because of a barbless hook, it is usually a jumper that shakes its head—a worthy opponent that deserves its freedom.

Tail Materials

Tails are designed to impress a fish in a number of ways: by adding life to the fly in the manner of movement, creating the existence of a trailing shuck, or by representing the presence of a tail filament or tails.

Life, in the form of movement, is the most important feature you can add to your fly patterns—without it, your fly is dead in the water, literally. When used for a leech pattern, a marabou tail sways and undulates in current and also during a slow retrieve in lakes, creating the almost irresistible impression of a living insect that is on the move. Marabou is a great choice for undulating nymphs, such as damsels during migration, leeches on the hunt, or Woolly Buggers that imitate everything!

Another superior tail material for nymphs, scuds or emergers is mallard flank barbs, which can be dyed or purchased from fly shops in a variety of colours: Callibaetis, olive, grey, summer duck and natural. Mallard feathers have a barred, sweeping look, and are my choice for imitating a trailing shuck on emerger patterns, tails on chironomids and scuds and for wings on adult mayflies.

Tails on dry flies need high-quality hackle barbs; those long, glossy stiff ones that you'll find on the ends of large feathers of dry fly capes and saddles. I use a variety of colours, but grizzly, brown, badger, white and blue dun are the most popular. Dry fly tails should be as long as the hook shank, because your fly sits on its tail when in the surface film.

When tying a fly that has a tail, abdomen and rib, and you want to keep the body slender, begin by tying the tail in at the three-quarter-shank point and take it down the hook, then return to the three-quarter point and take the ribbing material(s) down the hook shank under and with the body or abdomen material. If your fly has a tail, abdomen and thorax, start the tail at the two-thirds shank point. This will prevent those tying "lumps" of material when you stop and tie something else into the pattern at the bend, like a tail or rib.

Ribbing Materials

Ribbing on a fly is intended to highlight body segmentation; for subsurface patterns, wire ribbing has the added bonus of providing weight without bulk.

Fine, medium and large wires are available on spools in numerous colours and sizes: gold, copper, silver, red and green are the most popular. I use fine wire for hooks size 10 and smaller, and medium or large for size 8 and larger fly patterns. I purchase inexpensive bobbins (or use discards as I move up to ceramic) for my wire collection because they are handy to store it on, and you can use the bobbin for ribbing your flies if you can handle two bobbins on your hook shank.

Rod-building thread size A is an excellent ribbing material for patterns you tie without flash; unlike cotton thread, it holds a true colour when wet. Damsel nymphs and caddis pupae are some patterns where you will find this product useful. Some tiers use floss for this purpose, but I prefer thread because it doesn't fray and provides a thinner rib.

Saddle hackle stems, especially grizzly, black and brown, should be saved rather than discarded—they make excellent ribbing material and quill bodies for mayfly imitations and are the ticket for representing antennae on adult stonefly replications.

When you wrap a wire ribbing onto a nymph, it is sometimes best to counter-wrap; this means wrap the wire in the opposite direction you applied the body material, which gives highlight to the ribbing and strength to the primary barbs to prevent a fish's teeth from unravelling the abdomen.

Body Materials

The overall appearance of insects is "buggy"-looking—bodies that have tiny hairs that trap air bubbles and water. You can't get any material more buggy-looking than seal fur dubbing or its various substitutes. Back in the 1970s we used to be able to get seal fur easily, which isn't the case now, but there are many great-looking replacements on the market today, blended in all popular fishy colours: Hare-Tron, Hareline Rabbit Dub, Kaufman's Synthetic Living Fiber (SLF), Antron, Ligas and Soft Blend are a few that I use. Animal under-fur from beaver, muskrat, rabbit and squirrel is also a very good dubbing material. I don't use much dubbing on dry flies except for an enlarged thorax on mayflies, and on adult caddis patterns.

For abdomens on adult and emerger mayfly imitations, I like the look of and response from fish to primary goose wing barbs, which you can find dyed in many seductive fish colours: Blue-Winged Olive (BWO), Green, Callibaetis, numerous olives, white and black. Natural grey Canada goose primary is my favourite colour and body material for my Adams's and grey mayflies—you'll find lots of these in the summer in areas where geese congregate and moult their wing feathers. Pluck two feather barbs for most patterns, but only one barb for size 18 and smaller. When winding primary strips, tie them point first and use either hackle pliers or the fingers of both hands; use one hand to wrap and the middle finger of the other to hold the wrap on the far side of the hook.

Hackle feather stem wrapped as an abdomen is another method I use for dry flies, especially mosquitoes and quill dry patterns. Try them; they make interesting subs for any dry fly pattern.

Floss and nylon are available in dozens of colours, and have their place at the bench when you wish to tie adult patterns that have the appearance of smooth bodies (like stoneflies and adult spinners). I like both, floss which I use for smooth bodies on chironomids, adult spinner mayflies, stoneflies and many attractor steelhead and salmon patterns, and nylon for midges and may-flies smaller than size 18.

Underbodies of nymph patterns present a different problem—how to build an underbody that will "fatten" your fly without bulk? Embroidery thread lies flat, can be split into strands for small flies like size 16 scuds, and purchased in skeins of assorted colours from the sewing section of department or hobby stores.

Thorax Materials
Peacock herl is a favourite thorax material that adds colour, texture and a glossy buggy look that is impossible to imitate with synthetic products. For greater strength, trim and tie the points of two or three strands onto your hook, twist them around the tying thread six or eight times, then wind the thread onto the hook like dubbing.

Always versatile at the vise, dubbing is another preferred thorax material that is useful for offering a different colour than the abdomen to caddis pupae and adult mayflies.

Nymph Wing-Cases and Shellbacks
Back in the 1960s and '70s, fly tiers like Jack Shaw used ring-necked pheasant or turkey tail barbs for the majority of their wing-cased or shellback patterns. These materials are still popular today, but this is one of the major areas where modern synthetic materials have found their place on the bench. The revolution seemed to begin with the use of plastic bag strips for tying baggy shrimp patterns, and caught on from there, because you can now purchase clear plastics like Midge Flex dyed in a wide range of colours to suit every purpose and creative imagination.

Latex closed-cell foam is another product that is useful as a wing-case for terrestrial dry flies like ants and hoppers, because it floats like cork and doesn't absorb water. For a few dollars at Walmart, you can buy enough foam in a dozen different colours that should last a lifetime of fly tying.

Primary wing or tail barbs from pheasant, turkey, duck and goose are still good choices for nymph and pupa models, offering texture and natural colour that cannot be replicated by synthetic materials.

Wings

For the fly tier, wings are probably the most difficult features to replicate on insects, and likely the trickiest to get right because they are the crowning touch of well-tied dry fly patterns. If the wings don't look good, your patterns are not going to get accolades from your peers, regardless of how well tied otherwise. It does not, however, take fancy wings to catch fish, because what we are after at the bench is the *appearance* of wings.

Wings, along with good hackle, provide balance to a dry fly pattern—one that lands upright when cast and rides the currents like a natural insect. The most common and useful wing materials are mallard flank and breast feathers, select quality deer and elk hair and Antron or poly yarn.

For adult mayflies in sizes 10–16, dyed mallard flank or breast feathers are a good choice. These feathers are long, speckled in appearance and, like goose primary feathers, available in all of the popular mayfly wing colours. For wings, choose mallard that is flat across the top of the whole feather and about the correct size for the hook you are tying on. Study the next adult mayfly you see—the length of the posted wings should equal the shank and bend of the hook; in other words, slightly longer than the body of the fly.

A posted mayfly wing is one that sits upright at 90° on the hook. To post a mallard feather, first choose a feather that is flat across the top, strip the fuzz from the bottom of the stem and about half of the barbs, leaving about 5 mm of them, even on both sides of the stem. Measure the length at a little more than the shank of the hook, fold the feather once lengthwise and pinch it to the top of the hook at two-thirds shank length, with the stem toward the hook bend. Make four to five tight turns of thread behind the wing, then pull straight up on the wing and build a block of thread in front of it. Finish the posted wing by holding it upright in your right hand, and, with your left hand, make several turns of thread around the base of the wing on top of the hook shank. Whew, I hope you got that!

Tying a parachute wing uses this same method, but the wraps continue halfway up the posted wing to build a base for the parachute hackle, which is wound around the wing.

For winging adult mayflies smaller than size 16, Antron or poly nylon is easier to use than feathers. I often use yellow for wings on these little models as they are tough to see in river foam if you tie with white, and the fish don't seem to care.

A "spent" wing style means the wings are tied horizontally and perpendicular to the body; the spent female spinner dies, and lays her wings flat to the water surface after she has dropped her eggs. To tie this style, use a 5-mm-wide piece of Antron more than twice the body length of the hook. Centre it on top of the hook at the three-quarter-point of the shank; then make about six figure-eight wraps around and under the wing, leaving it perpendicular to the hook shank. When secure, take both sides of the wing between thumb and forefinger, pull straight up then back along the hook shank, switch hands to hold the wings, and trim them the same length as the mayfly body.

Deer hair is another excellent wing material. Use only select hair, which is available in either short or long and a variety of natural and dyed colours, and use a hair stacker to even the tips so you will produce consistent flies.

Tying stacks of deer hair for Mikaluk Sedge patterns is a little tricky, and takes practice to get it right. Most mistakes are made by using too much hair (a 4-mm width is about right) and by over-tightening the first wrap of hair, which causes it to spin on the hook. To correct this, make your first turn of thread a soft loop, and tighten progressively, finishing with very tight wraps. Monocord thread (review previous section on threads) is the best choice when working with deer or elk hair.

Elk hair is stiffer than deer, so for the novice tier elk is easier to work with because it is coarser and doesn't spin as much. For large flies like stoneflies and stimulators, elk is a better choice than deer; however, it has the same tying quirks: keep it sparse and don't over-tighten the first wraps of thread.

Gills (Chironomid)

There are as many ideas about what to use for gills on chironomids as there are patterns. I think as long as it is pure white and stays white when wet any material will do the trick: Antron, Glo-Yarn, wool, poly or nylon.

Many fly tiers post their gills in front of the thorax or wing-case on top of the hook—I don't, because chironomids have gills that surround their heads or protrude from both sides of their heads.

White steelhead Glo-Yarn is my favourite gill material for chironomids because it can be split and peeled into small sections, then tied figure-eight on top of the shank behind the eye of the hook and trimmed to length. Some tiers use beads in various metallic colours and also white for gill replicas, and I know they catch fish, but I think they are effective because they impart a bobbing action to the pattern more than being a gill representation.

Leg Hackle

Insect legs can be represented in a number of manners: as throat hackle, legs protruding from the sides, or appendages sweeping the body length of the bug. Throat hackles for nymphs can be taken from any cape or skin of the correct colour, but the feathers I find most useful are small wing feathers from grouse or partridge roadkill that I collect on my outings. I always keep an eye out for dead birds, and take them home to skin and borax them, which I leave in natural grey or brown, or dye them to colours using Rit brand fabric dye.

When tying a throat hackle, try this method: Use a whole feather, judging the correct size for the nymph. First, trim the fuzz and excess barbs, leaving about 5 mm of barbs each side of the stem. Spread the barbs backward toward the base of the stem, and clip out the tip of the feather with scissors, leaving a narrow V-notch. Turn the hook upside down on your rotary vise, place the "V" of the hackle toward the bend of the hook, and then anchor it with two or three firm turns of thread. Pull the stem to set the feather almost to the hook point and trim the waste—presto! Perfect throat hackle every time!

To imitate a struggling insect, especially mayfly and stonefly nymphs free-drifting in a stream, it's valuable to learn to tie legs protruding from the sides of the bug that will pulsate and wiggle with current action. Some tiers use rubber legs and yes, they do catch fish, but I prefer the look of natural feather hackle.

To begin, choose a wing feather from a grouse or partridge that will sweep back to the end of the nymph's body when extended. The leg hackle is tied after the wing-case on your pattern, and before the thorax material is applied. Strip and clean the fuzz, preen the barbs so they are perpendicular to the stem and tie the feather in by the tip, shiny-side up, and the stem pointing toward the hook eye. Apply your thorax dubbing, bend the hackle over the thorax, tie down, trim the stem, and bring the wing-case forward over the hackle and thorax. If tying a nymph such as a stonefly with multiple wing-case segments, perform the sequence in two steps of thorax and wing-case.

For stiff, sweeping legs such as those found on dragonfly nymphs that swim by expulsion and pull their legs under their bodies, moose or deer hair is an effective material. Tie the legs to brush backward and downward the length of the nymph's body, leaving a few hairs dangling out the sides.

Palmer Hackle

This style of hackling is common when tying Woolly Bugger and leech patterns. To "palmer" hackle, choose a high-grade saddle hackle about 1.5 times the hook gap, and tie it in by the tip at the bend of the hook, glossy (convex) side of the hackle on top pointing forward to the eye. After the body is applied, the hackle is wrapped over and through the body in five to six turns to the eye of the hook. Tied correctly, the barbs on palmered hackles sweep backward and will pulsate during a slow retrieve.

Dry Hackle

As you become seasoned at fly tying, your years of experience are reflected in your collection of dry fly capes and saddles (and the amount of money you have spent buying them). I couldn't afford expensive capes and saddles in my youth. My dry flies looked like my wallet—happy, but empty.

You simply cannot tie good-looking dry flies without high-quality hackle, at least #2 grade Whiting or Metz, which will set you back forty to fifty bucks for half a cape. And you'll need at least three of them: grizzly, brown and blue dun, which will cover over 90 percent of your dry fly tying. For your best dollar, choose capes or saddles that have at least 50 percent hackles that tie sizes 12 to 18. If in doubt, borrow a hackle gauge from the fly shop, open the package, and gauge the hackle—you'll be sorry if you don't. I prefer high-grade #2 or better saddle hackle to capes; they are about half the price and the fish don't seem to care at all.

To hackle a dry fly around a posted wing, first size the hackle with a hackle gauge. I begin by trimming the first four or five barbs on each side of the stem to 2-mm length with scissors to form an anchor for the thread. Dry flies are tied "dry" style—the flat (as opposed to shiny) or concave side of the hackle faces the hook eye, which aids the dry fly in its floatation. Tie the hackle by the stem in front of the wing and on top of the hook shank, with the hackle tip pointing away from you once anchored. The first half-turn is made in front of the wing, then carry the hackle immediately behind the wing; finally, take two full turns behind the wing and bring the hackle forward in front of the wing with three to four turns to the eye. If tying a double hackle, tie them in at the same time, but treat them separately when hackling the fly, winding the second hackle *through* the first.

To hackle "parachute" style, begin with a posted wing with thread built around and halfway up the wing base, for grip and support of the hackle. The hackle is bound by the stem in front of the wing, shiny-side up, wound up and down the posted wing in four to five turns, and tied off *on* the post. If you tie the hackle off on the shank, you'll bind barbules under the hook, making for a messy pattern. After hackling, finish the fly with dubbing or body material of choice by carefully lifting the hackle with a bodkin and sliding the body material under and to the hook eye to complete the pattern.

Chironomid

To develop into a competent still-water fly fisher, you must become proficient at fishing chironomids. They are the earliest insect to emerge after ice-out, continue to hatch until the heat of August, resume hatching as the water cools down in September, and will always be the last bug to hit the sack for winter. At most, there will be only a few weeks of the year when this insect will not be showing up on the lake in some form, and when they aren't hatching, the larva stage will be at its best for fishing success.

The adult stage of hatches should not be ignored either. During low light conditions—cloudy days, rain, early mornings and evenings—trout are often taking adults from the surface and totally ignoring subsurface pupae. This activity is signalled by dimpling surface rises; no fish are seen, just the circles left behind. I have extended many successful fishing days by switching to an adult pattern after the hatch has subsided, and because it is dry fly action, the result is more memorable. Such is fly fishing: the challenge of being constantly aware of changing conditions and using your powers of observation on the water.

When fishing chironomids, the ideal scenario involves setting up three fly rods: one with floating line and 6-m fluorocarbon leader, one with floating line and regular 4-m leader, and one with a full slow-sink line and 4-m fluorocarbon leader. These setups will cover all fishing opportunities from the surface to 8 m of depth.

Chironomids enjoy a complete life cycle: egg, larva, pupa and adult. The female deposits eggs in the lake after mating, which drift to the bottom and lie in the muck for a few weeks, soon hatching into tiny larvae. Eggs are too microscopic to be important as fish diet, but the larvae and pupae stages comprise more than 30 percent of a trout's still-water diet. Both of these stages are abundant in many colours, which are dependent upon their plant food sources: shades of green, tan and grey, but most often larvae appear in bright red or maroon due to hemoglobin entrapment (referred to as bloodworms). Pupae, on maturity, ascend to the surface to hatch into adult chironomids.

Chironomid

Order: Diptera
Family: Chironomidae
Larva: size 5–25 mm; colours: black, brown, olive, tan, cream, red—all translucent
Pupa: size 5–25 mm; colours same as larvae, also translucent
Adult and emerger: size 5–25 mm; colours same as larvae and pupae, except red

Chironomid Larva

Wormlike and segmented in appearance, larvae dwell in the bottom muck of lakes in depths up to 10 m, attached by an appendage to the lake bottom so they can hang in a vertical fashion and intercept decaying plant matter and drifting food substances swept by them from turbulence caused by winds and currents.

Larvae can be long-lived, up to two years in some species or as short as two weeks with others, and are found in various sizes depending upon their stage of development, beginning with emergence from the egg stage a few millimetres in length, reaching up to 25 mm at maturity. During growth stages, they are often forced to move their residence because of poor nutrient availability or changing conditions, which is a desperate time for larvae as they have poor mobility and become fish food as free-swimming organisms without defensive camouflage. Most larvae are a reddish colouration, which doesn't help their escape, as fish do see in colour! This travelling stage is an important time for the fly fisher: as the larva exits its case and drifts in search of new habitat, it is a sitting duck for eager trout and presents an opportune time for fly fishers to work their magic with a bloodworm pattern. As it reaches maturity the larva seals off its tube and spends the next few weeks developing into the pupa stage.

The best time to fish a larva pattern is through periods of low surface activity, as a general searching pattern when waiting for activity, or through summer doldrums and the fall feeding frenzy. I like to fish the larva with a #2–3 full-sinking fly line—choice depending on the maximum depth I want to fish—and 3–4 m of fluorocarbon leader tapering to a 4-X tippet. Your fly must sink within 30 cm of the bottom of the lake, because the larva is a deep dweller, and not very mobile. Tippet choice of high breaking strength is necessary, as there is a large possibility of catching a 2- or 3-kg fish when working a bloodworm through the deepest part of the shoal.

The retrieve is a slow hand-crawl action, interspersed with 30-second pauses and frequent changes in direction. Larvae patterns have long been a popular choice of fishers who like to troll, as they are a very good do-nothing fly requiring little attention or effort to use. The strikes of fish inhaling them is most comparable to a leech take—an unhurried, take-your-time stop of the fly, followed by a deep, violent run through the weed patch, which is another reason for using 4-X tippet. If you survive the first strike and run, you have a good chance of landing your trophy.

Jack Shaw deserves credit for developing bloodworm patterns, but I have modified and adapted Jack's original model into a pattern of my own design— the Bloodworm Translucent, which has been field tested over the past several seasons to the point where I have total confidence in it. The design uses an under-wrap of Johnson & Johnson dental floss; not the slick kind, but the flat, waxed type. The body for colour and wire ribbing for segmentation are then wrapped like ribbing over the dental floss, and the whole thing is lacquered with several coats of clear nail polish, which results is a translucent-looking body with a slick, glossy appearance that resembles the natural in its casement. Like Jack's pattern, a single turn of red pheasant behind the eye simulates movement; otherwise, the fly would be lifeless (see page 129).

Chironomid Pupa

I have a friend who tied a size 12 brown and copper chironomid pupa in April, and used no other fly for the entire fishing season. Sounds a little boring to me, but the pupa can be that effective, to the exclusion of all other insect hatches. Dragon Lake near Quesnel has a regular group of US fly fishers who arrive in May and stay until mid-June, only to fish the prolific chironomid pupae hatches. On the lake, there will be dry fly opportunities all around them—mayflies, caddis, damsels—but it's chironomid pupae fishing they relish.

To fish the pupa stage, it is important to recognize the adult, because the pupa will only be visible as a shuck left behind, unless you learn to scan the water 30 cm below the surface to see the ascending pupae. As you become a proficient chironomid addict, you will learn to recognize the shuck, and have the knowledge to instantly narrow the size range of ascending pupae. Adult chironomids resemble mosquitoes, but they don't bite. They are double-winged, with slender bodies and range in size from 2–25 mm, averaging about 20 mm. The small 2 mm pupa is more properly termed its cousin, the midge, another important insect dealt with in the next chapter.

Your successful choice of body and rib colour is often the difference between a few fish or a mess of fish, and the best way to determine colour, if the shuck doesn't give it away, is to somehow catch a trout, pump the stomach contents into a jar, and observe the live pupae. Many times there will be several colours in the mix—choose the dominant one, tie on one hook size larger than the mass, and go fishing.

Chironomid pupae are very short-lived, from a few hours to several days. In Chapter 2, I talked about the staging cycle that pupae undergo before the final ascent to the surface. Research indicates that, in prime lake habitat, there can be about 50,000 larvae per square metre of bottom, all in various stages of development. When we see a chironomid hatch of 50 individuals, there are up to a thousand times more waiting on the bottom, many of them milling around, organizing to begin their ascent, which indicates that we should concentrate our efforts mostly in the bottom zone of the lake.

Many fly fishers use float tubes and pontoon boats for chironomid fishing, basically mooching over an area because their watercraft are always moving around and impossible to keep still, even when anchored. This method is useful and I use it, but it's not as effective as a double-anchored boat that is motionless, because chironomid pupae don't move sideways; they wiggle a bit, stop, wiggle, and stop repeatedly on ascent to the surface. This action can only be represented from a stationary position.

The use of floating lines with strike indicators is the most popular and simplest method of fishing chironomid pupae, and there are several methods for rigging your indicator. The first technique calls for a strike indicator installed to your long leader at 1.5 times the depth of the shoal you are fishing, which allows for slow retrieval of the imitation and keeps the pattern in the same zone for a long period of time.

Another method some anglers use is a 6-m leader, a strike indicator 30 cm less than the depth of the water, a split-shot weight 30 cm above the fly, and the angler throwing the fly straight into the fishing zone. This method is cumbersome and not pretty to cast or watch, but effective.

Yet another popular system of rigging an indicator is to anchor on your favourite shoal, string your leader and tippet through a bobber, and then attach your fly pattern. To the hook bend of the fly, attach hemostat pliers and lower the line to the bottom of the lake; pull the line up 30 cm off the bottom, secure your indicator to the leader with a toothpick, and remove the pliers—you're 30 cm off the bottom all day long. If the shoal is deeper than 5 m, however, I think it's more effective to use my preferred methods of floating line/long leader or switch to a full-sink line.

For me, the main drawback to indicator fishing of any style is the strike of the fish; because indicators are bobbers, the take of the trout is visual and not felt until the hook is set. I prefer the feel of a good strike on a sensitive graphite rod to watching the bobber go down.

I learned to fish chironomids forty years ago using the floating line and long leader method before indicators were even thought of, and this is my preferred method. It requires a ton of patience to let the fly sink properly, but the reward is exhilarating. The retrieve is a slow hand-crawl, often stopping to rest as the natural will do, inching the pupa through the fishing zone. Many strikes and break-offs occur when your line is near the boat and the fly is perpendicular to the leader; the trout short-hits the fly with very little cushion from the fly line to absorb the impact, and parts the fly with a solid snap. Slow retrieves require patience—you can expect to spend ten minutes retrieving a 20-m cast; if you don't, you are working the pattern too quickly.

Other methods I often use to fish the pupa involve various full-sinking lines from #1 slow-sink to #3 fast-sink. Slow-sink lines are very similar to floating lines, but are more effective than dry lines in water deeper than 6 m, because they allow a pupa to be worked slowly on an ascent angle of 30° to the surface.

Chironomids will pupate in water as deep as 10 m; when this occurs, try the #3 fast-sink line equipped with a 3-m leader tapering to 3-X. Cast a line the full depth of water you are anchored in, let the line and leader sink to vertical, and slowly begin your retrieve; the fish should take right under the boat.

Trout will sometimes prefer to take the pupa just under the surface, an activity recognized by arcing head and tail rises as the fish comes up and over the pupa, taking it on a downward angle. On these occasions, fish the pupa with a floating line and the leader greased to within 10 cm of the fly. The key here is to not strike on the rise; be patient and wait to feel the fish take the fly down.

Jack Shaw came up with an original series of chironomid patterns for Kamloops lakes forty years ago, models that are still replicated or mimicked by fly tiers today. Jack used a lot of natural materials for his flies and, knowing him as I did, I have a feeling he wouldn't agree with bead heads used on chironomid pupae in today's imitations.

Jack used phentex yarn and straight Mustad 9671 hooks for his black patterns, which still works pretty well, but I prefer using curved hooks, which adds to the wriggling movement and overall shape I like to depict.

The translucent, red and silver patterns I'm showing you can be tied in many body colour combinations, including all black (no red floss underbody), olive, brown and grey complemented with ribbings of silver, gold and red wires or white nylon (see page 129).

Chironomid—Adult

Many fly fishers will argue with me on the importance of the adult stage of the chironomid—so be it, but I have enjoyed more days on the water using adult imitations than I care to admit, not catching the trophy fish of the bottom zone, but lots of 30–40-cm scrappy ones that want to make a game of it. Trout go to this stage later in the afternoon after the major hatch has waned for the day, when the random adult is still coming off and some of the bellies are not yet filled—or perhaps the trout are just in a frisky mood and decide to rise. Any excuse to use a dry line is good enough for me—one trout from the surface is worth ten from below, and I eagerly anticipate every opportunity to use a floating line, as if it's my last fishing day on earth.

Emerging adults have cinnamon-brown wings, which soon turn to grey when dry, with body colours of charcoal-grey and black most dominant, brown and olive sub-dominant. Chironomids don't skitter on the surface like a caddis, but will sometimes show a few false starts and jumps before becoming airborne. The aptly named 25-mm bomber resembles an aircraft bomber when taking off: slow, bulky and climbing quietly into the sky.

To fish the adult, target moving and dimpling trout. Simply cast, let it sit, and wait; if nothing happens, give it a few twitches to impart some excitement and action, and lift your rod the instant you see the rise, or the fish will be missed.

I've had my best success with a modified version of Brian Chan's Lady McConnell, a pattern that Brian originated in the 1980s, which I have named after that pretty little lake on the backroad to Lac Le Jeune. Other imitations that work are Tom Thumb and Humpy patterns in sizes 14–18 (see page 130).

Chironomid—Emerger

Alas, there will be days when both adult and pupa are refused, but fish are showing everywhere; it's during these frustrating occasions that an emerging adult could be what the fish are seeking. It's difficult to tell when the emerger should be used because the rise is the same as for an adult: dimpling trout.

My emerger pattern is similar to the adult, except that I've switched to a curved hook, used mallard flank for the tail, added a few turns of white ostrich herl at the rear of the body, eliminated the dry hackle and carried deer hair into my standard emerger "look," which I use on my emerging mayfly and caddis imitations. I use cinnamon deer hair to simulate the wet wings of an emerging adult, which will turn to grey within a few minutes. Because I want my emergers to penetrate the surface film and appear to be struggling to break free of the shuck, I grease only the deer-hair wing with floatant.

Fish the emerger dead drift on a floating line and regular leader, adding the occasional twitch if it's ignored (see page 130).

Midge

Midges

Order: Diptera
Family: Chironomidae
Larva: size 2–5 mm; colours: black, brown, tan, olive, cream, red—all translucent
Pupa: size 2–5 mm; colours: same as larva
Adult: size 2–5 mm; colours: same as larva and pupa, except red

Part 1—Still-water Lakes

Midges also belong to insect order Diptera and family Chironomidae, and are so closely related to chironomids that the only noticeable difference is size. Midges are the really little guys, just specks on the water when hatching. I wish I could say "Ignore them; they'll go away," but this is seldom true, only correct when there is a more significant emergence like chironomids appearing in conjunction with them. Thank God this miracle happens on a regular basis!

The midge life cycle is a replica of the chironomid: complete metamorphosis from egg, larva and pupa to adult, but in diminutive sizes. As larvae, they are often referred to as glass worms because of their transparency, which is hard to imitate on a hook. This larva stage, however, is among the 30 percent chironomid food source that a trout lake produces, so it is important to the fly fisher.

Midge Larvae

Tiny, wormlike and segmented in appearance like their cousins, the chironomids, the larva stage is found in multi-coloured assortments, but the most common is the transparent "glass worm." If you've pumped the throat contents of trout and noticed in the mix a green gob of minute, clear, wormlike larvae with a small dot at head and rear, these are glass worms. If they are the only content of the throat pump, you could be in for a tough day unless you can score with a good pattern. At these times, when you can't get action, try a blood leech for a change of menu. Spring, early summer and late fall are prime times because fish go to an exclusive diet of "ghost" larvae for a week or so.

Unlike chironomids, midge larvae do not build a case around themselves; they are free-roaming, which makes them an abundant and available food source in spite of their small size. The larvae's preferred habitats are weedy shoal areas, but they are also found mixed with chironomid bloodworm larvae in deep water. A prime year-round food source for other aquatic organisms such as shrimp, damselflies, mayflies, dragonflies and leeches, midge larvae deserve an important placement in the food chain of our still-water lakes.

I like a chironomid setup for fishing midge larvae: floating line and long 6-m fluorocarbon leader. They will often be found free-swimming in shallow water of less than a metre, which could necessitate a shorter leader, or perhaps resorting to a small paste indicator placed at 2–3 m from the hook on the 6-m leader. The fly should be inched slowly through the bottom zone, or dead drifted on the breeze, imparting only the occasional twitch.

Jack Shaw developed a glass worm larva pattern that used a silver tinsel body, a tuft of herl at each end, and a wisp of partridge behind the eye to simulate movement. I used this model with minor success for many years, but finally came up with one of my own that is similar to my bloodworm tie for chironomid larvae. The larvae, although transparent, take on a yellow-green hue because of their algae food sources, which is the "look" that I've attempted to mimic, using an underbody of green floss, clear Midge Flex over-wrap, and a sparse turn of partridge or grouse to impart some movement (see page 131).

Midge Pupa

A major difference between chironomids and midge pupae is that midge larvae pupate without the benefit of a protective tube, but they also exhibit stages of pre-emergence activity that is noticed by trout and likely rivets the fish's attention to the larva stage exclusive of other food sources.

Midge pupae are 2–5 mm long, larger and darker in the head and thorax area, with the appearance of two ear-like antennae protruding from the top of their heads. They move in a quick, wiggling, up-and-down motion, and rest in a vertical position. This stage of the insect is common in a number of colours: olive, tan, blood-red, dark brown, and even a fluorescent yellow-green, and shouldn't be overlooked by the fly fisher because of their diminutive size, as they are eagerly accepted by fish because of their abundance.

Midge pupa and chironomid patterns, because they require minimal movement by the fly fisher, lend themselves quite well to a two-rod setup: one cast and set out fishing the pupa, doing nothing, another deeply working a leech, scud or other pattern from the other side of the boat (see page 132).

Fish the midge pupa the same as the larva stage: floating line and 6-m fluorocarbon leader, again displaying the patience of Job to allow the line to locate the depth where fish are taking the natural. In the evening, it's common to find hoards of midge pupae suspended just under the surface film as they migrate upward during low light; this is the time to try the Suspender Midge pattern.

There is a multitude of midge pupa patterns on the market, every fly tying book offering mind-boggling discourses on which are best and how to fish them. I stick with several basic patterns: one of Brian Chan's when I see the "little green guy" coming off, another with a copper wire body and herl thorax, one with pheasant body and herl thorax, and the last a suspender pattern; all are simple to tie, and productive on lake or stream (see page 131).

Midge Adult

When still-water fishing, we don't get so overwhelmed with the significance of the adult midge hatch that we worry about developing patterns that will guarantee us a catch of fish from the surface, because larva and pupa stages are the most important to the fly fisher. Adults, however, are not to be ignored completely because trout will often feed on the surface at the end of a period of midge hatch activity, offering the patient and observant lake angler perhaps thirty minutes of dry fly action that is the most fun of the day.

At Cobb Lake last October, I was having a really tough day, catching only a brookie on my first cast with a Water Boatman pattern. There was a minor hatch of chironomid going on and an even more trivial emergence of midge in a minute size. The odd trout was dimpling the surface, but it was certainly nothing to get excited about that would tempt me to change my rigging to a dry fly. I wallowed through several fishless hours offering leech, scud and damsel to the quarry before I relented to the dry fly out of desperation. In the next half-hour, I caught and released three fine trout on the dry fly, a size 18 grey midge. Thinking about the day on the drive home, I realized that I could have probably caught every rising fish in the lake had I switched to a dry fly earlier in the day. That's fishing—ignorant style!

My midge dry pattern for lakes and still water is identical to my chironomid adult, except tied and presented in sizes 18–22. This pattern is effective because it represents the escaping adult that momentarily sits on the surface drying its wings before becoming airborne (see page 131).

Part 2—Rivers and Streams

Everything I have said about midges in lakes is adaptable to rivers, creeks and streams—except for the magnitude. Without the minuscule midge, rivers would be hard-pressed to support fish life. Lakes have an abundance of freshwater shrimp, dragonfly, damsel, chironomid and leech as staple food sources for trout; rivers rely on midge, mayfly, stonefly and caddis as their major grocery items. You need to be a clinger creature to survive the turbulence of spring breakup in moving water, and a quick, opportunistic fish to intercept moving targets.

Midge and chironomid insect order Diptera make up 50 percent of fish food sources in a freshwater stream ecosystem. Moving water is where colours other than the transparent glass worm larvae dominate the midge order: blood-red, dark brown and herl green imitated on hook sizes 18–22. They emerge at all times of year during open water, many species multi-brooded during a season, even hatching in the dead of winter during a snowstorm or a miserable rainy day.

Midge Larva

Midge larvae like back eddies, slow moving water and tail-outs in streams, areas where they can bury in silt and won't be swept away, but they also frequent the edges of fast water riffles if that's all they can get. Common larvae colours are red, olive, tan, cream and black, but when larvae bury in mud and are oxygen-deprived they take on a blood-red colouration, which I prefer to imitate because of its visibility.

In streams of Alberta, the US and other regions where you can fish more than one fly at a time, many anglers fish midge larvae as a dropper to a dry fly. In BC, our regulations prohibit the use of two-fly rigs, but we can use strike indicators with a floating line and 3-m leader, which is the most popular method. It's important to get the fly near the bottom of the stream to imitate drifting larvae that have become dislodged or are free-swimming, so many fly fishers will often add a split shot to the leader 30 cm above the hook, and sling the fly into a holding lie.

Other than floating line, I use a 2-m sink-tip and short 2-m leader for nymph, egg or larvae stream fishing, which I prefer to the strike indicator system at times when I need to fish the bottom of a river (see page 132).

Midge Pupa

The short-lived pupa stage of an insect is the most important phase to the fly fisher. As a larva begins to mature, it encapsulates, the thorax enlarges and gases form inside the pupa case, which are used to propel it to the surface. Vulnerable to their predators at this stage, pupae quickly split their cases and vamoose as adults.

This stage should be imitated with a floating line and regular 3-m leader tapering to 5-X tippet, often employing a Leisering Lift technique to replicate the rising pupa. To apply this method, begin with a short cast upstream of 5–10 m; maintain full contact with the fly through the float (no slack line or leader), and slowly lift your arm and rod vertically while following the drift of the fly with your rod tip. At the end or during the drift, you can drop your arm and rod tip to let the fly settle down, then begin the lift again, which simulates a rising and falling pupa, a very effective method on selective trout. At the end of the drift, permit the fly to "hang" in the slack water or current; many fish will follow it during the drift and lazily grab it as you lift the line to make a back cast (see page 132).

For a wet fly on a floating line, try the Soft Hackle Emerger; again using the Leisering Lift method with a short line. This pattern is very simple to tie; the tag end is matched to various colours depending on the hatch in progress. Trout like to intercept these on the swing, or when the fly is left hanging at the end of the drift. Again, challenge the fish by lifting and settling the emerger as it plays through the current (see page 133).

As in lakes, mature midges often travel to the surface of slack water during evening and low light conditions, which is an opportune time to try a Suspender Midge, the fly submerged except for the posted wing (see page 131).

Midge Emerger

During a midge hatch, many pupae get caught in the surface film, especially in the quiet water of streams that midges prefer, where there is limited friction of fast-moving water to aid the release of the pupa shuck. This is prime emerger time, and my favourite method to fish the adult midge is to cast a short line, pull back a little slack to keep drag from forming, and let the fly and current do the work.

Colours are varied—grey, black, olive, tan, blood-red and yellow-orange— all tied on curved hooks. Apply floatant to the front portion only because the two most important things to understand about all emerger patterns are that the rear end needs to sink, and the front end must float. On my emergers, I use deer hair for the emerger wing, tying the tips forward, extending the deer hair backward over the thorax to present a struggling adult midge trying to release its wings (see page 132).

Midge Adult

Once free of the shuck, the adult midge is airborne, allowing fish a small window of opportunity to target this stage of development. Even though the adult is gone in a fleeting moment, river and stream fish are vulnerable to a drifted adult pattern at almost any time of day. Enter the Adams—possibly the most widely used searcher of all midge patterns ever invented. When tied and fished in sizes 18–22, the Adams represents both midge and tiny mayfly; in larger sizes of 12–16, it also imitates the Callibaetis mayfly hatch, as the adult spinner stage. For river fishing, which many times calls for sizes smaller than 16, I now tie my little Adams parachute patterns with a pale yellow Antron post, which is much easier to see amidst foam and current on moving water than white, grey or black (see page 133).

During a heavy hatch, mating midges will often *cluster* in slack water, where you will see a pod of them in a ball of wings, hackles and legs. This cluster effect led to the development of another simple fly that has had great success over many years, the Griffith's Gnat by George Griffith (see page 134).

The adult midge is also a target for trout during the evening when females, which have hatched and mated over the past few days, return to the river at the spinner stage to deposit eggs. The spent, dying spinner will be visible drifting the current with outstretched wings, having completed its life cycle. Common colours for adult midge spinners are black, pale grey, charcoal-grey, olive and lime green, all tied with long sweeping tails, slim bodies and extended wings in sizes 18–28. Size 28s are beyond my current patience as a fly tier, but I've heard there are places in the world where you can't catch a fish without them—I would sheepishly learn to tie size 28s if I had to, I suppose… (see page 134).

Mayfly

Lake and river systems of the North Cariboo and Central BC abound with significant hatches of mayflies, which are available to fish throughout the open-water seasons. I think the high acidity and cooler summer temperatures of our water and the less crowded, unpolluted lakes and rivers play a part in this prolific and important insect's abundance in the North. When I arrive at my favourite lakes or streams to discover mayfly nymph shucks drifting near shoreline or adults hung in vegetation, my heart soars because I know the day's promise should be fishing a floating line with emerging duns or a nymph near shore. If spinner adults are present, clinging to trees and vegetation or flitting at the water's edge, I could witness the return of egg-laying females on my outing, begging for more dry fly fishing opportunities. What choices!

The importance of mayfly genera to the food chain of lakes and rivers is substantial, but varies in different regions of the province due to availability of the insect. Southern Interior lakes seem to have fewer mayflies than our Interior Plateau lakes, which have abundant quantities, where we often see daily hatches of mayfly families during early spring, summer and fall. Biologists estimate that fish-diet ranking of the mayfly is 10 percent for lakes, and up to 25 percent for rivers and streams.

Mayflies encompass an incomplete metamorphosis cycle: egg, larva (nymph), dun and adult spinner; absent is the pupa stage of the insect. They are multi-brooded, up to three per season, sizes diminishing from a hatch matching size 12 or 14 hook in early spring to an 18 or 20 during late summer or fall.

Mayflies belong to order Ephemeroptera, of which there are over 700 species. Several families of mayfly genera are most common in our area: Callibaetis of lakes and ponds, and Baetidae, Ephemera, Ephemerellidae and Tricorythodes widespread in streams.

In Northern lakes, Callibaetis mayflies begin to appear in late April, depending on elevation, or in May a few weeks after ice-out, and continue to hatch profusely through June, tapering in July and August; or they may hatch in hoards during a summer cool spell. In lakes of multi-genera families, a smaller

Callibaetis family appears during late summer.

Baetidae, known by fly fishers as Blue-Winged Olives, or BWOs, are stream dwellers consisting of several subspecies, whose adult stages are recognized by their pale grey, yellow-olive, black or, more commonly, olive-grey colours. River species of mayflies hatch year-round in open water, preferring weedy patches, corners, rocky riffles and soft runs.

The Ephemeridae family has genera known as Green and Brown Drakes, and the Ephemerellidae family as Pale Morning Duns (PMDs), Pale Evening Duns (PEDs), Sulphurs and Hendricksons. Around Central BC, the PMD has the more consistent presence of these two families.

Mayfly families prefer a warm, cloudy day to bright sunshine for their coming-out parties, with dun hatches typically beginning around noon and lasting until 3:00 p.m., and returning spinner falls occurring during both midday and in still evening hours.

Part 1—Mayfly Fishing Lakes

Callibaetis

Nymph: size 3–20 mm; colours: tan, green-olive, grey-olive and dark brown
Dun: size 6–20 mm; wing: mottled brown; body: brown-olive, grey-olive and light tan
Spinner: size 6–20 mm; wing: clear with grey mottled spots; body: medium brown or grey

Nymph

The nymph or larva stage matures from eggs deposited by the female adult spinner, which take only a few weeks to develop, allowing for several broods through the fishing season. Nymphs range in size from 3 mm at hatching stage to 20 mm at maturity, all sizes being available to fly fishers because of overlapping broods. They are quite stubby-looking with enlarged thorax and head area, short, tapered, gilled abdomens and three tail filaments the length of their bellies.

Aquatic insects feed on their environment, taking on the colour of the vegetation they devour. In dark tannin-coloured lakes, nymphs will be black, mottled brown tones or dark grey, whereas algae-rich and weedy water systems will produce light grey, pale green and yellow colourations of the nymph stage.

During development stages, the larva is a hider, preferring the safety and shelter of weeds, bottom debris, logs—or even burrowing into shoreline muck. They begin to appear as fish food as they mature: thorax darkening, their restless energy causing them to stage in preparation for emergence—prime fishing time for the nymph phase.

As the nymph matures, gases form between the skin and the body of the developing adult inside; this gas forms bubbles, and the added buoyancy carries the nymph to the surface for emergence. If not quite ready, the nymph can rise to the surface and swim to the bottom for several days, but eventually the pressure of increasing gas bubbles forces them to hatch into the emerging dun.

If I see shucks on the shoreline, I know they are staging on the bottom and have shown hatching activity the previous day. I'll typically begin with a size 12 nymph, fishing a #1 or #2 full-sink line over weedbeds and close to the bottom in 2–4 m of water using a slow, hand-crawl retrieve interspersed with quick strips and frequent resting stops.

By late morning, I expect to see the odd dun hatching close to shore, which will signal the beginning of nymphs rising to the surface. If fish are aggressively showing, I will switch to a floating line and work the shoreline with a nymph under the surface, or try a dun pattern on top. On bright sunny days, the hatch may not come or trout may not rise for the duns, but they will take the nymph at all depths—mayflies love a crappy day!

For my mayfly nymph and emerger patterns, I tie abdomens with primary quill barbs instead of dubbing, Antron or furry material blends, because I believe quill barbs, tied vertical to the body, impart the look of prominent abdomen gills. Being a natural material, the barbs also attract and hold tiny air bubbles that imitate gas-forming air in the nymphal case (see page 135).

Emerger and Dun

Drifting on the breeze of a lake surface like tiny sailboats, Callibaetis duns are impressive figures, and I enjoy watching them hatch while I fish, gazing with marvellous wonder at the joys of nature as they rest to dry their wings. During periods of low barometer and calm conditions, they shed their nymph case under water and "pop" to the top. Many fish gorge on floating nymphs as they struggle to free themselves of their enclosures, or on the duns as they ascend the water column or hesitate on the surface while drying their wings.

Emerging duns are prime targets for cruising trout. I have become a real fan of emerging patterns of any insect, because I sense the positive strikes and fewer misses indicate feeding trout that are less wary of predators. I also feel that larger fish are more comfortable taking food slightly below the surface than on it. Emergers will be taken with a swirl, perhaps allowing only a glimpse of the fish's tail as it whirls at the helpless insects.

The dun or sub-imago is not the true adult, but the hatching mayfly that we see on the water. Muted cinnamon-brown or grey-olive in colour, with brown mottled wings held in an upright position, they can be fished dry on a floating line, or subsurface and drowned without floatant, which imitates the "popping" dun. After hatching, the sub-imago will dry its wings, fly away and hang out around shoreline trees for a few days while it transforms into the adult spinner, which will mature within several weeks, return to mate and then die on the lake.

My emerger pattern is similar to the nymph in colour and material selection, except I want it to hang under the surface film, so I use a short-shank curved hook, tie a long trailing shuck, and do not apply floatant to anything but the deer-hair wing. A floating line and drifting fly imitates the struggling insect, with an occasional twitch to add stimulation. You can also fish a sink-tip line for this emerger, imitating the popping dun—no floatant, let your line take the fly under water, and give it a few quick strips while raising the rod tip (see page 135).

Adult and Spent Spinner

I fondly recall a day of unsettled, but warm June weather while fishing Hart Lake back in the late 1990s—perfect conditions for a mayfly hatch. Shortly before noon, adult females began to swarm over the shallows of the lake and males darted into the frenzy; they mated, and females began to dip the water to release fertilized eggs. During the next two hours, I released over 20 trout ranging in size from 40–55 cm, all on the Adult Spinner—a day to remember, not duplicated on the adult mayfly since. Days like these are etched in the mind forever: ideal temperatures, conditions, timing and circumstances.

Callibaetis spinners are recognized by their charcoal-grey colouration, long slender abdomens curved upward and ribbed with white, three body-length tails and transparent wings held upright over the thorax. When laying eggs, the female flits over the water, dipping in her abdomen—up again, and down, and up, many times—depositing her eggs over a large area, ensuring best odds of progeny survival by fully broadcasting her seed. Then she dies, dropping to the water with wings outspread, setting the stage for the Adult Spent Spinner imitation.

Adult upright and spent variations are equally effective, with trout occasionally preferring one over the other. I begin my quest fishing the upright adult, targeting rising fish, which often take as soon as the fly hits the water, because the female doesn't rest after mating as she carries on to another part of the lake. The spent version is most effective near the end of the spinner fall, the lake's surface littered with dead and dying adults, fish gorging on the easy pickings.

Many variations of patterns are tied to represent these stages of the Callibaetis life cycle, but I like the modifications I have made to my mentor Jack

Shaw's adult original from the 1970s: Tiemco 200R long, curved hook, speckled mallard wing, and long, parted tails. For the spent spinner pattern, I like to use glossy white Antron for wing material because the prominent transparency lying flat on the water has a better appearance than mallard (see page 136).

Part 2—Streams and Rivers

The importance of mayflies as a food source to fish—up to 25 percent—in river systems cannot be overlookedand on rivers like the Stellako, Blackwater, Crooked and McLeod, these hatches are significant, many of them overlapping with the emergence of midge and caddis throughout the day's fishing.

Not to be disregarded is the nymph stage of the mayfly, which is broadly categorized into four major groups that represent its adult families: crawlers, prowling the bottom and hiding in cracks and crevices of the stream bed; cling-ers, dwelling in fast water and hanging onto the underside of rocks; swimmers, undulating their tails and moving from place to place; and burrowers, residing in the bottom muck of streams. On bright sunny days when only sporadic mayfly hatches occur, the nymph can provide the best action of all stages, and is a good bet to start the morning.

Nymph

In stream environments, mayfly nymphs are generally hidden insects until matu-ration begins, when the fidgety nymphs become restless and, like their cousins the Callibaetis of still-water lakes, their thoraxes enlarge and wing-cases darken, gas bubbles begin to form and they come out of hiding to greet the world.

Mature mayfly nymphs of rivers and streams, with the exception of the drake family, are smaller than those of lake habitats, though identical in features: prominent gill structure on their abdomens, three tail filaments the length of their bellies, darkened and enlarged thorax areas and stubby appearances. They can be easily mistaken for smaller families of stoneflies; for example, the yellow sally genera. The best differentiating features are tail filaments (stoneflies have two; mayflies three) and wing-cases, (stoneflies have two distinct crescent-shaped pads). Most mayfly families are not good swimmers, so they inhabit slow sections of water or corners of pools where debris settles, providing cover that they can hide under and cling to.

Rivers and streams lend themselves to several methods of fishing the nymph stage: floating lines and strike indicators, floating lines and 3-m leaders, and 2-m sink-tips with 2-m leaders. Your choice will vary with the pace of the stream—soft, shallow water is covered nicely by floating line and leader twice the depth of the average water, whereas runs of quick velocity and deep pools are best worked with floating line and indicator set at 1.5 times water depth, or my preferred method of mini-tip line and short leader.

Pattern selections are simple—the Hare's Ear Nymph in sizes 16–18 has long been the choice for small Baetidae family insects found in rivers. Use the Pheasant Tail Nymph sizes 10–14 for matching the cycles of Green and Brown Drakes and PMDs (see page 137).

Emerger

In the past ten or twenty years, emerger imitations have played an important role in the evolution of fly fishing patterns. I think many wet fly patterns of the early 20th century, using primary quill as wing material, tinsel for body structure and saddle hackle for movement inadvertently mimicked the effect that emerger models should impart—they move, they glisten, and are buggy and natural enough in design to look like struggling insects about to surface.

Large fish are wary creatures, needing to expend as little effort as possible to camouflage their resting spots and secure their existence. The constant search for food consumes a great deal of their time and energy; they're always watching for insects drifting through their window, patiently waiting for the opportunity to dart from cover to intercept. Emerging nymphs wake them up—something visible, active—the chance to make a decision and be fulfilled. A trout will make many of these assessments during a day—take it or leave it—and emergers make it easy for them. A struggling insect, not yet able to fly away, is an easy target for sure. That's why the emerger imitations work so well; they make the decision a no-brainer.

During the past several seasons on the rivers, I have fished emergers two to one over traditional dry flies. When fish are rising, but not taking the visible insect, emergers are the ticket. They can be parachute, cripple or floating dun style: all emerger variety as they partially sit under the surface film, not on top. And don't forget soft-hackle nymphs, matched with a tag the colour of the current hatch.

All parts of the river—fast and slow water, long corners, tail-outs and edges of seams—can be fished with emergers with a floating line and long, 4-m leader. I prefer using a lot of short casts, downstream mends and parachute casts, giving slack line, allowing the fly to work the current undisturbed, and permitting the fish to get a good look at the offering.

When tying emerger patters with deer hair that protrudes forward of the body, the pattern also passes for a cripple, one that cannot free itself of the shuck. The only floating image that fish see is the wing, and these flies are so durable and resilient they can usually be fished for a full day without destruction.

Dun and Spinner

Hatches of duns, emergers and cripples coincide in river systems; emergers and cripples being clear winners when it comes to hook-ups because of the greater length of time that fish get to see them. Duns of some families often emerge under water, becoming airborne immediately after they break the surface film of a river. I will always have dun patterns on me, but the obvious choice is to try the emerger first, and even if fish are feeding on duns, usually they will not pass up the easy pickings of a struggling, emerging insect or a cripple that will never hatch.

The dun is the hatch we see on the water, rising from river currents and escaping into shoreline trees. Along with cripples and late emergers, they collect in back eddies and corners of the stream as they dry their wings, becoming easy targets for trout that casually sip and snout their way through the hatching hoard of insects.

It's important to be able to recognize different families of duns, because they are the first clue to the hatch in progress, each family's genus having its own colouration and size; to confuse matters more, some hatch differently.

A floating line and long, 4-m leader tapered to 6-X and even 7-X is the rule of thumb for fishing adult stages of mayfly hatches, where hatching duns and dying spinner adults will stack up in back eddies and soft water. Learn to spot foam lines, and throw short lines into them as trout know these are safe spots to circle under to pick up hatching and spent adults. Use slack line methods, wiggle casts, pile casts—anything to gain valuable, free drift time, and above all, avoid line drag.

When tying adult spinner patterns of mayfly, I use either a single strand of flat floss, nylon or a stripped quill feather to represent the now-glossy ribbed abdomen of adult stages; but don't overbuild the slender belly, a characteristic necessary to create a realistic replica. Tying these little guys down to size 24 is not fun, but essential if you want to be successful.

Blue-Winged Olive (BWO)

Genus: *Baetidae*
Nymph: size 4–12 mm; colours: dark brown, brown-olive, grey-olive
Dun: size 4–10 mm; colours: wing: blue-grey; abdomen: grey-olive, brown-olive, tan and black
Spinner: size 4–12 mm; colours: wing: clear; abdomen: brown-olive, grey-olive or red-brown

BWOs are tiny, and recognized by their colouration, which is usually olive-green or olive-grey, with blue-grey tails and wings—the largest gracing hook size is 16, even down to 22 later in the season—and because they are the most prolific and reliable hatch of all mayflies in rivers, they induce nostalgia in even the most seasoned fly fishers.

BWO nymphs are swimmers, and are great early season or winter fish catchers, inhabiting slow water, often found migrating through the water column to find new digs, which makes them more vulnerable at this stage than other mayfly families. Match the nymph with a Hare's Ear size 14–18, not being afraid to go one size larger than the insect (see page 137).

Although they are called olives, BWOs are a multi-genus family, and also common in tan, grey and even black—best to have a sampling of each colour tied. Blue-Winged Olives are the first mayfly to appear in early spring, and never really disappear from streams, continuing to hatch through the most miserable days of winter if the water is open. Unlike some families that pop to the surface, the hatching BWO nymph and emerging dun is vulnerable to fish for a long period of time during emergence, often riding the current for 50–100 m before becoming free, which sets this insect up nicely for emerger patterns.

Some fishers say spinner falls are not important—but I beg to differ. One August evening many years ago, I fished the Stellako through a BWO spinner fall without a reasonable pattern in my fly box, and was badly trounced by the fish. Trout were rising everywhere on the bridge run, hundreds of them, all in union; so many it was unnerving. Needless to say, I tied some up the next morning expecting the same hatch to occur during the evening. It never came, and that's why it's called "fishing"—be prepared, another lesson learned (see page 138).

Green Drake and Slate-Winged Olive

Genus: *Drunella*
Nymph: size 11–16 mm; colours: brown, brown-olive
Dun: size 11–16 mm; wing: blue-grey; abdomen: yellow-olive, brown-olive, grey-olive
Spinner: size 11–16 mm; wing: clear; abdomen: yellow-olive

Green Drake duns are muddy olive, presenting upright grey wings, three body-length tails and yellow belly ribbing best represented on size 8–12 hooks. In the North, we see both hatches, but the smaller Slate-Winged Olive (SWO) duns are more prolific than the big Western Green Drake, and I tie the patterns identically, but prefer the SWO tied in matching sizes 12–16. They are summer flies in our slow-to-warm waters of the North, where you can expect the hatch to begin in July, and continue sporadically until the first frosts of late August. Being a larger morsel than the little BWO, Green Drakes and SWOs cause quite a stir when they begin to show—fish like them and because they are often the "new" hatch on the water, trout will key to this and refuse other offerings.

Nymphs of the family are strong-legged crawlers, inhabiting moderate flows, riffles and runs, hiding under rocks and bottom debris. Trout will sometimes knock them loose with their tails, returning for the prize, but they are more abundant during maturity when the nymph migrates to slower flows to begin adult development.

Duns take a long time to emerge and dry their wings, becoming a leading target for surface-feeding fish, so if the emerger won't take them, fish the dun. My emerger pattern is the same as the BWO Emerger, tied in sizes 12–14 (see page 139).

Brown Drake

Genus: *Ephemera*
Nymph: size 14–21 mm; colour: yellow-brown
Dun: size 10–20 mm; wing: grey-brown; abdomen: yellow-brown
Spinner: size 10–20 mm; wing: grey-brown; abdomen: yellow-brown

The Brown Drake is the largest of the mayfly order and not an abundant hatch on northern streams, but because of the insect's size, it creates a big impression when it decides to pop. The Stellako in mid-July is a good place to look for this hatch, and you'll recognize them by both their hefty size and distinct rusty-brown colouration, sporting grey upright wings and yellow belly markings similar to the Green Drake genus.

The nymphs are burrowers, living in up to 30 cm of mud, fine gravel or silt, so are not an easy morsel for fish to locate until they come out of hiding during the evenings or early mornings to hunt other insects. As they mature and become more active during the day, fly fishers get the chance to test a Hare's Ear or Pheasant Tail in sizes 8–12, bouncing one on the bottom of the stream.

The dun is not as important as the spinner stage to the fly fisher because they emerge quickly, offering scattered opportunities to fish this stage of the insect. The dun pops through the nymphal case under water, and is strong enough to be airborne once it hits the surface. The hatch and spinner fall is strongest during evenings, often into darkness, which again makes for difficult fishing, but emergers and cripples worked through pools, tail waters and back eddies are usually my best producers for this elephant of a mayfly. Great fishing when they are on (see page 139 and 140)!

Pale Morning Dun (PMD)

Genus: *Ephemerella*
Nymph: size 7–12 mm; colours: olive and rusty-brown

Dun: size 7–12 mm; wing: blue-grey; abdomen: pale yellow or tan

Spinner: size 7–12 mm; wing: clear; abdomen: rusty-brown

Pale Evening Dun (PED)

Nymph: size 6–12 mm; colour: dark brown-olive

Dun: size 7–15 mm; wing: pale yellow; abdomen: pale yellow, tan

Spinner: size 7–15 mm; wing: clear; abdomen: pale yellow, tan

Hatching through hot summer months right into the last fishing days of fall, PMDs and PEDs are two of my favourite mayflies; not only because they are one of the prettiest, but because they elicit a trigger response from feeding fish. They are the classic gentleman's (or lady's) hatch: on time and on schedule during summer afternoons and evenings between 5:00 and 8:00 p.m. I'm sure there have been more missed dinner bells for this hatch than all others combined—when they come on, you don't want to be away from the river during the evening's hatch or spinner fall.

Nymphs of this family are small, represented by sizes 14–18 Pheasant Tail Nymphs, and are members of the crawler family. When mature, they migrate to the soft water of shoreline, and should be targeted in less than 30 cm of water, swinging the fly through rock crevices and quiet runs with short casts and Leisering Lift methods.

Duns are reddish-brown; spinner adults have brown backs with pale yellow underbody—the yellow a stark and visible contrast to the fading light of late afternoon. All adult stages: dun, spinner and spent spinner are excellent fishing, but I have found that the little PMD Emerger fishes this hatch like a true champion, captivating the interest of even the most wary of quarry. It doesn't take a cloud of PMDs to get the trout moving; a few are often enough, and I think the bright yellow colouration of adults arouses the trout's predatory response, much like the colour red gets a bull going in circles.

I recall one July day in 2006 fishing the Livingstone in Southern Alberta, a classic east-slope cutthroat stream, with my son Kevin, who is a size 20 Parachute Adams kind of guy on small streams. The PEDs began hatching on schedule at 5:00 p.m. or so, sporadic but mixed with the odd small Slate-Winged Olive. Kevin had done well all day on the Adams, but trout snubbed it through every run during the evening, as they were keyed on only the PED, and I fished the runs behind him, taking rising fish after fish on the emerger until Kevin stopped fishing and just came along to watch—a classic learning moment for both of us.

PMDs and PEDs often hatch on the same day; the adults are so similar in size and colour that patterns can be interchanged—perhaps not on the chalk streams of England, but surely in the remote and under-fished streams of the BC Interior. PMDs are a tad larger, so I will use a size 14 emerger during the day, switching to size 16 in the evenings. Spinner adults and spent stages are often the ticket also, imitated on size 16–18 hooks with yellow quill abdomens (see page 140-141).

Trico Dun and Spinner

Genus: *Tricorythodes*

Nymph: size 3–10 mm; colour: dark brown

Dun: size 3–6 mm; wings: pale grey; body (females): olive abdomen/dark brown thorax; body (males): dark brown, charcoal

Spinner: size 3–6 mm; wing: clear; body (females): grey abdomen/black thorax; body (males): all black.

Also known either affectionately or in distaste among fly fishers as the "white-winged curse," this smallest of mayfly families ranks only below the BWO in significance as a contributor to mayfly hatches. But be warned that the competition is fierce—size 20 is the largest hook that you can get away with. When they are coming off there are literally clouds of them; when fishing the Stellako many years ago, I managed to join the 20/20 club with my Trico dun pattern—a 50-cm fish on a size 20 fly. The 22/22 and 24/24 clubs still elude me, but this is the fly that will surely take me there, and with all probability it will be on the Stellako, or perhaps Dragon or Hobson Lakes, as these little guys are also present in lake systems.

Slender mayfly abdomen, charcoal colouration, pale ribbing, three body-length tails, white upright wing—all captured on a size 20–24 hook. That's the curse! Worse yet, 7-X tippets are mandatory.

Trico duns hatch and spinners return to the softest of water, females emerging in the mayfly-like fashionable hours of late morning, males at night. The transformation from adult to spinner occurs during the same day as the hatch for females, and the mating and egg-laying fall begins in the afternoon. Fish take hatching duns and spent spinners equally well; the trick is long, fine leaders and drag-free drifts—difficult with a fly you can barely see.

Nymph stages are not important per se, but on any occasion that you search water with size 18 Hare's Ear or Pheasant Tail Nymphs, you are on target for imitating the larva stage of Tricos, BWOs or small PMDs. During early morning hours, I also fish the Soft Hackle Emerger (olive, grey or golden-orange tag) in sizes 16–18, using short casts and the Leisering Lift method to search slow runs along shoreline, as precursor to the pending hatch (see page 142).

Chironomids

Bloodworm Translucent—Smith's

Originator: Brian Smith 2004
Hook: Tiemco 200R, #10–14
Thread: UTC red
Tail: none
Underbody: Johnson & Johnson waxed dental floss
Body rib: red floss, 6–7 turns over underbody
Rib: copper wire, 6–7 turns in front of red floss
Topcoat: clear nail polish, 2 coats over body and ribbing
Hackle: pheasant rump reddish phase; hook length, 1 turn only
Tying tip: To eliminate bulk, this is a method you can use for any pattern that requires more than two materials tied at the hook bend (see following chapters).

Begin by tying in red floss, copper rib and dental floss (in that order) 5 mm behind the eye. Wrap all materials to the bend of the hook with the first wrap down the shank of dental floss and return the dental floss to the tie-in point. When wrapping the body of red floss, treat it as a rib, leaving a gap of underbody showing through the process. The copper wire then follows the red floss as a rib in front of each wrap back to the tie-in point.

Chironomid Pupa
Translucent Blood—Smith's

Originator: Brian Smith 1999
Hook: Tiemco 200R, #10–16
Thread: UTC black
Tail: mallard flank barbs, sparse
Rib: silver wire, fine; 1 wrap in front of each abdomen rib
Underbody 1: red floss, ½ abdomen length
Underbody 2: Johnson & Johnson dental floss, flat, waxed
Abdomen rib: black floss, single strand
Wing-case: dark turkey, laid over thorax and gills
Gills: white Glo Yarn, clipped short
Thorax: peacock herl, 2 strands
Throat hackle: partridge feather, grey phase
Topcoat: 2 coats clear nail polish over abdomen only

Tying tip: Tie the tail in first at two-thirds shank point, and follow with instructions for bloodworm pattern. It's easier to tie in and clip the gills *before* you begin the wing-case and thorax.

Chironomid Red & Silver—Smith's

Originator: Brian Smith 1993
Hook: Tiemco 2487 #12–16
Tail: none
Rib: fine wire, red and silver combination; 5–6 turns over abdomen
Abdomen: black floss single strand; slim at the rear, build up behind thorax

Wing-case: Midge Flex black, laid over thorax and gills
Gills: Antron white
Thorax: peacock herl, built up 2x abdomen

Chironomid Adult—Smith's

Originator: Brian Smith 1993
Hook: Mustad 94840 #12–16
Thread: UTC grey
Tail: deer hair, natural, body length
Back: deer hair, natural
Body: goose primary barbs, olive or charcoal-grey

Hackle: grizzly, 3–4 turns

Chironomid Emerger—Smith's

Originator: Brian Smith 2001
Hook: Tiemco 2487 #12–14
Thread: UTC clear
Tail (as shuck): mallard flank feather barbs natural; body length, tied down and past the gap of the hook
Gills: ostrich plume herl white, tied in front of tail at hook bend

Abdomen: goose primary barbs, charcoal-grey
Thorax: peacock herl, 4–5 turns
Wing: deer hair, cinnamon, body length; tied and posted at 45° in front of thorax, and clipped to thorax length

Midge

Chaoborus Larva—Smith's
Originator: Brian Smith 2004
Hook: Tiemco 200R #16–18
Thread: Uni-Mono clear
Tail: none
Rib: gold wire fine; wrap over Midge Flex 6–8 turns
Underbody: floss, pale lime green
Over-wrap: Midge Flex clear, wrapped over underbody
Hackle: partridge feather olive; body length, 1 turn only
Tying tip: This pattern is tied in the same manner as my translucent chironomid, except for using an under-wrap of coloured floss instead of dental floss.

Chaoborus (Midge) Pupa
Originator: Brian Chan (tied by Brian Smith)
Hook: Tiemco 2487 #16–22
Thread: UTC olive
Rib: gold wire fine; 5–6 turns over abdomen
Abdomen: floss, light lime green
Wing-case: duck primary, light grey
Thorax: rabbit dubbing, natural grey

Suspender Midge
Originator: unknown, (tied by Brian Smith)
Hook: Tiemco 2487 #16–18
Rib: gold wire fine; 5–6 turns over abdomen
Wing: Antron white, posted
Abdomen: goose primary barbs, grey
Thorax: peacock herl, 2–3 turns
Hackle: grizzly; parachute style, 3–4 turns around posted wing

Midge Adult
See tying instructions for Chironomid Adult opposite page.

Midge Larva—Smith's
Originator: Brian Smith 2004
Hook: Tiemco 200R #16–18
Thread: UTC red
Rib: red wire fine; 5–6 turns over Midge Flex
Underbody: Mylar, pearl
Body: Midge Flex red; wrapped over pearl Mylar
Hackle: grouse feather, 1 turn only

Midge Pupa—Smith's
Originator: Brian Smith 2001
Hook: Tiemco 2487 #16–20
Tail: none
Rib: silver wire, fine
Abdomen: goose primary barbs, grey
Thorax: peacock herl, 2 turns
Gills: Glo Yarn white; posted at eye, trimmed short

Tying tip: It's always easier to tie in the Glo Yarn gills after the abdomen and before you tie in the thorax; then use the thorax material to cover the ends of the Glo Yarn and clean up the pattern.

Adams Emerger—Smith's
Originator: Brian Smith 2004
Hook: Tiemco 2487 #16–18
Thread: Uni-Mono fine
Tail: mallard flank barbs natural; body lengths, sweeping down past hook bend
Rib: gold wire, fine; 5–6 turns over abdomen
Abdomen: goose primary barbs, natural grey

Thorax: rabbit dubbing, natural
Wing: deer hair, natural, body length; tied in front of thorax, posted at 45°, butt to the rear.

Tying tip: The only trick here is the deer-hair wing, where you must leave enough room in front of the thorax at the hook eye to tie in the wing; about 2 mm will suffice. You need about a 2-mm width bunch of deer hair; more is hard to work with. Measure the length on the body so the wing tips will extend about body length in front of the hook, where you will cinch it down in front of the thorax, and trim to thorax width and length.

Soft Hackle Emerger

Originator: unknown (tied by Brian Smith)

Hook: Tiemco 2487 #14–18

Thread: UTC orange

Tail: none

Butt: floss, yellow-orange; about ⅓ of hook shank

Thorax: rabbit dubbing natural

Hackle: grouse feather grey; body length, 1 turn only

Tying tip: When I say 1 turn only, it means prepare the full feather hackle by stripping off loose fuzz, tie in the hackle by the tips and wind 1 turn of hackle around the shank. This pattern can be tied using many different butt colours: grey, olive, lime green, red, cream and black.

My Adams—Smith's

Originator: Brian Smith 1992

Hook: Mustad 94840 #12–18

Thread: UTC black

Tail: grizzly and brown mixed hackle barbs, body length

Wing: mallard breast feather; folded, posted at ⅔-shank point

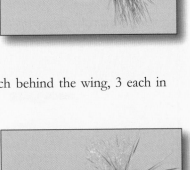

Abdomen and thorax: goose primary barbs, grey

Hackles: grizzly and brown, 1 each; 2 wraps each behind the wing, 3 each in front of wing

Parachute Adams—Smith's

Originator: Brian Smith 1996

Hook: Mustad 94840 #14–18

Thread: Uni-Mono clear

Tail: grizzly and brown mixed hackle barbs, body length

Wing: Antron yellow, posted at ⅔ body length

Abdomen and thorax: goose primary barbs, grey

Hackle: grizzly, parachute style

Griffith's Gnat

Originator: George Griffith, founder of Trout Unlimited, (tied by Brian Smith)
Hook: Mustad 94840 #16–24
Thread: UTC black
Tail: none
Hackle: grizzly 1½ x hook gap, palmered through body
Body: 2 peacock herls, wrapped as dubbing

Midge Adult

Originator: unknown (tied by Brian Smith)
Hook: Mustad 94840 #18–24
Thread: UTC black
Tail: grizzly and brown mixed hackle barbs, body length
Body: UTC black thread, built up
Hackle: grizzly and brown mixed, 3 turns of each

Midge Spinner, Olive

Originator: unknown, (tied by Brian Smith)
Hook: Mustad 94840 #18–24
Thread: UTC olive
Tail: badger hackle barbs; cream colour, body length
Wing: Antron white; body length, tied at ⅔ hook shank, spread flat
Abdomen: olive hackle stem, 6–7 turns
Thorax: olive dubbing wrapped around spent wings

Tying tips: Tie the tail first, then the wing, which is clipped to length after you figure-eight it onto the shank. Follow with the abdomen and thorax to finish the fly. This exact same style and pattern can be used to imitate Mayfly Trico. Tie abdomens in many colours: black, grey, cream, olive and rusty-brown—whatever your home water dictates.

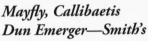

Mayfly

Callibaetis Mayfly
Nymph Olive—Smith's

Originator: Brian Smith 1991

Hook: Tiemco 200R #12–16

Thread: UTC olive

Tail: grizzly hackle, dyed olive; abdomen length

Rib: gold wire, fine, counter-wrapped over abdomen 5–6 turns

Abdomen: goose primary barbs, grey-olive

Wing-case: peacock herl, over thorax

Thorax: goose primary barbs, grey-olive; built up larger than abdomen

Throat hackle: grouse feather, dyed olive

Mayfly, Callibaetis
Dun Emerger—Smith's

Originator: Brian Smith 2004

Hook: Tiemco 2487 #10–14

Thread: Uni-Mono clear

Tail: mallard flank barbs, colour Callibaetis; body length to imitate shuck

Rib: gold wire, fine; 6–7 turns over abdomen

Abdomen: pheasant sword barbs, colour reddish-brown; wrapped to ¾-point of shank

Thorax: dubbing ball, SLF 37 Rust Brown

Wing: deer hair, reddish-brown; posted at 45° body length in front of thorax, rear clipped thorax length

Mayfly, Callibaetis Dun—Smith's

Originator: Brian Smith 1994

Hook: Tiemco 200R #12–16

Thread: UTC brown

Tail: grizzly hackle barbs; body length, spread

Wing: mallard flank feather colour Wood Duck; folded and posted at ⅔-shank point, clipped to round shape

Rib: gold wire, fine; 4–5 turns counter-wrapped over abdomen

Abdomen: pheasant sword barbs, reddish-brown
Thorax: dubbing SLF 37 Rust Brown; behind and in front of wing
Hackles: grizzly and brown, 1 each; 3–4 turns each, 1 behind wing, 2–3 in front
Tying tips: I spray my dry flies with clear boot silicone—it won't change the colour, sheds water like a duck and keeps them floating high. I tie a batch, then stick them into cardboard and give them a good dousing.

Mayfly, Callibaetis Adult Spinner—Smith's

Originator: Brian Smith 1994
Hook: Tiemco 200R #12–16
Thread: UTC black
Tail: grizzly hackle barbs; body length and spread
Rib: grizzly hackle stem, 5–6 turns counter-wrapped over abdomen
Wing: mallard flank feather natural; folded, posted upright, clipped to round shape
Abdomen: fine nylon, colour charcoal
Thorax: dubbing Hare-Tron HT 7 black
Hackle: grizzly hackles (2); 1 wrap each behind wing, 2 in front

Mayfly, Callibaetis Spent Spinner

Originator: Brian Smith 1994
Hook: Tiemco 200R #14–18
Thread: Uni-Mono clear
Tail: hackle barbs, white; body length and spread
Rib: grizzly hackle stem, 4–5 turns counter-wrapped over abdomen
Wing: Antron white, tied spent style
Abdomen: fine nylon, colour charcoal
Thorax: dubbing Hare's Ear Plus #4 black; built up around wing, finish at eye
Tying tip: Fly pattern recipes should be listed in the order they are put onto the hook—if you follow this advice with my recipes, the materials will be tied in the easiest sequence to achieve the best-looking patterns.

Mayfly Nymph, Hare's Ear

Originator: very early pattern, originator
unknown, (tied by Brian Smith)
Hook: Mustad 94840 #12–16
Under-wrap: lead wire 0.20 mm, 6–8 wraps
at front of hook
Tail: rabbit guard hairs, body length
Rib: gold rope or wire, fine; 5–6 turns
counter-wrapped over abdomen
Abdomen: rabbit dubbing, natural
Wing-case: mottled turkey; over thorax and throat hackle
Thorax: rabbit dubbing ball, larger than body
Throat hackle: grouse feather grey

Mayfly Nymph, Pheasant Tail Bead Head

Originator: unknown, (tied by Brian Smith)
Hook: Mustad 94840 #12–16
Bead head: gold bead
Tail: pheasant sword barbs, colour reddish-
brown; abdomen length
Rib: gold wire, fine 5–6 turns counter-
wrapped over abdomen
Abdomen: pheasant sword barbs, reddish-brown
Wing-case: pheasant sword barbs, reddish-brown, over thorax and throat hackle
Thorax: peacock herls; built up larger than abdomen
Throat hackle: grouse feather, brown
Tying tip: When tying bead-head patterns, the bead goes onto the hook first, small
opening toward the eye. Crimp the hook barb flat, insert the bead at the point and
slide it up the shank; begin your thread behind the bead, building up a thread ball
that will secure the bead, and prevent it from sliding down the shank.

Mayfly, BWO Emerger—Smith's

Originator: Brian Smith 2004
Hook: Tiemco 2487 #16–18
Tail: mallard flank feather barbs, olive; body lengths below hook bend, as trailing shuck
Rib: gold wire, fine; 5–6 turns over abdomen
Abdomen: primary goose barbs, grey-olive
Thorax: dubbing clump, Hare-Tron H 15 Pale Olive
Wing: deer hair, natural grey; body length, posted upright and forward of the eye at 45° angle, butt ends clipped length of thorax

Mayfly, BWO Dun—Smith's

Originator: Brian Smith 2004
Hook: Mustad 94840 #16–18
Thread: Uni-Mono clear
Tail: hackle barbs, blue dun; body length, spread
Wing: mallard flank feather, dyed grey; body length, posted at ⅔ hook shank
Abdomen: primary goose barbs, grey-olive
Hackle: blue dun; 2 turns behind wing, 3–4 turns in front

Mayfly, BWO Spent Spinner—Smith's

Originator: Brian Smith 2005
Hook: Mustad 94840 #18–22
Thread: UTC olive
Tail: hackle barbs, blue dun; body length, spread
Rib: hackle stem, olive; wrapped over underbody
Wing: Antron Poly, white; tied spent style
Underbody: floss, black; single strand as abdomen
Thorax: dubbing, Hare-Tron HT 7 black; behind and in front of spent wings
Tying tips: To keep the body slim, first tie in the tail, then the rib and wing. The poly or floss for the abdomen is next, which is tied behind the wing and taken down and back up to the wing point. Bring the rib hackle forward over the abdomen, and the thorax is last.

Mayfly, Slate-Winged Olive Dun—Smith's

Originator: Brian Smith 2005

Hook: Mustad 94840 #10–14

Tail: blue dun hackle barbs; body length, spread

Wing: mallard flank feather dyed grey; folded, posted upright

Abdomen: primary goose barbs, grey-olive

Thorax: dubbing Hare-Tron H 15 Pale Olive

Hackle: blue dun; 2 turns behind wing, 3 in front

Tying tip: The abdomen and thorax are a similar colour on the natural insect, but when I tie dun patterns, I like to add sparkle to the emerging insect with a high-lighted thorax colour. First I tie in the tail and wing, and then wrap the abdomen and the thorax, which is built a little larger around the wing using a highlight of dubbing colour; lastly, I hackle the fly.

Mayfly, Slate-Winged Olive Spent Spinner—Smith's

Originator: Brian Smith 2005

Hook: Mustad 94840 #14–16

Thread: UTC olive

Tail: hackle barbs, blue dun; body length, spread

Wings: Antron white; body length, spent style

Abdomen: UTC threads, colour olive

Thorax: peacock herl; tied behind and in front of spent wings

Mayfly, Brown Drake Dun—Smith's

Originator: Brian Smith 1993

Hook: Tiemco 200R #10–12

Tail: moose mane hairs; body length, spread

Wing: mallard flank feather, dyed grey; folded and posted

Rib: rod-building thread, yellow-gold; 5–6 turns over abdomen

Abdomen: pheasant sword barbs, reddish-brown

Thorax: Hare-Tron dubbing HT 10 Golden Stone; behind and in front of posted wing

Hackles: grizzly and brown, 1 each; 1 turn each behind wing, 3 turns in front

Mayfly, Brown Drake Spent Spinner—Smith's

Originator: Brian Smith 1993

Hook: Tiemco 200R #10–12

Tail: moose mane hairs; body length, spread

Wings: Antron grey, spent style

Rib: rod-building thread, yellow-gold; 5–6 turns over abdomen

Abdomen: pheasant sword barbs, reddish-brown

Thorax: Hare-Tron dubbing HT 10 Golden Stone; behind and in front of spent wings

Mayfly, PMD Emerger—Smith's

Originator: Brian Smith 2005

Hook: Tiemco 2487 #14–16

Thread: Uni-Mono clear

Tail: mallard flank barbs, dyed Callibaetis; body length, tied below the hook bend as trailing shuck

Rib: gold wire, fine; 5–6 turns over abdomen only

Abdomen: pheasant sword barbs, reddish-brown

Thorax: dubbing ball, Hare-Tron #8 Pale Yellow

Wing-case: deer hair, bleached; tied emerger style posted at 45° angle, clipped thorax length

Tying tip: I also use this pattern for my Pale Evening Dun Emerger, tied in sizes 16–18.

Mayfly, PMD Quill Dun—Smith's

Originator: Brian Smith 2004
Hook: Mustad 94840 #16–18
Thread: UTC cream
Tail: hackle barbs, blue dun; shank length, spread
Wing: mallard flank feather, natural; folded and posted upright at ⅔-shank point
Abdomen: cream badger hackle stem, wrapped as body
Thorax: dubbing, Hare-Tron #8 Pale Yellow; built up around posted wing
Hackle: blue dun; 1 wrap behind wing, 2–3 in front
Tying tips: I use a similar pattern for tying a Pale Evening Dun Spinner, substituting a wing of mallard dyed Callibaetis-colour, brown tail and hackle instead of blue dun.

The trick to tying quill patterns in small sizes is to use only the slim end of the hackle stem, which keeps the abdomen slender. Some fly tiers soak their hackle stems in water for a few hours before tying, which softens the stems and will prevent them from splitting.

I save my stripped hackle stems when I'm tying flies, and have amassed quite a collection for tying quill patterns.

Mayfly, PMD Spent Spinner—Smith's

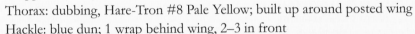

Originator: Brian Smith 2005
Hook: Mustad 94840 #16–18
Thread: UTC tan
Tail: hackle barbs, brown; shank length, spread
Wing: Antron white, tied spent style
Abdomen: hackle stem, brown
Thorax: dubbing ball, SLF 37 Rust Brown; behind and in front of spent wings
Tying tip: I use this same style of pattern for a PED Spinner, substituting light tan nylon for the abdomen, and Hareline dubbing HE 4 for the thorax.

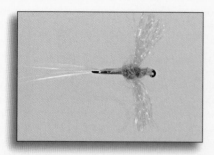

PED Spent Spinner
Originator: Brian Smith 2005
(for tying instructions, see *tying tip* page 141)

Mayfly, Trico Dun (Male)—Smith's
Originator: Brian Smith 1999
Hook: Mustad 94840 #20–24
Thread: UTC black
Tail: hackle barbs, white; hook shank length, spread
Wing: Antron white; body length, posted upright
Abdomen: fine nylon, charcoal
Thorax: dubbing, Hare's Ear Plus Black #4; behind and in front of posted wing
Hackle: grizzly; parachute style, around posted wing
Tying tip: This pattern imitates the male Trico dun; for the female stage of the dun, substitute an olive abdomen and dark brown thorax. I believe an Adams in size 20–22 is a fine choice as a searching pattern for this hatch.

Mayfly, Trico Spent Spinner (Male)—Smith's
Originator: Brian Smith 1999
Hook: Mustad 94840 #20–24
Thread: UTC black
Tail: hackle barbs, white; hook shank length, spread
Wings: Antron white, spent style
Abdomen: fine nylon, charcoal
Thorax: dubbing Hare's Ear Plus Black #4; behind and in front of spent wing
Tying tip: Male Trico abdomens are all black; sometimes it's important for those very selective trout, so after many skunk lessons, I resort to carrying all of the different colours and patterns of the Trico that I can think up.

Damsel Nymph—Smith's

Originator: Brian Smith 1988

Hook: Tiemco 200R #10–12

Thread: UTC olive

Tail: grizzly hackle, dyed olive; 12–16 barbs, short tail, spread

Rib: strand of yellow-gold rod-building thread; 5–6 turns over abdomen

Abdomen: dubbing, Hare-Tron #24 brown olive

Wing-case: grouse feather, dyed olive

Head: Larva Lace, olive; lashed figure-eight at head, trimmed 2 mm wide each side of hook, and then burn ends

Hackle: grizzly feather, dyed olive; laid over top of thorax

Thorax: dubbing, Hare-Tron #24 brown-olive

Head: dubbing Hare-Tron #24 brown-olive; figure-eight dubbing turn around Larva Lace

Tying tips: This pattern can be tied in many abdomen and thorax colours—tan, yellow-olive, dark olive—all with yellow-gold rib. I like to use a single strand of floss or better yet, yellow-gold rod-building thread, because these materials keep their vibrant colours when wet.

For the wing-case, I use a whole feather. Trim the fuzz and use the tip of the feather trimmed to 5 mm on each side; tie in the feather by the tip, then attach the head of Larva Lace and burn the ends so the eyes are dominant and protrude from each side of the hook.

The leg hackle procedure takes a little practice, and it's one that I use for many nymph patterns, described in Chapter 7.

Damsel Nymph, Marabou—Smith's

Originator: Brian Smith 2003

Hook: Mustad 9671 #10–12

Tail: marabou, grey-olive

Rib: gold wire, small; 6–7 turns over abdomen

Wing-case: Midge Flex olive, over thorax and hackle

Head and eyes: Larva Lace olive, burned

Hackle: grouse feather dyed olive; laid over back and thorax (see previous instructions for last pattern)

Thorax: marabou grey-olive

Head: marabou grey-olive; 1 figure-eight turn around Larva Lace

Tying tip: Tying with marabou takes a little practice. Make sure you purchase only "select" brands, because working with inferior, webby marabou is difficult and produces poor patterns. If in doubt about quality of marabou hackle, choose a bag that has long and full filaments.

Stump Lake Damsel

Originator: Jack Shaw circa 1970s (tied by Brian Smith)

Hook: Mustad 9672 #10–12

Rib: gold wire, fine; 6–7 turns

Body: wool, olive-gold

Wing: mallard flank natural, laid over and extending past body

Hackle: ginger, 1 turn wet style

Head: chenille, fine olive-gold; 1 turn

Dragonfly

Dragonfly Nymph, Deer Hair Darner—Smith's

Originator: Brian Smith 2000

Hook: Tiemco 200R #4–10

Thread: Uni-Mono clear

Tail: deer hair, natural; trimmed to end of hook bend

Rib: copper wire, medium; 5–6 turns over abdomen

Underbody: deer hair, natural; clipped and tapered

Abdomen: seal fur, dark olive; wrapped over and through the underbody

Wing-case: pheasant sword; laid over thorax

Thorax: seal fur, dark olive

Legs: deer hair; extend body length, sweep down and back

Eyes: Larva Lace olive; body width, burned, over-wrapped with seal fur, olive

Tying tips: See the Gomphus (opposite page) for tying tips on spinning and clipping deer hair. The darner's body is not as fat or short as the Gomphus, but is fatter at the rear of the fly. These patterns take a lot of time to tie, but are very durable and will take many fish before they are destroyed.

Dragonfly Nymph, Darner—Smith's

Originator: Brian Smith 2008

Hook: Tiemco 200R #4–10

Thread: UTC grey-brown

Tail: moose hair; stacked, tied short, only to bend

Rib: copper wire, medium; 5–6 turns over abdomen

Underbody: wool, dark green; built up thicker at rear of abdomen

Abdomen: dubbing, Ligas #43 dark olive

Wing-case: Swiss straw, dark olive; over thorax, tied off behind eyes

Eyes: Larva Lace olive; body width, burned, over-wrapped with peacock herl

Thorax: peacock herl, 3 strands; twisted as dubbing

Legs: moose hair stacked; body length, tied under shank behind eyes, swept down and back

Tying tips: Eyes are attached after the wing-case, then thorax and legs, with final procedure wrapping peacock herl over and around the eyes.

Dragonfly Nymph, Gomphus—Smith's

Originator: Brian Smith 1991 (adapted from Jack Shaw's original circa 1970s)

Hook: Mustad 9671 #8–10

Thread: Uni-Mono clear or Monocord

Body: deer hair, natural; spun in many clumps around the hook and trimmed to shape

Legs: deer hair, natural; tied in front of the thorax, sweeping to the sides and downward

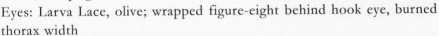

Eyes: Larva Lace, olive; wrapped figure-eight behind hook eye, burned thorax width

Tying tips: This pattern uses only deer hair, an opportunity to use ragged second-rate deer hair that I beg from hunting buddies, because it will be trimmed to shape. I find this is one pattern that is more productive to tie clumps onto batches of a half-dozen hooks before I begin to shape the nymphs.

Dragonfly, Adult—Smith's
Originator: Brian Smith 1990s
Hook: Tiemco 200R #4–6
Thread: Uni-Mono clear
Tail: deer hair, olive; extend ½-shank length past bend, and trim
Rib: floss, black; 6–7 turns over abdomen
Abdomen: deer hair, olive; spun and trimmed to shape, tapering to rear
Wings: Antron pale grey; tied spent at ¾-shank point
Thorax: peacock herl; built 2 times body width behind and in front of wings
Hackle: grizzly; 2 turns behind wings, 2 in front, bottom trimmed flat to shank
Eyes: Larva Lace, olive, burned; peacock herl wrapped over and around eyes

Caddis

Woolly Worm
Originator: unknown, dates back to 1700s, (tied by Brian Smith)
Hook: Mustad 9672 #4–12
Tail: hackle barbs, brown; ½ body length
Hackle: brown saddle; palmered over body, trimmed to gap of hook
Body: medium chenille, brown

Kamloops Sedgefly Pupa
Jack Shaw original (tied by Jack Shaw)

Caddis Pupa, Traveller—Smith's

Originator: Brian Smith 1991
Hook: Tiemco 200R #8–12
Thread: UTC olive
Rib: rod-building thread, yellow-gold; 5–6 turns over abdomen
Underbody: lead wire 0.20 mm; wrapped on the rear half of hook shank, followed by wool or embroidery thread to "fatten" it
Abdomen: dubbing, Hare-Tron HT 19 Dark Olive
Wing-case: pheasant tail sword barbs, tied over thorax
Thorax: dubbing, SLF 37 Rust Brown
Swimmerets: golden pheasant tippet barbs; under shank as throat, swept to hook point
Hackle: pheasant rump, red phase; body length, 1 turn only
Head: peacock herl; 2 strands, 3 turns

Tying tips: Weighting the pupa at the rear is dual purpose: it helps sink the pattern and can also add an enticing movement by allowing the pattern to bob when retrieved, which simulates a pupa that is making false starts at emergence.

Alternate colours for abdomen and rib of this pattern are Naples yellow/green rib; cinnamon/yellow-gold rib; insect green/yellow-gold rib.

Sedge, Mikaluk Traveller

Originator: Walter Mikaluk, Calgary Alberta (modified by Brian Smith 1992)
Hook: Mustad 9671 #6–14
Thread: Uni-Mono clear
Tail: deer hair, natural; ½ body length, stacked
Body: dubbing, Hareline HE 5 Dark Hare's Ear; 2–3 turns between stacks of deer hair
Wings: deer hair, natural; stacked, 3 sections in front of dubbing turns
Hackle: grizzly and brown mixed, 2–3 turns each

Tying tips: Refer to Chapter 7—Fly Tying for tips on working with deer-hair wings.

"Stacking" your hair means to use a stacking tool, which is a tube that evens the tips of deer hair for the tier. This pattern can be tied in a multitude of colours. Some good ones for me are SLF 37 Rust Brown (cinnamon), Hareline HE 4 Hare's Ear, Hareline HET 2 Dark Hare's Ear Plus, Ligas 21 Pale Olive, and Brian Chan's Soft Blend Olive. I use brown hackle for tan and cinnamon flies, grizzly and brown mixed for olives and grey.

Tom Thumb

Originator: unknown (tied by Ralph Shaw)
Hook: Mustad 94840 #6–18
Thread: black
Tail: deer hair, natural, body length
Shellback (wing-case): deer hair, natural; over body
Body: deer hair, natural

Wing: deer hair, natural, body length; posted at 45° over the eye of hook

Tying tips: The original pattern calls for black thread, but my preference is Uni-Mono clear, which I think improves the original pattern.

Begin the fly by tying the tail in at the ¾-point of hook shank, and follow it down the shank with your thread. A soft loop will hold the tail at the bend without spinning it; tighten progressively. For the shellback, choose deer hair twice the length of the body. Tie it in at the hook bend, butts forward. Spiral the thread forward, bring the shellback over the body, and tie off at the hook eye, hair tips forward and posted at 45°.

Caddis Pupa, Cinnamon—Smith's

Originator: Brian Smith 1993
Hook: Tiemco 200R #14–16
Thread: UTC brown
Rib: gold wire fine; 5–6 turns over abdomen
Underbody: tan embroidery thread, fatter at rear
Abdomen: dubbing, Whitlock's SLDW02 Red Fox

Wing-case: pheasant tail sword barbs, tied over thorax
Thorax: dubbing, Kaufmann's SLF 37 Rust Brown
Swimmerets: golden pheasant tippet barbs; tied as throat, length to hook point
Hackle: pheasant feather, red phase; 1 turn only
Head: peacock herl, 2 turns

Caddis Adult, Cinnamon—Smith's

Originator: Brian Smith 2001
Hook: Mustad 94840 #14–18
Thread: UTC brown
Tail: elk hair, cinnamon; ½-body length
Body: Kaufmann's SLF 37 Rust Brown
Under-wing: red squirrel; length to end of tail

Wing: elk hair, cinnamon; length to end of tail

Hackle: brown, 5–6 turns

Tying tip: I use this style for many of my small caddis now—varying my colours to suit the hatches—because it has very clean lines, and sits low in the water. The Mikaluk also works well, but with dwindling eyesight, I find I have trouble tying a Mikaluk in hook sizes smaller than 14, so this one is easier to tie for us old guys.

Elk Hair Caddis

Originator: unknown (tied by Brian Smith)

Hook: Mustad 94840 #12–24

Thread: UTC brown

Hackle: brown; length to hook gap only, palmered through body

Body: dubbing, Hareline HE 4 Hare's Ear

Wing: elk hair, natural; length of body, stubs left trimmed over hook eye

Caddis Larva, October—Smith's

Originator: Brian Smith 2006

Hook: Tiemco 2487 #10–12

Rib: gold wire, medium; 5–6 turns over abdomen

Underbody: cream embroidery thread, tapered thinner to front

Abdomen: dubbing, seal fur natural (cream colour)

Collar: dubbing, Whitlock's SLF 37 Rust Brown; 2 turns only

Throat hackle: grouse feather, tied as throat in front of collar

Head: peacock herl, 2–3 turns

Caddis Adult, October—Smith's

Originator: Brian Smith 1994 (adaptation of Mikaluk Sedge)

Hook: Mustad 94840 #10–14

Thread: UTC brown

Tail: deer hair, cinnamon; stacked, tied short (about ⅓ body length)

Body: dubbing, Whitlock's SLF 37 Rust Brown; 3 clumps, alternated with deer hair

Wing(s): deer hair, cinnamon; 3 stacks, Mikaluk style
Hackle: brown, 5–6 turns
Tying tips: Tie this pattern the same way the Mikaluk Traveller is tied—use sparse clumps of deer hair, stack them one on top of the other between 2 turns of body material, trying to not have visible separation between the clumps of hair. For tying the October Caddis pupa, use the recipe for my Cinnamon Caddis Pupa—guaranteed to work.

Caddis Larva, Spotted—Smith's
Originator: Brian Smith 2006
Hook: Tiemco 2457 #12–14
Thread: UTC brown
Rib: gold wire, fine; 5–6 turns over abdomen
Underbody: embroidery thread, tan: tapered to front
Abdomen: dubbing, Hareline Plus HET 2 Dark Hare's Ear

Collar: peacock herl, 3–4 turns
Throat hackle: small grouse feather

Caddis Pupa, Spotted—Smith's
Originator: Brian Smith 2006
Hook: Tiemco 200R #14–16
Thread: UTC brown
Rib: gold wire, fine; 5–6 turns over abdomen
Underbody: embroidery thread, tan; fatter at rear
Abdomen: dubbing, Hareline Plus HET 2 Dark Hare's Ear

Wing-case: duck primary barbs, light colour
Thorax: dubbing, Hare-Tron HT 14 Caddis Green
Swimmerets: golden pheasant tippet barbs; swept under to hook point
Hackle: pheasant rump body length; 1 turn only
Head: peacock herl, 1 turn only

Caddis Adult, Spotted—Smith's
Originator: Brian Smith 2006
Hook: Mustad 94840 #16–18
Thread: Uni-Mono clear
Tail: deer hair, natural, ½ body length
Body: dubbing, Hare's Ear Plus HET 2 Dark
Hare's Ear
Under-wing: beaver guard hairs; length over tail
Over-wing: deer hair, natural, over under-wing
Hackle: grizzly, 5–6 turns dry style

Tying tip: This is my pattern for the little guys, size 16 and under; for size 14, I tie
the Mikaluk-style caddis using the same colour combinations: natural deer hair,
HET2 dubbing, with grizzly and brown mixed hackle.

Caddis Adult, Green—Smith's
Originator: Brian Smith 2008
Hook: Mustad 94840 #16–18
Thread: Uni-Mono clear
Tail: deer hair, natural, ½ body length
Body: dubbing, Hare-Tron HE 14 Caddis Green
Under-wing: red squirrel hair; length over tail
Over-wing: deer hair, natural
Hackle: brown, 5–6 turns

Caddis Adult, Grannom—Smith's
Originator: Brian Smith 2004
Hook: Mustad 94840 #12–14
Thread: UTC brown
Tail: deer hair, dark brown; ½ body length
Body: dubbing, Rabbit Dark Olive
Wing: deer hair, dark red-brown
Hackle: brown; tied dry style 5–6 turns

Stonefly

Stonefly Nymph,
Salmonfly—Smith's

Originator: Brian Smith 1993

Hook: Tiemco 200R #6–10

Thread: UTC black

Dubbing ball: Hare's Ear Plus #4 Black

Tail: goose biots, 2; one each side of dubbing ball

Rib: copper wire, 5–6 turns over abdomen

Underbody: lead wire 0.20 mm and black wool, built over thorax only

Abdomen: dubbing, Hare's Ear Plus #4 Black

Wing-cases: Midge Flex black; tied to simulate 2 wing pads

Eyes: Larva Lace, grey; tied figure-eight at head, burn ends to thorax width

Leg hackle: dark grouse wing feather; sized to sweep body length, whole feather tied over thorax, separated by 2 wing-case sections

Thorax: dubbing Hare's Ear Plus #4 Black; 2 turns each between sections of leg hackle

Antennae: 2 black hackle stems; ½-body length each side of eyes

Collar: peacock herl, wrapped around and behind eyes

Tying tips: Refer to Chapter 7—Fly Tying for instruction on tying legs for these nymphs.

To set tail biots apart so they appear on each side of the abdomen, begin with a dubbing ball of body colour at the hook bend of the hook, and then tie the biots on each side in front of the ball.

Stonefly Adult, Salmonfly—Smith's

Originator: Brian Smith 1995

Hook: Tiemco 200R #6–10

Thread: UTC orange

Tail: elk hair, natural; short tail, slightly past hook bend

Ribs: rod-building thread, yellow-gold; 5–6 turns, followed by a turn of peacock herl in front of thread wraps

Body: floss, orange

Wing: elk hair, natural; extended over body to end of tail

Antennae: brown hackle stems; body length, 1 each side of head
Hackles: brown (2); 5–6 turns through dubbing base of Hareline HE 17
Rusty Orange

Stonefly Nymph, Skwala—Smith's

Originator: Brian Smith 1998
Hook: Tiemco 200R #8–10
Thread: UTC Brown
Tails: biots, brown; 1 each side of dubbing ball,
Hare-Tron HT 16 Dark Brown
Rib: copper wire, 5–6 turns over abdomen
Underbody: lead wire 0.20 mm and brown wool;
built over thorax only
Abdomen: dubbing, Hare-Tron HT 16 Dark Brown
Wing-cases: dark pheasant tail sword barbs; 2 sections over thorax and legs
Eyes: Larva Lace, brown; tied figure-eight at head, burn ends to thorax width
Leg hackle: dark grouse feather; whole feather tied over thorax, separated by 2
wing-case sections
Thorax: dubbing, Hare-Tron HT 16
Antennae: brown hackle stems ½-body length, 1 each side of eye
Head: dubbing, Hare-Tron HT 16; wrapped over and around eyes

Stonefly Adult, Skwala—Smith's

Originator: Brian Smith 1998
Hook: Tiemco 200R #8–10
Thread: UTC Olive
Tail: elk hair, natural; short tail, slightly past
hook bend
Ribs: rod-building thread, yellow-gold; 5–6 turns
over abdomen, followed by 1 turn peacock herl
in front of thread wraps
Abdomen: floss, brown-olive
Wing: elk hair, natural, over body and tail
Antennae: brown hackle stems; body length, 1 each side of head
Hackles: brown (2); 5–6 turns through dubbing base of Hare-Tron HT 10
Golden Stone

Stonefly Nymph, Golden—Smith's

Originator: Brian Smith 1998
Hook: Tiemco 200R #8–10
Thread: UTC Brown
Tails: biots, brown; 1 each side of dubbing ball,
Dragonfly KB 121 Golden Stone
Rib: copper wire, 5–6 turns over abdomen
Underbody: lead wire 0.20 mm and brown wool;
built over thorax only
Abdomen: dubbing, Dragonfly KB 121 Golden Stone
Wing-cases: Midge Flex Summer Duck; 2 sections over thorax and legs
Eyes: Larva Lace, brown; tied figure-eight at head, burn ends to thorax width
Leg hackle: dark grouse feather; whole feather tied over thorax, separated by 2
wing-case sections
Thorax: dubbing, Dragonfly KB 121 Golden Stone
Antennae: brown hackle stems; ½-body length, 1 each side of head
Head: dubbing, Dragonfly KB 121 Golden Stone, wrapped over and around eyes

Stonefly Adult, Golden—Smith's

Originator: Brian Smith 1998
Hook: Tiemco 200R #8–10
Thread: UTC Hopper Yellow
Tail: elk hair, natural; short, slightly past hook
bend
Ribs: rod-building thread, yellow-gold; 5–6
turns over abdomen, followed by 1 turn of pea-
cock herl in front of thread wraps
Abdomen: floss, brown-gold
Wing: elk hair, natural; over body and tail
Antennae: brown hackle stems; body length, 1 each side of head
Hackles: brown (2); wrapped through dubbing base, Hare-Tron HT 10 Golden Stone

Stonefly Nymph, Little Yellow—Smith's

Originator: Brian Smith 2007
Hook: Tiemco 200R #14–16
Thread: UTC Hopper Yellow
Tails: mallard flank barbs, dyed Wood Duck:
tied each side of dubbing ball, Hare-Tron HT
10 Golden Stone

Rib: copper wire, small; 5–6 turns over abdomen

Abdomen: dubbing, Hare-Tron HT 10 Golden Stone

Wing-cases: mottled turkey wing barbs

Eyes: 20 lb. mono, burn ends

Leg hackle: grouse wing feather, small; 2 sections tied over thorax

Thorax: dubbing, beaver under fur (muddy brown)

Antennae: brown hackle stems; 1 each side of head, ½-body length

Head: dubbing HT 10 Golden Stone; wrap over and around eyes

Stonefly Adult, Yellow Sally—Smith's

Originator: Brian Smith 2008

Hook: Tiemco 200R #16–18

Thread: Danville's Chartreuse 6/0

Tail: deer hair, bleached; short tail, ½-body length

Tag: floss, golden stone; small tag, 1 mm width at bend of hook

Body: nylon, chartreuse colour

Wing: deer hair, bleached; over body and tail

Hackle: grizzly, 5–6 turns

Stonefly Nymph, Little Olive—Smith's

Originator: Brian Smith 2006

Hook: Tiemco 200R #12–14

Thread: UTC Olive

Tail: biots BWO Olive; 1 each side of dubbing ball, Superfly SLF 05 Medium Olive

Underbody: lead wire 0.15 mm; under thorax only, over-wrapped with olive embroidery thread

Rib: copper wire, medium; 5–6 turns over abdomen

Abdomen: dubbing, Superfly SLF 05 Medium Olive

Wing-cases: goose primary barbs, BWO Olive

Eyes: V-rib Olive; burned thorax width

Leg hackle: grouse wing feather, olive; 2 sections over thorax

Antennae: hackle stems, olive; ½-body length, 1 each side of head

Thorax: dubbing, Superfly SLF 05 Medium Olive

Head: dubbing, Superfly SLF 05 Medium Olive

Stonefly Adult, Little Olive—Smith's
Originator: Brian Smith 2006
Hook: Tiemco 200R #14–16
Thread: UTC Olive
Tail: deer hair, bleached; short tail, ½-body length
Rib: peacock herl, 1 strand; 5–6 turns over body
Body: floss, medium olive
Wing: deer hair, bleached; over body and tail

Antennae: hackle stems, grizzly; 1 each side of head
Hackle: grizzly, 5–6 turns

Shrimp

Opalescent Shrimp, Shaw's
Originator: Jack Shaw circa 1960–1970 (tied by Jack Shaw)
Hook: Mustad 94840 #10–14
Thread: Mono clear
Tail and shellback: pheasant tail sword barbs, over-wrapped with 5–6 turns of clear mono as rib
Hackle: pale dun, palmered 5–6 turns over body

Body: pink and blue knitting fabric
Comment: Good luck finding that fabric for the body! Jack gave me a ball of it many years ago (about 1977, I think), and said, "Guard it with your life because I bought all there was." If I had to replicate it, I think pale blue dubbing with a touch of pink and white would do the trick.

Shrimp, Gammarus—Smith's
Originator: Brian Smith 2008 (revised from 1985 pattern)
Hook: Tiemco 2487 #10–14
Thread: Uni-Mono clear, fine
Tail: mallard flank barbs, dyed olive; length of hook gap

Rib: gold wire, fine; 6–7 turns over body and shellback
Underbody: lead wire 0.20 mm; middle section of body only, over-wrap with embroidery thread for a smooth body

Shellback: Midge Flex, tan
Dubbing: Stillwater Soft Blend, olive
Legs: dubbing, picked out of body
Antennae: mallard flank, dyed olive
Tying tips: This pattern is tied "baggy" style—pick out the legs from the dubbing body material. Use a little more body dubbing than normal, which will give you a better simulation of legs.

Pregnant Shrimp, Smith's
See page 195 for pattern and comment on tying instructions.

Leech

Leech, Blood Bugger—Smith's
Originator: Brian Smith 1993
Hook: Mustad 9671 #8–14
Thread: UTC black
Underbody: lead wire, 0.15 to 0.25 mm; 10–12 turns wrapped on front half of hook shank
Tail: marabou, black; body length
Hackle: hackle, black saddle; 1½ x hook gap, palmered through body
Body: Dazzle Dubbing BC Blood

Tying tips: There is a trick to wrapping lead on a shank. Using the spool, poke the loose end through the eye of the hook on the bottom side of the eye, and spiral the lead back to where you want it placed on the shank. Trim the front off, drop some head cement on the lead, and wrap through it several times with your tying thread—done.

Mohair Blood Leech
Jack Shaw original (tied by Jack Shaw)

Water Boatman and Backswimmer

Water Boatman, Smith's Original

Originator: Brian Smith 1990 (adapted from Jack Shaw original)

Hook: Mustad 94840 #10–14

Thread: UTC Brown Olive

Shellback: packing foam, 3-mm wide strip; tied in at hook bend, coloured with felt marker

Overbody: thin strip of plastic bag, wrapped over body material to give appearance of lustre

Rib: Mylar, fine silver; 4–5 turns over body

Underbody: embroidery thread, cream colour; tied in middle third of hook shank to "fatten" body

Body: Poly-yarn cream, over-wrapped with plastic

Hackle: pheasant tail sword barbs, tied as throat

Swimmerets: stiff peacock herl strand; needled through body at ⅔-shank spot, glued in place with a dab of Krazy Glue, trimmed to slightly past hook bend

Water Boatman Floater—Smith's

Originator: Brian Smith 2006

Hook: Mustad 94840 #12–14

Thread: UTC Tan

Underbody: Antron: any colour, built up in the middle of shank only

Wing-case: foam strip, brown; overlaid with Midge Flex Tan

Body: Antron, pale yellow; over-wrapped with Midge Flex clear

Swimmerets: stiff peacock herl strand, needled through body at ⅔-shank spot, glued in place with Krazy Glue, trimmed to slightly past hook bend

Hackle: pheasant sword fibres tied as throat

Tying tip: I buy my foam strip at Walmart in the hobby section; you can purchase sheets of foam in a variety pack of colours for a few dollars, and cut it into the strip width you need. Other patterns that you'll find foam handy for are ants and hoppers, covered in the next chapter on terrestrial insects.

Backswimmer Floater—Smith's

Originator: Brian Smith 2006

Hook: Mustad 94840 #10–12

Thread: UTC Brown

Underbody: Antron, any colour; built up in middle of hook shank

Wing-case: foam strip, brown, 3-mm width; overlaid with Midge Flex Brown

Body: dubbing loop peacock herl, 3 strands; over-wrapped with Midge Flex clear

Swimmerets: stiff peacock herl strand, needled through body at ⅔-shank spot, glued in place with Krazy Glue, trimmed to slightly past hook bend

Hackle: pheasant tail sword barbs, tied on top of hook

Terrestrials: Ants, Termites and Grasshoppers

Daddy's Ant—Smith's

Originator: Brian Smith 2006

Hook: Mustad 94840 #14–18

Wing: calf tail, white; body length, tied and posted at mid-section of shank

Abdomen: dubbing ball, Hare-Tron HT 17 black

Hackle: grizzly; tied in front of abdomen and posted wing, palmered over thorax section

Thorax: floss, orange

Foam Ant Black—Smith's

Originator: Brian Smith 2007

Hook: Mustad 94840 #12–18

Abdomen: foam, black

Shellback: foam, black; over abdomen

Wings: 2 dun hackle tips; 1 each side over abdomen, cocked at 45°

Hackle: brown, 3–4 turns in front of wings

Thorax and head: dubbing ball, Hare-Tron HT 17 black

Tying tip: My red ant and termite patterns are tied the same way, substituting abdomens of orange foam for the red ant and white for the termite, maintaining orange floss on the thoraxes, but palmer dry fly hackle through the thoraxes.

Termite

Red Ant

Grasshopper

Hopper, Foam
Yellow/Brown—Smith's
Originator: Brian Smith 2006
Hook: Tiemco 200R #8–12
Thread: Uni-Mono clear
Abdomen, body and thorax: tan foam over yellow, tied at ¾-point of hook shank, extended ½-body length past hook bend
Wings: mottled turkey feather strips; 1 each side of body, extended past hook bend
Legs: deer hair; tied on top and bottom of hook behind head, extended to end of wings
Head: deer hair, spun and trimmed bullet style
Tying tips: For the foam overlay of tan on yellow, use Krazy Glue to spot-cement the 2 strips together. Tie the foam onto the shank at the ¾-shank point, then spiral mono thread tightly over the foam, binding it to the hook shank; continue to twirl the thread to the rear of the extended foam body, and finally back to tie-in point. To reinforce the body to the hook, make an additional spiral wrap of thread on the foam to the hook bend and back to the tie-in point.

Damselfly

Family: Coenagrionidae

Nymph: size 15–50 mm; colours: tan, brown-olive (dun), green-olive, and yellow-olive
Adult: size 25–50 mm; blue, olive and brown; dark bands on abdomen

Damselflies emerging on Interior lakes signals the beginning of the first major "big insect" hatch of the summer, and prompts fly fishers with truck and camper, tent or RV to roll up the highway in droves, heading for the BC Interior lakes to intercept fighting trout. For two to four weeks every June and early July, the intense early damselfly nymph migration from deep water to shoreline will rouse the most suspicious trout from its deep water lair onto the shoals in deliberate pursuit of the tasty morsels. Migration occurs again late in the year, after the first fall frosts, when the nymphs move from shoals to deep water for overwintering.

One of the few insect hatches that is visible to the observant angler, damselfly nymphs emerge from their nymphal shucks by climbing onto reeds, sedge grass, branches or twigs, and also by clambering onto the shoreline of lakes and ponds. They require something solid to attach onto with their strong legs as they split their nymph cases, from which emerge adult insects of such beauty and grace that witnessing the transformation will leave you breathless at the marvel of nature. The curious adults zoom around the lake, landing on boats, fly rods, fly lines, hats, whatever—almost as if they were carrying out inspections.

Male damselfly adults are bright blue with black bands; females are olive-green or olive-brown with black bandings. Unlike adult dragonflies that hold their wings perpendicular to their bodies, damsels fold their wings over their back when at rest. As adults, they are copy-cats in size, all about 50 mm in length, and one-half the size of the big dragonflies, having an incomplete metamorphic life cycle that is similar to the mayfly and dragonfly—egg, larva or nymph, and adult.

As a food source for fish, damselflies rank about sixth place in importance to the Interior angler, comprising about 6 percent of a trout's diet, with most of the consumption occurring during daylight hours when nymphs are most active.

To the fly fisher, the appearance of the blue insects swarming the shoreline on warm spring days signals either an emergence or adult females returning to lay their eggs. If damsels are active, you are a lucky angler because you've hit one of the best times of the year, and should be rewarded with a few trophy trout.

Damsel Nymph

Damselfly nymphs are available to fish year-round, but are usually an inactive insect, preferring to hide under vegetation, or sit motionless in wait for their foods of preference—freshwater scud, mayfly nymph and other prey smaller than themselves. Camouflaged perfectly within its environment, the nymph is a stalker and hunter, and is rarely found free-swimming until time of emergence beckons.

Damsel nymphs, like their close cousin the dragonfly, belong to order Odonata, but the suborder of damselflies is Zygoptera and the family is Coenagrionidae. Nymphs have a life stage of up to three years, during which they moult their outer skin up to twelve times. Jack Shaw enjoyed raising damsels in his home aquarium, noting that during the various stages of growth and moulting the nymph would go into hiding, as its case is soft, its colour a pale watery-green and its camouflage betrayed during these growth stages. He found that he had to raise them with dragonfly nymphs separated from other insects, because they would quickly devour the contents of the aquarium if scud or mayfly nymphs were introduced.

Nymphs average about 25 mm in length at maturity, and are found in a range of muted colours: both pale and dark olive, Naples yellow (which is a yellow-gold) and tan. They have a much slimmer profile than dragonflies, with prominent bulbous eyes, and three tail filaments that act as a rudder when they swim. As with most insect orders, nymphs assume the colouration of their environment—if the weeds are green, the nymphs will most certainly be a shade of green as well.

Look for nymphs to become active a few weeks before emergence, usually late May or early June depending on elevation, and fish them before the adults begin to emerge. They commence their shoreward migration by raising themselves to within a few inches of the surface, and swim in an undulating motion, stopping frequently to rest. Many take the wrong direction, get turned around, and swim away from shore, where they become easy pickings for marauding trout, which relish the opportunity to snatch a meal with ten times the protein of their normal diet of scuds, chironomids and other small larvae.

To fish the nymph stage, pick an area of extensive weedbeds, preferably lined with reeds, anchoring near shoreline in 1–2 m of water, and fish the migration with a floating line and long, 4-m leader by casting the nymph to deep water (the far shore), and slowly hand-crawl the pattern onto the shoal. During the retrieve, allow frequent pauses to let the nymph relax and drift in the water column, imitating resting periods that will often provoke a strike from cruising fish.

Damsel nymphs are nicely imitated with fine chenille, dubbing or marabou. Because the swimming motion is difficult to imitate when retrieving any fly pattern, I prefer marabou with its natural flow and movement, and when tied on a 3-X long-shank hook and retrieved with a twisting hand-crawl, it gives the model a sweeping, undulating motion that is difficult for fish to resist. Prominent eyes are important, which I imitate with Larva Lace or V-rib, lashed figure-eight around the top of the hook shank, trim to body width, and each end burnt to create two stumpy looking posts.

Emerging damselfly adults will climb and attach to anything solid to pull themselves from their nymph cases...even a rope. *Photo Brian Chan.*

The damsel nymph is an excellent trolling pattern to use on outings with the young family, the child's line on the shallow side of the boat. Dad or mom can fish the transition shelf of the lake; junior can fish the weeds with a floating line, and cut down on child maintenance a little! When a youngster catches a trout in shallow water, the fish will probably go ballistic on the surface for a real thrill for everyone aboard (see page 143).

Damsel Adult

Trout don't key on adult damsels as they do on caddis, midge and mayflies because fully developed damsels hatch off the water. There are, however, occasions when trout will randomly target them, which is during both hatching and egg-laying periods—not the pretty adult versions while in flight, but the insect while drying its wings after emergence, or the fertilized female that climbs down the weed stem to lay her eggs under water. If you're fortunate to be on the lake when either of these events are presented, get out your dry line and begin searching the shoreline for cruising trout.

When the nymph climbs a stem to hatch, the transformation to a flying adult takes twenty to thirty minutes depending on the warmth of the day. The young adult must first dry its wings, and then pump body fluids into its abdomen, which lengthens the body into the familiar adult shape. Trout recognize this vulnerable time for the adult, and will actually hunt down these emerging damsels, knock them off the weeds while they are weak, and grab a quick meal on the surface.

Jack Shaw wrote an article for *BC Outdoors* (January/February 1990) that covered his experience while fishing the damsel hatch one day on Stump Lake. Trout were scavenging the shoreline, knocking hatching adult damsels off their perches, and causing great commotion while feeding on the emergence. From this incident, Jack developed the Stump Lake Damsel, which represents the emerging stage of the adult (see page 144).

When egg-laying females return to deposit their eggs, they once more become a welcome morsel for foraging trout. If you notice damsels coupled and mating, females will deposit their eggs immediately after fertilization, so be on lookout for "moving" vegetation along the shoreline, which could signal the opportunity to fish the adult damsel as Jack Shaw did back in the 1970s.

Dragonfly

"Helicopters" of lake and stream is a distinction reserved for the largest order of insects that hatch from lakes and slow-moving streams. What else can you say about an insect that can fly in two gears, reverse and forward, plus straight up and down, and hover like a chopper?

Dragonflies hovering around fly fishers and their watercrafts, generally making a nuisance of themselves, are welcome attractions and offer interesting and thoughtful breaks during fishing outings. Like damselflies, they are curious by nature. Thank God they don't bite, or have the vicious meat-hunting temperament of horseflies, because I'm certain they would strike fear into the most courageous fisher's soul and probably keep a lot of people away from the sport. It's interesting to watch dragonfly nymphs in their freshwater surroundings, where they are ferocious hunters and kings of their insect environment, feeding on everything they can catch: leeches, scuds, mayfly nymphs, snails, caddis larvae and even small fishes. My friend and editor, Bob Graham, says that fossils of extinct dragonflies have been discovered that had wing spans of up to 90 cm—that's a serious predator!

Dragonflies belong to order Odonata, suborder Anisoptera. In Interior BC lakes and streams the common abundant families are Aeshnidae, the Darners, and Libellulidae, Gomphus nymphs. Their life cycle is incomplete; nymphs hatch from eggs deposited under water on lake vegetation and bottom debris, or buried in muck. Adults emerge from nymphs—there is no pupa stage of development—and during their two- to four-year lifespan as nymphs they moult through a dozen growth phases, or instars, before reaching maturity.

Comprising about 7 percent of a fish's diet in Interior lakes, dragonflies rank fourth in importance as a food source. As nymphs, they spend most of their time in hiding, preferring to ambush their prey rather than stalk it. Because of their size and high protein value, these nymphs are the "big meal deal" of lakes, where they are preferred table fare for trout should they find them migrating or straying from their protective hiding spots.

Adults are rarely a meal for fish because emergence occurs on land, and they are far too quick when travelling over water to present an easy target. On a few occasions I have seen trout leaping clear out of the water, trying in vain to snatch them out of the air. The best opportunity for fish to capture an adult is when females return to shoreline vegetation to lay eggs after mating, when they'll drop eggs anywhere they will stick: lily pads, bullrush stems, sticks or debris; the pre-occupation of egg-laying affording fish an opportunity to grab a huge meal of wings and meat.

Darner Dragonfly

Family: Aeshnidae
Nymph: size 1–80 mm; colours: olive-brown, dark brown, pale olive (young)
Adult: size 50–80 mm; abdomen blue, olive, brown with dark bands

Nymph

Darners, the climbers and scramblers, are the most commonly found nymphs and adults. If they are not on the move—migrating from deep water to weed-beds in early spring, scrambling to shore to hatch during early summer, or travelling on a return ticket to deep water in fall—you will rarely see the nymph out and about. However, venture into the water and turn over a log, or snorkel around some weedbeds, and you'll surely see what trout can seldom locate—a mouthful of protein.

Dragonfly nymphs hatch directly from eggs, and can be observed as very small insects when young, incredibly large when mature and any size in between during their four-year growth cycle to maturity. An abundance of newborns and immature nymphs are always present in the fall; your choice of pattern size should reflect this fact, and be two or three sizes smaller (hook sizes 12–14) than in spring, when the predominant profusion of mature nymphs will dictate that hook sizes 4–8 should be offered.

Darner nymphs are recognized by size, shape and colour. They average 25–40 mm in length, abdomens triangular in shape, flat on the bottom, tapering from widest at the midpoint of the abdomen back to the anus, and slimmer forward to the beginning of the narrower thorax. The only other insect that you could mistake for the darner is the damselfly nymph, but once compared you won't make the error again, because the dragonfly is much stubbier than the dainty, slim-bodied damsel and more menacing-looking. Eyes are prominent

166

features on both insects, but the dragon's eyes are much more ominous than those of the damsel.

Colouration of the darner is subtle: grey-black, ruddy green, muted brown and dark olive. As with most insect orders, the colour of bottom vegetation and clarity of water will dictate the colour and shade the insect will take for camouflage—if in doubt about colour, always begin with a muted match to the weed growth in a lake, and consider that colours darken when they are wetted.

During instar stages, nymphs shed their exoskeletons and are a pale watery-green for several frantic weeks until the new shell hardens and darkens. Having lost their protective disguise of muted colourings, they feel vulnerable to predators; fish recognize this liability, and embark on exclusive hunts for the fresh, soft nymphs. It's always prudent to have a few large, pale green patterns with dark portentous eyes in the fly box arsenal—they can sometimes save a day or trip, and become another gimmick in the bag of tricks that a seasoned fisher should have for those tough days on the water.

Dragonfly nymphs are always fished on the bottom layer of the lake, and at all times around weedy shoals and areas laden with obstructions, cover and structure. Because they are present in all sizes and at all times of year, they are favourite searching patterns for many fly fishers and can be trolled effectively as long as they are fished deeply, with fast-sinking type 3–6 lines.

The early spring migration from deep overwintering water to shoals is the prime time to expect fish to focus on nymphs as they progress to their preferred habitat areas, crawling along the bottom looking for cover and concealed places to spend the summer feeding, growing and moulting as they mature. Relocation begins after spring turnover, a few weeks following ice-out. Floating, intermediate and slow-sinking lines effectively imitate the unhurried progression, the fly fisher anchored in the drop-off zone over a weedbed in less than 2 m of water, casting to the far shore, slowly working size 4–8 nymphs onto the shoal. Takes can be violent, with your line screaming from your hand into the backing, or as soft as a loving kiss, requiring only a tightening of the fly line.

During early summer, usually late June to mid-July depending on elevation, mature nymphs scramble to shore along the bottom, climb onto any structure they can find, and begin their transformation to adult insects. This migration brings the best trout in the lake into shallow water, onto the transition shelf in search of the worthy prey. During hot summer days warm shoal water is uncomfortable for trout, and it often pays to anchor right on the drop-off, casting a full-sinking type 3–6 line as far as possible to deep water, and crawl your nymph to the ledge; most often a strike will occur directly under your anchored station. Many dragonfly nymphs hatch under cover of darkness, often at their best during a full moon; trout will gorge in the cooling shallows all night long, leaving the fly fisher a lake full of very contented and lazy fish the next day.

As fall approaches, shoal water cools, and dragonfly nymphs migrate back to deep water to overwinter. With an abundance of immature nymphs available at this time, anchor on the drop-off, and fish your small patterns from shore outward to shelf water—deeply, crawling through the lake's bottom zone. If you aren't picking up weeds, you are not fishing the nymph deep enough to fool the fish. These are the opportunities to make the best use of deer-hair-body dragons that will bounce along the lake's floor in weed-less fashion.

Jack Shaw was intrigued with finding the right impression to imitate the darner nymph. Until the 1960s, before Jack became serious about aquarium studies, many insects were represented by attractor flies, and the dragonfly nymph was one of the most popular insects imitated for freshwater fishing. Bill Nation, another Kamloops fly fishing pioneer of the 1920s and '30s, became famous for his thoughts and impressions of the dragonfly nymph with a venerable list of patterns: Nation's Fancy, Nation's Red Dragon, Nation's Blue, Nation's Special—all attractors representing various dragonfly nymph possibilities. Doctor Don Spratley from Mt. Vernon, Washington, gave us the venerable Doc Spratley, originated by his friend Dick Prankard circa 1949—God knows how many Kamloops trout have met their fate with this top-producing fly made popular during early days when chironomids were not yet understood, and general purpose flies were the order of the day. Many veteran Interior fly fishers, especially trollers, still swear by the Doc Spratley, which can best be described as general purpose depending on size offered. Small Spratleys in hook sizes 10–14 can even be trimmed to mimic a chironomid!

Jack used a lot of natural, dyed seal fur to create his imitations, materials that are now becoming difficult to find. He felt that seal fur did the best job of holding tiny air bubbles that natural insects gather and have clinging to their bodies. I use seal fur if I can get it, but also like some of the new synthetics like Hare-Tron, Ligas, and Chan and Rowley's Soft Blend that blend a small amount of sparkle into the fur, passing on that elusive look of air pockets, so necessary when crafting worthy fly patterns for trophy trout. I also incorporate deer hair for my Darner imitation, which I can shape and build into a good body for the nymph by spinning the hair on the hook, shaping and tapering the body, and then spiralling dubbing through the abdomen to give it some colour. An added benefit from deer hair is buoyancy; you can fish the pattern with a full-sinking type 6 line, cast and drop the line to the bottom, and literally bounce the fly through weeds and debris without many foul hook-ups (see page 144 and 145).

Gomphus

Family: Libellulidae
Nymph: size 1–50 mm; colours: brown-olive, grey-brown
Adult: size 40–50 mm; olive-brown, red shoulders

Nymph

The Gomphus dragonfly nymph in the adult phase is the Red Shouldered Dragonfly—if you see adults out and around, give the nymph a try because they are a favourite of trout. Shorter than the Darner, and more portly in shape and appearance, Gomphus nymphs are burrowers, preferring to hide in the muck bottom of the lake, their reclusive attitudes rarely providing a target for marauding fish, but taken greedily when discovered.

Gomphus enjoy the same life cycle as all dragonflies: egg, nymph and adult. Mature nymphs are 20–30 mm long, stubby and almost spider-like in appearance, with abdomens much wider than the front end, flat on the bottom and tapered to a teardrop shape at the rear. They are drab in colour, tinged with muted shades of yellow and green-olive, similar to their environment, with eyes that are prominent, but not as dominant as those of darner nymphs.

Even more cautious than darner nymphs, Gomphus like to live in concealment in the bottom muck of lakes, and that's where you will find them, happy to ambush passer-by insects, larvae and small fish. They exhibit all of the traits of the dragonfly family: many growth stages through instars, migration patterns and timing, and hatch schedules. The methods to fish them are also common, most importantly the ability to get your patterns to the bottom layer of the lake and to hand-crawl the fly onto shoals and through weedbeds.

Darners and Gomphus can move rapidly when they need to, by a method of propulsion used to relocate from place to place or to jump out to snatch food that is casually wandering through their feeding lane. They intake and expel water through their anus, which propels them for short bursts of several centimetres. To mimic this action, use a slow hand-strip method, ending with a short twitch of the line, followed by a rest period. Sometimes varying this twitch retrieve with the hand-crawl method will attract fish to the imitation they might otherwise not see when it is retrieved slowly. Fishing methods are never a given—sometimes unorthodox style will produce best results, especially when appealing to finicky trout. It pays to vary your style until the right combination is found.

I tie my Gomphus pattern with all deer hair, using a shorter shank hook than the Darner. This is a pattern developed in the 1970s by Jack Shaw. The use of deer hair allows you to shape and trim the body in proportions to the natural that are not achievable with seal fur or dubbing. Another benefit is the buoyancy of deer hair, discussed in the section on darners, which increases your retrieval time with a minimum of bottom hang-ups.

I was re-reading my copy of Art Lingren's book *Contemporary Fly Patterns of British Columbia*, and came across an insertion by Hermann Fischer that sheds more light on the Gomphus Nymph. Apparently, early authors Jack Shaw and Alf Davey have been incorrect in the identification and naming of the Gomphus which, according to researcher Loucas Raptis, is not a Gomphus but rather the *Sympetrum* genus. Loucas is probably right, and kudos to him. However, the fly pattern works, and I'll keep calling mine a Gomphus because it sounds a lot better than trying to come up with another name for the bug.

The secrets to tying this pattern are the quantity of hair per clump, and the use of strong thread like Monocord. A pencil-width portion of about 5 mm is about right; more is difficult to handle. Deer hair will spin better if you do not build a base of tying thread on the shank—it needs to spin freely. Begin by binding a section of deer hair at the rear on top of the hook with tight wraps of cord, wrapping the thread through the hair, allowing the hair to spin freely around the shank. Keep binding and jamming sections of deer hair tight to the last section with your thumbnail, finishing the abdomen portion at the thorax, about ¾ distance up the shank.

Begin trimming the fly; the shape of the pattern needs to be flat on the bottom, rounded over the top and tapered to the sides, with an overall appearance of oval, fatter at the rear. I find it easiest to take the fly out of the vise, and begin trimming from the rear with the hook eye pointing away; trim the top first, flatten the bottom, and then taper it from the rear of the hook, leaving a trailing portion to represent tail filaments.

The eyes and legs are attached, and then deer hair built around them, trimming to achieve an impression of segmentation at the thorax and head of the fly (see page 145).

Dragonfly Adult

If you could have an insect for a pet, I think the dragonfly would be a great pal: friendly, curious, courageous and outgoing—fine attributes for a companion. Problem is they can fly; sadly we cannot, thus the relationship can never be on equal footing, and the best we can hope for is to see them for a season. When I am fishing my favourite lakes, I swear I see the same adults every time. They are always the welcoming committee when you unpack the boat and gear (as long as you don't arrive too early), and the insect to inspect your lunch bag and teacup at noon hour. This familiarity is in my own mind of course, and I'm likely mistaken because dragonflies of a family all look pretty much the same; they just act like inquisitive old friends when they see you.

Adult dragonflies are the most conspicuous insect on the water during July and August. Easily the largest bug to hatch from still-water lakes and ponds, darner adult males are about 80 mm in length, showing blue abdomens banded with black. Females are also blue, toned with olive and brown abdomens and black bands. Gomphus adults are shorter than darners, about 50 mm long, red-shouldered, with dark olive-green abdomens that taper to a club shape at the rear. When at rest, dragonflies hold their wings perpendicular to their bodies, distinguishing them from their cousins, the damselflies, which hold their wings parallel to their bodies. It would be interesting to clock them on a speed gun as they whip across the water; I'm thinking 30–40 km/hour is not unrealistic.

Adults live several months, until first frosts, and are capable of breeding multiple times during open-water season. My curiosity was aroused by this mating fact, and I sourced Assistant Professor Dezene P.W. Huber, B.Sc., Ph.D. at UNBC to find an answer that was not available through my Internet research, periodicals or extensive collection of books by fly fishing gurus about the dragonfly life cycle. Dr. Dezene says this about the interesting mating habits of dragonflies: "Dragons and damsels do live long enough to have several broods in a season. It is well known that they mate multiple times, which is why you often see males guarding females in flight—the male has mated with her and stays with her until she lays eggs. The male's copulatory apparatus includes a scoop-like portion that the male can use to scoop out a prior male's sperm from the female." Devils, aren't they?

The adults present very few opportunities for the fly fisher, but it is always a good idea to have a few patterns in your box for that memorable day that fish make fools of the fisher and decide against all odds to pick a dead adult off the surface (see page 146).

Caddis

Several times larger than chironomid, midge, and most mayfly species, caddis is one of the big meal tickets of Interior lakes and streams, and a delicious treat for trout when they find one. When a fly fisher unlocks the secrets of caddis fishing, a whole new world of trout fishing evolves, because there isn't a trout alive that can refuse a well-presented imitation of the caddis, or sedge fly. When no hatch is present, or during times of overlapping hatch activity, and if trout are looking up, a caddis can spur aggressive feeding action that no other insect can duplicate, except perhaps the giant adult stoneflies of rivers. Many fly fishers opt for an Adams as their first choice for a searching dry pattern, but mine is a caddis for probing any stream June through late August; and always a caddis when hunting shorelines of lakes during summer.

Caddis belongs to order Trichoptera of class Insecta, which consists of multiple levels of species and families numbering in the thousands, the genera dwelling in both lakes and streams. In our Interior lakes, the most common families are those of Traveling Sedge (Phryganeidae), Northern Case Maker (Limnephilidae) and Longhorned Case Maker (Leptoceridae), whereas in streams you'll find other varieties present: Green Caddis (Rhyacophila), October Caddis (also Limnephilidae), Grannom (Brachycentrus), Spotted Caddis (Hydropsyche) and the pesky little Microcaddis (Hydroptilidae).

In spite of the varied assortment of families, caddis identification is pretty simple and falls into three categories: big ones (hook sizes 8–12), little ones (14–18) and the minute microcaddis (20–24). Adults have two pairs of wings held tent-like over their abdomens, are clumsy flyers and appear to look like their cousins, the moths. Mature adult Traveller Sedges can be as large as 40 mm long, but average 20–25 mm in the Interior, most commonly a mousy-tan body colour with brown wings, but also present in shades of pale and olive-green, or cream with light grey-coloured wings. Most Interior lakes also contain minor hatches of sedges that are of the smaller 10–15-mm variety, the Longhorned and Northern Case Makers, which I have seen in bright green, pale cream and cinnamon. You don't want to be caught without a pattern when these little guys show up. In river systems, adult caddis are found in smaller sizes compared to still water; right down to 2 mm, which is really tiny.

Adults live up to eight weeks, hanging around lake or streamside foliage, and are capable of producing multiple generations during a season when conditions are right. They are taken by fish in several stages: as drifting larvae, as pupae during staging and emerging exercises, as egg-laying female adults as they skim the surface or dive under water and lastly, during their living cycles as they return to water for a drink.

Caddis display a complete metamorphosis—egg, larva, pupa and adult. Larvae look like the grub worms you find in your vegetable garden, and can be free-swimming as found in some river-dwelling genera, or the web-cased variety that build encasements from pebbles, weeds, sticks and bottom vegetation. In river systems, cased larvae live in little cigar-shaped objects clutched onto rocks and stumps, whereas lake-dwelling cocoon larvae will be found clinging to bottom debris, weeds, rushes, or anything they can attach to.

Colours of the larva stage ranges from pale green to various shades of tan, cream and brown with darker thorax and head areas. After several growth stages and renovations of its case, the larva will encase itself and pupate in the closed cavity, making ready for its emergence over the coming weeks.

Pupae shucks, observed drifting lazily in a lake's surface film, can easily be mistaken for dragonfly nymphs on first glance, but dragonflies—without exception—hatch on land, whereas sedge pupae emerge in several fashions: under water, popping to the surface as adults; on shore, crawling onto vegetation; or on the surface, by discarding their shuck. On close inspection, you'll notice that caddis pupae have two body-length antennae, two immature pairs of wings, and a pyramidal shaped posterior that is widest at the rear. They can move through the water column very quickly and, when they are ready to hatch, ascend the water column, often travelling great distances a few inches beneath the surface as they struggle out of their pupae cases before becoming airborne. This is a wonderful time for the fly fisher, the emerging adult presenting a worthy target for trout as the caddis pursues its freedom—floating line, shallow shoal water and the biggest fish in the lake coming undone over a caddis hatch!

Look for caddis flights to take place on Interior lakes and rivers anytime after the May long weekend, depending on elevation. Low-lying lakes, such as Dragon near Quesnel, have a strong hatch of cinnamons (Northern Case Makers) that occurs during mid-May, coinciding with the best mayfly and chironomid hatches of the year, and rivers like the Blackwater, Stellako, Crooked and McLeod have strong hatches every day from early June until the first frosts of late August, or sometimes September.

Caddis in all stages of development account for a huge proportion of a fish's diet, up to 20 percent, even more in river systems, which ranks them right up there with freshwater shrimp, midges and mayflies as the prime sources of protein for our finned friends. Evenings are best for sedge activity, but because they are long-lived, trout are always on the lookout for them. Caddis imitations should be among the best arsenal in your fly box for those days when you're wondering what to use.

Part 1—Caddis Fishing Lakes

Caddis Eggs and Larvae

Adult caddis flies mate either in a swarm during a heavy hatch or individually in shoreline vegetation and cover when the opportunity presents itself. Females take flight and return to water soon after breeding and, depending on the species and mood of the insect, either "run" over the lake, dive to the bottom, or sit on the surface while depositing their eggs, which are bright green and laid in strands that drop to the lake bed or attach to foliage, developing into larvae within weeks.

Larvae are found in multiple colours: tan, brown, olive-green, cream and Kelly green, depending on the species and colour of lake foliage. Their size range is also variable, from as small as 2 mm to as large as 40 mm, owing to various genus and levels of maturity encountered. Some river species of sedge larvae are free-swimming and don't build a case; however, other species spin a sticky silk web which they use to draw sticks, stones, weed growth or debris into a cocoon-like case that becomes their seasonal home and camouflage for pupae development. This "stick" stage is an important part of fish diet during winter, early spring and late fall when hatches and other food sources are minimal or dormant.

As cased larvae grow to maturity, they leave their cases to rebuild their homes, and become fish food during these short renovation times. Woolly Worm imitations are a favourite pattern used to represent these free-swimming moments. When Jack Shaw taught his fly tying courses, the Woolly Worm was the model for his students' first attempt at tying flies, because it is perhaps the most simple of patterns that, even when tied in a scruffy-looking manner (which is best for this fly), will fool the largest of trout if fished correctly. Hurrah for the students;

their untidy first attempts work (see page 146)!

Fish larvae patterns in less than 5 m of water, on full-sinking type 1–3 lines in the very bottom zone of the lake, where most strikes will occur when your line is perpendicular to the rod, your fly slowly inching and twitching through bottom muck. Many hang-ups are encountered and flies are lost or snagged on weeds, but the result is always worth it.

Caddis Pupae

As a sedge larva reaches full maturity in its cocoon, the urge to reproduce begins the pupation process, a major transformation from worm to adult-looking pupa. After pupation is complete, the pupa, or pharate adult, is a fully formed caddis fly, lacking the ability to fly only by the restraint of a thin exoskeleton that surrounds its body. It's this skinny layer that the struggling adult splits to allow escape, leaving the shuck that we recognize as the transparent pupa case. Pupae will flee their cases "en masse" during a good hatch, causing great commotion under water, invisible to the fisherman who ponders the day away trying to resolve which pattern will be successful. Caddis are mainly evening emergers, but it may take several days of staging, swimming around and false starts before the pupa is ready for the evening's activity—these are the fly fisher's times, when trout will seek out restless pupae. More joyfully for the fly fisher, trout will key on the pupa during its ascent as it swims a few inches below the surface, the fish reacting in a violent whirling manner as they take the insect, creating a tail swirl and exciting dry line options.

Fish caddis pupae with fly lines that can be controlled for depth, delivery and retrieve: type 1 full-sinking intermediates, #2 sink-tips, or floating lines, all with fast-sinking fluorocarbon leaders and tippets. Pupae begin activity on shallow shoals during emergence, most often in less than 2 m of water, but during the bright sun of a typical summer afternoon, trout will be holding off the shoals in up to 6 m of protective depth. Envision trout cruising in and out of the shoal areas in a circular fashion. They will feel safer intercepting your offering in 4 m of water than they will in 1–2 m, this behaviour dictating that the pupa is best fished from deep to shallow by casting to the far shore with a type 2 sink-tip line, allowing it to sink fully, and retrieving up onto the shoal area. If the shoals are flat and long, defer to an intermediate or floating line, which will allow you to keep the fly travelling at the same depth for a long steady retrieve through the shallow zone. The key to success is to keep your fly off the weedy bottom, and to manoeuvre it through all of the feeding zones effectively. On cloudy days of low light conditions, or during evenings, fish will abandon the security of deep water and often glide into just inches of shoal water to pick up pupae and hatching adults, which necessitates the use of a dry line exclusively during these occasions.

Caddis Adults

As I get longer in the tooth, I realize that my best fishing days are probably behind me—that's life after sixty years of age, and over forty fishing with only a fly. These days, every time I go out on a lake or river, I look for dry fly opportunities, and from June to September it's usually caddis adult patterns that I turn to when fish start rising on the shoals, or when trout are cruising, because fish can't seem to refuse one. Even on lakes not known for sedge activity, feeding trout recognize caddis as a hearty snack, and will not hesitate to chase one down and devour it. I've become so preoccupied with finding dry fly action on my outings that I'll choose my lakes based on their quality of insect reproduction rather than size of fish, and constantly watch the shoals for signs of surface feeding, humbly subscribing to that sometimes foolish mindset that "I'd rather catch one trout on top than five below."

Adult caddis flies are taken on the surface at several different stages: while shedding the pupa skin and drying its wings, during the egg-laying rendezvous of the female adult, or when thirsty adults dip the surface for a drink. In the first and third cases—a hatching or feeding adult—this becomes a hunt-and-seek method: you track the shoal with a kick-boat and target an individual rising fish, trying to anticipate its direction of travel and entice it by casting your offering in front of it. You know where the fish is, you anticipate the take with a quick rush of adrenalin, and focus intently on the drifting offering. The positive response is exhilarating; it's a feeling of total immersion in your sport.

Females that have mated act in a different manner than hatching adults. They fly out of the bush to the lake and flop to the surface in their cumbersome flights, often several times before they get their bearings, and begin to "skitter" or "run" along the water while depositing eggs. For the fly fisher mimicking the female's activity, the searching routine is best reproduced by positioning or anchoring your craft on a likely shoal area, making certain that you can cover deep water as well as the edge. Your fly is cast in quartering segments to cover all depth zones, and you wait...until you can wait no longer, and you raise and jiggle your rod tip to simulate a travelling caddis skimming the surface. If there are trout in the area, you'll wake them up without question, and the best is yet to come as a cruising fish clobbers your offering.

Traveling Sedge

Family: Phryganeidae
Genus: *Banksiola*
Larvae: size 20–40 mm; colours: tan and grey-brown, pale green
Pupae: size 20–40 mm; tan and grey-brown, green, yellow-gold
Adult: size 20–40 mm; tan and grey-brown, pale green, yellow-gold

These are big boys, bugs that cause heart-stopping moments on Interior lakes, but they are not confined to lakes, as the family can also be found in the quiet backwaters of streams and beaver ponds. Fly fishers who target this species can create havoc on a marriage when they become obsessed with catching the first major caddis hatch of the summer season: lunar periods are studied; charts and historical diaries document the place, date and time the heaviest hatches occurred; work and family are set aside for a few weeks—the angler's passion is uncontrollable. There are a few lakes on the Interior Plateau that foster such a hatch of these giant bugs that to miss it is considered a sin: especially Dragon, Fir, Marmot, and Bishop lakes of the North Cariboo; and in the Central Interior, lakes with generous weedbeds like Hobson, Eena and Vivian, Junkers, Wicheeda and Carp, the trout are foolish enough to take a Traveller anytime you offer it.

Larvae of this family are case makers, brown or green in colour, and the most free-swimming of all caddis species, thus the easiest for fish to target. The Woolly Worm works well to imitate active larvae, trolled with type 3 full-sinking lines or cast and settled on the bottom, then painfully inched along with a hand-crawl retrieve. I have seen patterns tied using clipped deer hair to simulate debris and sticks of caddis case, and I'm sure they work on occasion, but my preference is to imitate the juicy worm of the wandering larva stage.

Pupae imitations can be most effective for the fly fisher because their movements coincide with hatch activity, their restless commotion and staging acts before emergence triggering fish to hunt them on the shoals. Depending on the clarity of their habitat, pupae can be found in a variety of colours: tan, grey-brown, olive and bright shades of green, golden yellow and sometimes grey, with wings of muted brown held close to the body. Two features the fly tier cannot overlook are the thorax, which should depict a sharp contrasting colour to the abdomen, and the ribbing of the abdomen, which is highlighted with bright green or yellow-gold. Common thorax colours are ginger on green specimens, darker brown on muddy-coloured pupae, and rich rust colour on golden yellow imitations. Long antennae and swimmerets are prominent, adding life in the form of movement when represented with Golden Pheasant tippet and a single turn of pheasant rump. The Kamloops Sedge Pupa was one of Jack Shaw's favourite patterns, which Kamloops fly fishers credit Jack for developing back in the early 1960s, but fly patterns like the Knouff Lake Special and Green Carey are reasonable imitations, still in use by many old-timers to emulate the pupa stage of this important insect (see page 146).

The pupa pattern I tie is modelled on the pupa Jack invented, which was a feature in Art Lingren's book *Contemporary Fly Patterns of British Columbia*, and it has been a mainstay of my fly box for many years, especially when I dip my fly line in those fertile Interior lakes.

The adult stage needs only one fly to imitate the Traveller Sedge—the venerable Mikaluk Sedge. What a pattern Walter Mikaluk of Calgary designed when he came up with this one! I've lost count of the number of trout this fly has fooled over the years, and for a deer-hair pattern, it's durability is remarkable—I've had twenty-fish days on a couple of flies, changing them only to dry and shake off the fish slime (see page 147).

The Mikaluk Traveller is tied in a myriad of colours and sizes from 6–12; shades of pale green and olive, yellow, tan, and grey are some of my favourite lake colours. Pale green caddis, common in the Southern Interior, are not often seen in our more northern waters—we find our big travellers are not so large, and are usually mousy-grey or warm tan, with wings a muted dark brownish-grey, tones that are well matched with natural grey phase deer hair or natural elk. Some tiers like elk for Mikaluk wing (the original calls for elk), but I prefer select deer hair because I find it less stiff to work with, and it gives me the full-wing impression I like to see on my caddis adults (see page 147).

My friend Ralph Shaw of Courtenay, BC, swears by another revered all-purpose caddis pattern, the Tom Thumb. He ties them by the dozens in all sizes, and fishes them through every hatch. I admit the Tom Thumb has a place; it is everything an *emerger* caddis should be, which is where I feel it has unwittingly found its place in Kamloops lore for over five decades. The Tom Thumb lacks durability, but it's got that roughed-up look an emerger needs—a struggling, stuck-in-the-shuck insect that craves to be free, and not only imitates caddis, but also mayflies, chironomids and midges when offered in small sizes (see page 148).

Northern Case Maker

Family: Limnephilidae
Genus: *Dicosmoecus*
Larvae: size 18–25 mm; colour ginger-brown (cinnamon)

Pupae: size 18–25 mm; cinnamon abdomen/tan shroud
Adult: size 15–18 mm; cinnamon/pale brown wing

I admit it took my research into caddis families to discover which genus our very common Cinnamon Sedge falls within. Caddis worldwide looks the same, with size and dominant colour the major determining factors between families. Our prevalent Interior family appears to be Limnephilidae, the largest and most varied caddis family in North America, which is about half the size of the Traveller Sedge and hatches a month or so earlier, eagerly taken by trout from mid-May to September. I enjoy them because I can't wait to fish caddis, and they are the first hatch to show, usually around the May long weekend in low elevation lakes, a few weeks later in higher altitudes.

Egg, larva, pupa and adult stages are ginger-brown in colour, making them highly visible to both fish and fisher, and they will often overlap with heavy mayfly and chironomid hatches, so trout will happily take them as a "new" hatch, welcoming a change of diet.

I have also enjoyed many days of fishing with this family on Central Interior rivers, as all of my favourites—the Stellako, Crooked and Blackwater—have produced really good days for me on what I call my Cinnamon Sedge. This family also includes the prized October Caddis, which steelhead will pound on the surface in the Skeena system on warm September days. The Mikaluk-style pattern in size 14 works the same in river or lake: positively, and without hesitation. Larva and pupa stages are also important, using the same pattern styles as the Traveller, but matching the ginger colour, reducing the hook size to 12–14, and altering the hair and hackle style a little (see page 148).

Longhorned Case Maker

Family: Leptoceridae
Genus: *Oecetis*
Larvae: size 7–15 mm; colours: black, dark brown
Pupae: size 7–15 mm; black, tan-brown
Adult: size 7–15 mm; black, tan-brown, cream, bright green

While fishing Hart Lake many years ago, I witnessed this diminutive, flopping, caddis-like insect getting sandbagged by trout along the north shoal, which upon close inspection was indeed a caddis, recognized by its distinctive tent-shaped wings, but it had antennae twice the length of its cream-coloured body. I had never seen a still-water caddis so small, and those long antennae were unusual.

Finally, many years later I decided to write this book, which led me into hours of research trying to figure out what our Interior lakes contain for insect variety and hatches. Imagine my delight and surprise when I found this little fellow (or lady) to be from family Leptoceridae, the second most common sedge family.

You can find this little caddis in an array of body colour combinations, all with dark brown or black wings. Their larvae, like all caddis in lake environments, are case makers, represented by the Woolly Worm in dark brown or black. Pupae patterns should be either tan or dark brown, tied size 10–12 curved pupa hooks.

The adult is a different matter, and perhaps the most important to the fly fisher when imitating this family of caddis. The largest specimen you'll find is tied on a size 16 hook, which is where the popular river pattern Elk Hair Caddis (EHC) becomes my fly of choice because it can effectively be tied to hook size 24. The EHC, with its palmered hackle and extended wing style, has a lot of "suggestion" for a small fly, and is really simple to tie (see page 149).

Part 2—Caddis Fishing Rivers

Next to mayflies, caddis is the prime source of protein for river-dwelling fish; probably an even greater proportion when you factor in the size of caddis, many times larger than our most common mayfly species. On many occasions, especially at our seldom-fished wilderness rivers like the Crooked, Blackwater or McLeod, I've found a size 10 Stimulator or Mikaluk in a hot-orange colour will take fish at all times, regardless of hatch activity. Caddis hatches of individual families overlap in river systems; trout will often see all of the home-river families at different times in the same day, so they are very hard to beat as a river-searching pattern when you stand a chance of fooling fish with any family. I believe if you begin your summer day searching with a caddis, either pupa or adult, and fish are looking for food (as most river fish do constantly), you'll find and catch receptive fish.

October Caddis

Family: Limnephilidae
Genus: *Dicosmoecus*
Larva: size 15–30 mm; colour: pale yellow or cream/rusty-orange shroud
Pupa: size 15–30 mm; cinnamon
Adult: size 15–30 mm; hot orange or cinnamon/red-brown wing

Also known as Giant Orange Caddis—and to me, Cinnamon Caddis—this family is found in both lakes and streams, but the two genera are different; in this case river dwellers are the larger insect. During late August, walk the shoreline of any fertile Interior river and you'll see cases of this family's larvae clinging on almost every large underwater rock near the shoreline, where larvae build their cases of small pebbles, which can often be multi-coloured and lavishly decorated depending upon the river's mineral resources. The larva stage of this family is a prime target for fish, because during growth cycles they are often forced into free-swimming adventures as they search for new home-building materials to rebuild their cases. Larvae, available during the entire fishing season and also active during winter, present an opportunity for the fly fisher who enjoys drifting patterns with a floating line or strike indicator. This is a productive pattern for searching shallow rocky riffles and soft sections of moderate flows for most of May and June in Central BC (see page 149).

The hatching period is concentrated into a three- to four-week time frame during late August and September, and is usually the only major hatch of large insect going on at this time, making it a focus for marauding trout. Pupae patterns are occasionally taken eagerly, but the adult is the one that fish wait for and feed on with aggression. Because the insect is large, impart some fluttering action when fishing the adult: skitter it, drag it, splat the water—create some excitement.

In mid-August 2007 my wife, Lois, and I spent a week's vacation at the Stellako River. We love the river at this time: weather is usually decent, heavy fishing pressure is over for the year and Saskatoon berries are at their finest eating stage. Sockeye salmon are gathering in the Nechako and Nautely rivers and in Fraser Lake, but haven't ascended the Stellako; the native trout have rested almost a month from the most intense angling pressure, and are ready to tackle the fall feeding frenzy, especially the Cinnamon Caddis.

I invariably witness several species of caddis hatching at this time: often the little Grannom during the evenings, and usually the Spotted Caddis at midday, but the major day-time hatches are always the big Cinnamons. It's definitely caddis time, and I love it!

Fishing had been spotty, and Lois and I struck up a friendship with our cabin neighbours, a visiting French couple, Doctor Joel Sarkissian and his wife, Martine. Joel had been catching the odd trout during the past few evenings, but not stirring much activity through the day. However, I was able to pick up several nice trout during the first day on my #14 Cinnamon Caddis. I shared the pattern with Joel, who also began to catch a few fish on it. But the week's big moment was during a squall that rushed down Francois Lake. With the wind came dark, ominous clouds, warm rain and a high pressure weather front that turned on the big fish of the Bridge Run. Dripping wet and scantily clad in only a T-shirt and waders, I had to roll and spey cast my way through the shallow pocket runs in the driving wind, but in that hour of inclement weather the big fish felt secure, and nine of them from 40–50 cm came to the Cinnamon Caddis. That's why I like late August vacations at the Stellako (see page 149)!

Spotted Caddis

Family: Hydropsychidae
Genus: *Ceratopsyche*
Larva: size 10–16 mm; colour: tan-green/dark green shroud
Pupa: size 10–16 mm; tan/pale green thorax
Adult: size 10–15 mm; tan/mottled brown wings

This family is clearly the most abundant caddis fly species of Interior streams, and is the first sedge pattern I turn to for searching runs and riffles in June and July. The larvae are not case makers, but net spinners that secrete a silky substance to weave their nets in logs, rock crevices and stream obstructions. A larva may build several nets, and farm them like a planter tending his crop, constantly surveying its land claim for the captured stream organisms that it feeds on. Because of this free-swimming larva's mobility and availability to fish at all times, this stage is a leading choice for the fly fisher. Use a floating line to dead drift or bounce a larva pattern through soft, rocky runs and riffles (see page 150).

The pupa stage should not be overlooked by the fly fisher, as the pharate insect may drift a long time in the current before breaking the surface film, and this is the best opportunity for bright sunny days. You know the time is right; insects are hatching, but where are the fish? Usually they are waiting for the dim light of cloud cover or nightfall. Using a pair of Polaroid glasses, you'll often witness silver flashes on or near the stream bottom as you quietly work through a run, and wonder why fish aren't rising, or when they will surface feed. These flashes are feeding trout scouting the river bottom, darting and turning as they quickly pick off insects drifting through their feeding vision, then swiftly returning to their cover. These are the times to try a pupa, or a Soft Hackle Emerger using floating or sink-tip line until the adult hatch is more evident, or conditions are more conducive to dry fly prospects (see page 150).

The adult caddis—what fish can refuse an insect that looks this good? Most anglers don't use enough of them, and I don't know why, because they are deadly ammunition. It doesn't matter where I go—Kootenays, Alberta, the Okanagan or Montana—trout relish being fooled by caddis imitations. This little fellow in sizes 14–18, tied either Mikaluk method (if your eyes are still good), or using my Spotted Caddis Adult in small-hook style, both with mousy-grey body and brown deerhair wing, usually turns the trick for me (see page 151).

I reason that if 25 percent of a river trout's diet is caddis, then I'm going to use a caddis in some form at least 50 percent of the time. The adults of this genus are "divers," witnessed when egg-laying females return to the river and dive to the bottom to deposit their eggs, then float or drift back to the surface and die. At this time, even a sunken or poorly cast and scuttled imitation is a target for greedy fish. Keep your fly in the water; good things are often the result.

Green Caddis

Family: Rhyacophilidae
Genus: *Rhyacophila*
Larva: size 11–18 mm; colours: green/tan shroud, tan/green shroud
Pupa: size 8–16 mm; green body/tan thorax, tan body/green thorax
Adult: size 8–16 mm; green or green-grey body, grey wing

This caddis is similar to Spotted Caddis in most respects: free-swimming and caseless, therefore always available to fish. Even the differentiation in colour—this family being brighter green—is not enough to warrant separate discussion. I suggest the fly fisher will get by with having some larva and pupa patterns tied with a visible green body and contrasting shroud and thorax, and adult imitations also in green with a grey wing.

The adult caddis that I tie for this imitation is a credit to A.K. Best of Boulder, Colorado. I've altered A.K.'s Sparkle Wing Caddis from his book, *A.K. Best's Advanced Fly Tying*, by changing body colour, substituting guard hair that I have available, and adding a short tail of deer hair to assist with floating the fly. This is an experimental pattern that I haven't yet fished with, but it looks like a winner (see page 151).

Grannom

Family: Brachycentridae
Genus: *Brachycentrus*
Larva: size 12–17 mm; colours: cream or green/tan shroud
Pupa: size 6–12 mm; bright green body/tan thorax
Adult: size 6–12 mm; muddy olive-brown/dark brown wing

Other common names for this little caddis are Mother's Day Caddis and Black Caddis, and they are the darkest coloured sedge that you'll see. I've come across them in lakes as well as rivers, mostly during evenings in late August, the hatch intensifying as the sun dips lower on the horizon. I've witnessed prolific flights of this insect, so many coming off that the air is full of them; fish are rising all over the place and you, as a fly fisher, are confused as hell.

Grannom larvae are case makers, building their homes out of weeds and grass material, living in riffle water and soft flows of moderate speed. All stages are trout food, especially adults because they hatch near shore, gather and mate in swarms or in overhanging foliage, and the female returns to deposit eggs later in the day. She crawls or swims into the water from shore, releases her seed, and drifts away in the current. This hatch activity can be so intense that feeding trout don't need to move from their station, rather just sit and wait for dying adults to cross their position.

The Grannom adult is a productive fly early (when most of our rivers are closed) and late in the year, not seen by fish as often as Spotted or October Caddis. As with all species of caddis, however, the Grannom is available year-round in the larva stage and this is the phase that you should target with a floating line during periods of non-hatch activity (see page 151).

Microcaddis

Family: Hydroptilidae
Larva: size 2–5 mm; colour: dark brown
Pupa: size 2–5 mm; dark brown, cream/tan shroud
Adult: size 2–5 mm; dark brown, cream/dark wing

Some say they are so small, they are insignificant, but I think not. There are hundreds of genera in the family; all are tiny, and because of their comparative size, are often mistaken for midge family Tricorythodes (Trico—also known as the "White-winged Curse"). In some fertile rivers like our Stellako, there are so many of these little buggers you can't overlook them as an important food item, because the fish don't.

The adult stage is most significant to the fly fisher, which is where those size 22 and 24 Elk Hair Caddis you tied last winter, wondering at the time if you will ever need them, are your best and only friends. And never rule out an orange or cream-tagged Soft Hackle Emerger in size 22, swung lazily through a quick run—this is the hatch matcher for diving, egg-laying Microcaddis (see page 133 and 149).

Stonefly

In the 1990s, I think every budding wannabe fly fisher was captivated by the movie *A River Runs through It*, and the imagery of the Maclean brothers casting adult stoneflies in the Big Blackfoot River. Stonefly fishing can sometimes be magical, just like the love story of a river that chased a generation of yuppies off the sofa, motivated them west to Montana for a little soul-searching, and introduced them to one of the finer sports in life—fly fishing.

When work transferred me north in 1992, I thought I was already a pretty good all-around fisherman. I quickly confirmed that I was as good a lake fisherman as I knew I was; rivers, however, were a different matter. The fly fisher's season on a trout river is short in the Central Interior, barely three months long, but from opening day in July (some are mid-June) to the end of September (in the best years) our rivers are in their prime. Every living thing that uses the stream competes for its own dominant act: insects to mate and regenerate; fish for food and spawn; animals for sustenance; and fly fishers for sport. Everything must balance and work in unison for the river and its life forces to succeed: water levels, temperatures, spawning, nurturing and the critical timing of each.

For a fly fisher to contend with all of these natural forces and learn the ways of a river, he or she must be successful—find a way to catch some fish, gain confidence and *then* study the intricacies of the stream over a period of years. In the beginning of my northern sojourn, I had a love affair with the stonefly nymph, which was my most successful pattern during the first five years here because I worked it the hardest in every river I fished. Oh, I tried other searching patterns: mayfly nymphs, caddis larvae and pupae, and an assortment of dry flies, but none caught fish consistently like the Black Stonefly Nymph (see Salmonfly Nymph pattern, page 152). Problem was, I caught a lot of coarse fish by nymphing the bottom, and I prefer trout; but I didn't turn diehard dry fly fisherman on rivers until about 1997. The pursuit was not easy; there was a lot to see, learn and experience before I could understand the way of rivers because each is different, taking decades to uncover its secrets. As I say to one of my fishing partners, Danie Erasmus—a fine fly fisherman and partner newly trans- planted in the North from Vancouver—when the Stellako is a bit off and gives us a spanking: "Danie, you have to pay your dues in this river." I'm still learning, and hope to continue the education for a few more years.

This takes nothing away from the stonefly nymph, which is probably the best nymph I know for searching rivers and still the ace-in-the-hole for those "one-in-ten days" when I need to use a nymph because I'm exasperated and can't bring trout up for a dry fly. Stoneflies can be a fish's largest single meal ticket in the river, or one of the smallest, depending on the species hatching, which can range from a diminutive Yellow Sally that is 2–7 mm long to the humungous Salmonfly measuring 50 mm. A Salmonfly whacking you in the back of the neck while wading hip-deep down a river can be pretty unnerving, akin to that of a horsefly trying to relieve you of some meat. I'm glad they are not cannibalistic, but I bet these huge insects have caused more calamities for river- wading fly fishers than all other bugs combined.

Though the adult stage is more romantic, as I like to think of all dry fly fishing opportunities, the nymph stage probably constitutes over 90 percent of the stonefly diet for trout, ranking third in importance to river-living fish behind mayfly and caddis species. In terms of quality of dining experience, a single stonefly nymph of 30 mm constitutes several times the volume of a mayfly nymph or caddis larva. In spite of being a "filet mignon" of river insects, very few stonefly nymphs make it into the fish's belly because they cling tenaciously to their hideaways under rocks and cover, but they do come out of hiding when mature and nature urges them to procreate the species. At this full-grown stage, they clamber along the river bottom toward shore under cover of darkness— twilight or early morning—to find suitable habitat: a dry rock, log or tree branch on which to dry and split the nymph's skin so the adult can emerge. This process can take several hours, which renders the nymph prey to all sorts of predators: fish, birds, reptiles and animals seeking an easy meal. Some smaller species of stoneflies don't migrate; they hatch in the stream, similar to mayfly or caddis.

The families of large-sized stonefly nymphs are easy to recognize because they are huge at maturity, up to 40 mm long with several distinctive features: two long tails and antennae; three pairs of long, clinging legs; two separate pairs of wing pads; and eyes that are widely separated. Stoneflies are similar in appearance to still-water dragonfly nymphs, but are mostly river dwelling. Smaller species of lesser families, sizes less than 10 mm, are more difficult to recognize because they can easily be mistaken for mayfly nymphs, which is why a Hare's Ear Nymph size 12–14 fishes well, passing as a general impression for both. The most noticeable differentiation is the presence of three tail filaments on the mayfly, and only two on the stonefly. Colours are varied, two-toned with bright yellow or orange in muted body colour combinations: dark or chocolate-brown with yellow or orange; olive-green with black and yellow; black with orange; and rusty-brown with dark brown and yellow. Nymphs develop within the mating year, live up to three years before maturity, and moult twelve to twenty times before reaching full-growth stage, which means they are a valuable and constant food source for fish at all times and in many sizes. Fish find them hard to come by, but seldom pass one up when offered the chance.

There are many fishing methods for nymphs. I prefer to not use indicators or split shot, so my favourite technique is to fish a well-weighted nymph with floating line, using an upstream cast and mend, which tumbles the nymph through the current pockets, over rocks, and through feeding lanes. Strikes are usually a "stopping of the drift," much like steelhead fishing, where the fish mouths your offering while it is in its path; if you don't gather your slack line through the drift, the fish will be gone! Another option, using the same tackle, is to cast at 45° downstream and let the fly swing through the run on a tight line; fish will often follow it and again, like steelhead fishing, pick up the offering at the end of the drift while the fly line is directly below you. And let's not forget the migrating nymphs: floating line, parachute cast below you over feeding lanes and boulder runs; let the fly tumble through pockets close to shoreline to intercept

Stoneflies are river dwellers, and can be up to 40 mm at maturity. *Photo Brian Chan.*

those big trout lying in wait for mature nymphs travelling to land to mate.

An adult stonefly looks like the nymph stage, except for two wings slightly longer than body length folded flat over its back. Its features are the same: two short tails and two body-length antennae. Adults of different genera comprise a variety of mottled colour combinations: orange with brown, brown with yellow, and olive with green and fluorescent yellow with yellow.

Contrary to popular opinion that adult stoneflies splat the water and cause a ruckus, I don't feel they do so. Perhaps on windy days their landings are a little rough because of their size, but generally they land softly on a cushion of air, and then flutter their wings as they deposit tiny nymphs. These nymph-laying routines in combination with the adult stonefly habit of staying close to stream-side vegetation during its few weeks of maturity are the fly fisher's opportunities to catch a few fish. When casting a stonefly, allow it to land gently, then give it some twitches, or what I call "skitters," to simulate the seed-laying routine; or when fishing close to the bank, use parachute casts and short downstream drifts to imitate adults that have blown or fallen from their perches in trees.

There is one obstacle to contend with when fishing our Interior stonefly hatches: the big genera (Salmonfly, Skwala and Golden Stone) begin to mature at high-water time in early June when most years some of our best rivers like the Blackwater (open June 14) and Stellako (June 1) are difficult to fish until the beginning of July when water levels drop a few feet. You'll find trout almost living in the bush during June, right on the banks. Wading can be treacherous, but you have to chance it because the reward may well be worth the trouble. Major stonefly hatches often occur during the full moon phases of June, July and August, and sporadically through the rest of those months.

Stoneflies belong to order Plecoptera; the common families in our waters are: Salmonfly (Pteronarcyidae), Skwala (Perlodidae) Golden Stone (Perlidae), Little Yellow (also Perlodidae) and Little Olive (Chloroperlidae).

Salmonfly, Skwala, and Golden Stone

Salmonfly (see page 152)

Family: Pteronarcyidae
Genus: *Pteronarcys californica*
Egg stage: incomplete for entire family (no stage)
Nymph: size 25–50 mm; colours: black, chocolate-brown
Adult: size 30–50 mm; dark brown topside, dark grey wing; mottled brown and orange underside, orange-banded head

Skwala (see page 153)

Family: Perlodidae
Genus: *Skwala*
Nymph: size 20–40 mm; colour: dark brown, mottled with light patches
Adult: size 20–40 mm; olive-brown topside, dark grey wing; mottled olive-brown and yellow underside, yellow-banded head

Golden Stone (see page 154)

Family: Perlidae
Genus: *Hesperoperla Pacifica*
Nymph: size 20–40 mm; colour: rusty-brown mottled with yellow
Adult: size 20–40 mm; golden brown topside, brown wing; mottled golden brown and yellow underside, yellow-banded head

These three, the largest genera of stoneflies, appear late May through late July on our Interior rivers, beginning with the Skwala, then Golden Stones and finally the Salmonfly. Easiest identification that differentiates the genera are bright orange or yellow markings on the underside and head areas. They will often overlap in their breeding cycles as one hatch wanes and the next intensifies, but not to the extent that they will interbreed.

I find all insect breeding a remarkable act of nature. You can find three similar-sized but different genera of one insect in a river system, but the insect's genetic strain is not diluted by mating, insurance that survival of subspecies is constant and foremost to the order. Like the Pacific salmon that grace our streams, their sole purpose is procreation of the genus; they live a short life of maturity to die in sacrifice so that the strain may survive.

I love stonefly hatches because it's an opportune time to cast a big fly and raise a big fish, similar to but shorter-lived than caddis hatches. The size 6 and 8 hair-winged flies can be cumbersome to throw with 2-and 3-weight rods, but often that's all you have in your hand, and you have to make the best of it. Ideally, a 5-weight outfit is standard fare when you're on the river at stonefly hatch time, and forget fishing slack water—stoneflies live in boulder gardens, riffles, and broken pocket-water sections of streams. That's where females will return to lay seed, usually in the middle of the flow where the deposits will settle to the bottom, find a seam or crevice, and mature to reproduce three years hence.

Stimulators work as all-purpose flies during a hatch or for searching water, and I used to use them extensively, but I think the stonefly deserves a place of its own on the fly tier's bench. If mine are modelled after a standard pattern, it's the Sofa Pillow. When I tie my big stoneflies, I keep a common theme: mix the colours by adding a yellow rib for highlight, use peacock herl with the rib to introduce contrast and glitter, and complement the pattern with golden yellow or rusty-orange for head markings.

The Salmonfly Adult pattern that my tinkering produced became a fixture in my fly box after Blackwater River opening day in June 1997, when the fish god smiled on me with great favour—I released sixty-seven wild rainbows one afternoon, fishing only three runs of the river. It has not let me down since, so I developed the Golden Stone and the Skwala along the same line, with similar successes.

Little Yellow Stoneflies (Yellow Sally)

Family: Perlodidae
Genus: *Isoperla*
Nymph: size 7–12 mm; colours: mottled tan/light yellow
Adult: size 7–12 mm; fluorescent yellow/pale wing
This is the family of smallest stoneflies that you'll discover on Interior streams, but not the least important, because it's just another one of those frustrating "little fly" hatches that can turn you into a good fly fisher, or leave you on the bank after a day's fishing wondering "What the hell went on out there?" I've learned lessons from both situations, and prefer the former. Come across this hatch on a river, and you'll find it's similar to that pesky little fluorescent yellow bugger that you can barely see but is a regular contributor to the midge cycle on lakes. Adults are small, less than 7 mm, and it's one of the stonefly species that will hatch either in the river flow or migrate to shore. On the Stellako, they often hatch in the river and are a regular sight on summer afternoons during the Salmonfly hatch.

Turn over some rocks in a river and you'll surely find the nymphs of this family, marked with a soft yellow-coloured abdomen, tan thorax, and two tail segments. Nymph patterns are a good choice for those summer days when hatches are non-existent or during mornings while waiting for the afternoon's pending activity. Patterns that work universally are the Hare's Ear Nymph in pale colours or, as an emerger pattern, the Soft Hackle with a yellow or chartreuse tag, but I've developed a nymph for this insect that is a consistent producer using Hare-Tron dubbing and the previously mentioned hackle and leg style. Bounce it through some riffles, dabble it over a boulder run, or fish it close to the bank under overhanging tree branches; give it a chance and I'm sure it'll produce well for you (see page 154).

The adult pattern is another matter. Yellow Sally models are listed in fly tying manuals, and I have tried some of them for this hatch, but without success because I don't think they are close enough to the insect we see up here. Recipes call for a golden yellow imitation, which is way off for our streams, so I've decided to come up with my own, using a #16 hook and cutting back on materials to give it a clean and simple look. Our Little Yellow Stone is very fluorescent, the colour more chartreuse than yellow, and it's a very small size with pale wing, and should be dressed to float high. I mimic the seed-laying female by adding a tag of bright orange to the abdomen.

If I can catch the hatch on the Stellako this summer, we'll see if this model pans out—I bet it will. Fish nymph-laying females right in the riffles and any adults close to the bank, using a short-line parachute cast and 6-X or 7-X tippet, letting trout see the fly before the line and leader—it must float freely on the current without drag (see page 155).

Little Green (Olive) Stonefly

Family: Chloroperlidae
Genus: *Alloperla*
Nymph: size 10–16 mm; colours: dark brown, olive-green
Adult: size 10–16 mm; olive-green body/pale wing

Little Olive and Little Yellow Stoneflies are similar in many respects: small sizes, adults ranging from 7–16 mm; brightly coloured, chartreuse to olive-green; both available for trout in July and August; and they command attention from fish as a prime food source both as nymphs and adults. River systems that contain them are clean and unpolluted, always rocky and boulder-strewn, as is every one of our Interior rivers. Little Olive nymphs and adults are about twice the size of the species of Yellows at maturity, but are available in many size ranges as nymphs because of their long life-stage of three years (see page 155).

Olives are fished the same as all stoneflies, paying close attention to where adults are hatching or depositing. In our rivers, I've seen Little Olives hatching in midstream the same as Little Yellows, so the myth of stoneflies migrating to shore for their mating run is likely only true for the large species. Regardless of where they are hatching, observation and timing are the keys to success, remembering that stoneflies prefer to move in subdued light, so early morning and evening and cloudy days will be favourable to their migration habits (see page 156).

Freshwater Shrimp

Family: Gammaridae
Genus: *Gammarus* and *Hyalella*
Gammarus: size 10–25 mm; colours: yellow, all shades of green, tan, opalescent blue
Hyalella: size 3–7 mm; pale olive-green is dominant

When I lived in Kamloops for ten years during the 1970s and early '80s—the heyday of trout fishing legend Jack Shaw and other pioneer fly fishers—there was no Coquihalla Highway. It took about seven hours to get to the Kamloops lakes from Vancouver, then setup time—a fly fisher needed a three-day weekend to catch a few fish and return home to the Lower Mainland. We had the lakes mostly to ourselves in those days, but since the mid-'80s, with the new highway system, you can leave Vancouver at 5:00 a.m. and be fishing on any lake in the South Thompson Region by 9:00 a.m., fish until after dinner, and be home in bed by midnight.

The freshwater shrimp, or scud, was the number one go-to pattern in those days, and still is. The Baggy Shrimp had not made its debut; scud patterns of the day (and still popular) were the Werner Shrimp and Dexheimer Sedge, a caddis pattern that became more revered as a shrimp imitation than sedge. I fished and tied Werner-style deer-hair scud patterns religiously in those days, using chenille for the body, deer hair for the tail and shellback, and palmered brown saddle hackle for the scuds' legs. They caught trout, lots of trout, and they kept catching trout until the deer hair was torn from the back, the body was frayed and falling apart and the hackle was unwound—and they still do. Were fish more stupid in those glory days? Perhaps they were, or maybe it's just my imagination that takes me back to those simple but effective patterns of the 1960s and '70s.

Alas, but the shrimp isn't a glory pattern in the Central Interior. I think the pH of water in most of our lakes is too low (acidic) to support healthy populations of scud, but that doesn't mean they aren't here, because many of the North Cariboo region's best lakes that support trophy trout rely heavily on them as a food source: Dragon, Hobson, Marmot and Chief Gray to mention a few, but not to the extent of the Southern Interior. In the south, lakes are more alkaline (higher pH) and therefore calcium-rich, which scuds require for the formation and maintenance of their exoskeletons. *Hyalella*, the little genus, is more common than *Gammarus* in lakes of high elevation and cold water.

In the Southern Interior, shrimp comprise up to 40 percent of the food source for trout, ranking it the most important aquatic organism in their food chain. In spite of our lower pH water they are, nonetheless, an essential food organism on the Plateau, because fish are instinctive in their feeding habits— they rely greatly on past experience (in the fish tank), repetition and natural response. If the insect (or crustacean in the case of shrimp) looks like a shrimp, and acts like a shrimp, it'll get eaten as a shrimp by automatic selection whether or not shrimp are in the water. This is a great advantage for the fisherman. You can't overlook the importance of scud to fish, even when they don't exist in the water you are fishing, which leads me to another basic rule when fly fishing lakes: if perplexed and you can't think of anything else to try, tie on a scud. Scud populations are not limited to lakes; they are also present in beaver ponds and the slow-moving backwaters of creeks and rivers.

Shrimp are crustaceans—they don't hatch like insects, but are born looking like shrimp, only smaller versions of their adult form. Both species, *Gammarus* and *Hyalella*, appear exactly the same: curved bodies, 14 pairs of legs, four antennae, and 11 body segments. The *Hyalella* is much smaller, and a paler colour than *Gammarus*. Scuds feed on decayed vegetation, taking on the colour of plant life in their environment, which accounts for the huge variations of colours they assume. They are also opportunists, and feed on animal matter if available; a moose, deer or cow falling through winter ice and drowning is a welcome addition to their larder, the rotting carcass readily consumed by shrimp and other underwater insects and organisms, including fish.

Shrimp mate several times a year, which accounts for the abundance of different sizes and colours, and for the peak times of availability during the fishing season. A key time is ice-out in early spring when lake water begins to warm and circulate, because scuds have been on the dinner plate all winter, and are among the first organisms to become active when the ice melts. Another is in late spring, about the middle two weeks of June in the Central Interior and North Cariboo, between insect hatches, when mayfly and chironomid decline and caddis are waiting. Still another is through the doldrums of midsummer, about the first two weeks of August, when caddis hatches wane, and the short, fall hatches of midges and chironomids are waiting to develop. Finally, late fall, about mid-September, after the last flights of water boatmen and back-swimmers, shrimp is the banquet ticket for trout to "fatten up" for their winter layover, and they continue to feed on scud as their staple food source through October until freeze-up.

Scuds are the acrobats of the underwater world. You fish them where they live—on the bottom whether in 1 m of water or 10 m, because they live and scavenge for food in vegetation, using their colouration as defensive camouflage. Your pattern should match the colour of the vegetation, your choice of fly line able to cover the zone you are fishing with a painstakingly slow retrieve, interspersed with stop-and-go delays.

The fishing method for scuds is summed up like this: fish it deep and slow in spurts of 15–30 cm, with erratic movement and frequent "rest" periods. During early spring and again in late fall, floating or intermediate type 1 full-sinking lines and weighted scud patterns fished over weedbeds in 1–3 m of water is often the ticket for success, and through warm summer months, vary your depths and

Freshwater shrimp (*Hyalella*) are usually 3–7 mm, and are easily identified by their dominant pale olive-green colour. *Photo Brian Chan.*

defer to type 3 full-sinking lines, fishing over weedbeds in deep shoals of less than 10 m.

Many fly patterns and trimmed originals such as the Woolly Worm work well for *Gammarus* scud imitations as long as they are available on small hooks, sizes 10–14. The model needs to imitate the appearance of 14 pairs of legs and many segments, with appendages at the rear and antennae in front of the head. Scuds are transparent, their digestive tracts showing through their exoskeletons; their backs or shellbacks at maturity are darker than the body colour, and they have definite body segments, one for each pair of legs.

Early shrimp patterns developed by pioneers such as Jack Shaw used dubbing for the body, pale palmered hackle for legs, and cock pheasant tail sword barbs over the back as a shellback. Today, many patterns are of the "baggy" shrimp origin, incorporating strips of plastic bag (I now use Stillwater Midge Flex) for the shellback, and dubbing for the body that is "picked out" with a dubbing needle to simulate scud legs. I find these simple to tie, realistic in appearance and my choice for the style that I like to tie. Hooks have come a long way since the '60s—I like to use curved caddis pupae or scud hooks such as Mustad C-49 or Tiemco 2487 (see page 156).

Hyalella shrimp, when imitated on the fly tier's bench, needs no differentiation from *Gammarus* other than size and paler colour tones. When young shrimp are expelled from the female egg sac, they are less than 1 mm in length, and will grow and moult through many stages to reach the average length of 3–7 mm. There is no need to imitate the *Hyalella* as a separate genus, because as long as a fly fisher has scuds of hook sizes 8–18 in his box, and ties small imitations in paler colour tones, both families are represented.

The Hyalella scud is also tied in this manner, but use a size 16 hook and substitute a pale chartreuse green dubbing for the body and natural mallard for the tail and antennae.

After mating, females carry an egg pouch slightly behind the midpoint of their body until giving birth. This pouch is orange in colour during development, and important to the fly fisher using scud patterns, as trout will key on females carrying eggs, often ignoring other imitations. When you tie a fly that imitates this egg sac, simply add a few turns of yellow-orange floss to your regular pattern, and you'll have the Pregnant Shrimp pattern (see page 157).

Leeches

Phylum: Annelida
Subclass: Hirudinea
Family: Glossiphoniidae
Size: all sizes up to 150 mm; average 35–40 mm
Colours: solid and mottled shades of black, maroon, brown and olive

A still-water fly fisher can't be successful without a good selection of leech patterns. Lowly and ugly as they are in real life, you can't discount them as fishing arsenal on any lake in British Columbia, or in the world. On many occasions, especially through summer doldrums, I have salvaged a near-skunking by anchoring on a weedy shoal, tying on a leech pattern, and mooching the bottom to come up with a fish or two. They are also productive trolling patterns, ideal for people who enjoy catching fish on flies but can't master the art of casting a fly and, because everyone in the boat can fish when trolling, for teaching children and non-fishers the wonderful sport of fly fishing.

Leeches are recognized by their wormlike flattened and segmented bodies and undulating motions when swimming. A common opinion is that they are parasitic "blood suckers," but our freshwater leeches are toothless and do not have the ability to suck blood from their hosts. They are carnivorous scavengers, feeding on decaying organic matter, insect life and their preferred diet of snails. Their habitat is the shallow zone of lakes, places where vegetation and cover is plentiful and their favourite foods are readily available. Leeches are more plentiful in lakes that are dark-bottomed and ringed with lily pads, generally indicative of acidic lakes that we find in the Central Interior, but they cannot inhabit water of extreme acidity.

Like earthworms, leeches are hermaphrodites; both have male and female sexual reproductive organs, but do not reproduce asexually (by themselves). They replicate by reciprocal sperm transfer during copulation with another leech, each secreting a ring-like cocoon to carry their eggs until they are deposited on vegetation or bottom debris. Early spring is mating time for mature leeches; young are born during late spring, grow and develop through the prime open-water season and mature for reproduction the following year.

Leeches are great fishing tools. Similar to my affair with black stoneflies for river fishing during the first years I spent in the North, leeches dominated my fly choices when I began to fish our remote lakes. Wherever I fished, they were present in good numbers and trout were more than happy to feed on them. During April through late June, chironomid hatches rule Interior lakes, but this is also prime season for mature leeches to roam the weedbeds looking for mates, and a good time to present the largest leech patterns in your fly box. After the young are born, there is an abundance of smaller-sized leeches roaming the weedbeds, presenting the best opportunities to fish leeches as small as hook size 14 through the summer months, increasing the hook sizes to 10–12 later in the fall.

Trout relish a few good leeches after a feeding session on chironomids; don't leave the lake at 3:00 p.m. without trying one. Who knows? Maybe those slippery, slimy leeches are dessert—chocolate ice cream after a meal of steak and potatoes? Summer evenings is another active time for leeches, and as the summer season fades into fall they become a highly sought-after food source for trout to bulk up on before winter.

A still-water smorgasboard. L to R: A leech, a *Gammarus* shrimp, two cased caddis larvae and two darner dragonfly nymphs. What choices! *Photo Brian Chan.*

The size of the leech pattern you are fishing is important. When trout are taking leeches, they typically circle them and approach from behind, taking a long suck on the posterior of the prey, which pulls the leech backward into their mouths; if the pattern is too large, they'll grab the tail, discover their mistake, and expel it quickly, never setting the hook. I think small leeches are ingested in a gulp, resulting in more positive hookups. Many times when fishing leech patterns, you'll experience short hits—often your size is wrong, and you should drop two hook sizes, because fish can be very selective of size when feeding on this food source.

Leeches are found on the shoals, in less than 6 m of water, where a type 1 slow-sinking line is usually the ticket, occasionally reverting to a type 2 medium-sink when you have to get deeper than 5 m, or when mooching a fly with a float tube or pontoon boat. For trollers in boats, I recommend a type 3 full-sinking line because your trolling speed is always quicker than an anchored or mooching fly fisher's retrieve, and your 3-weight line will fish the depth of types 1 or 2 full-sink being mooched. When anchored or mooching, fish them with a slow and steady hand-crawl retrieve, pausing occasionally to let the fly drop.

Tying leeches should be like gluing hair on a stick, the slimmer the better. Over the years, fly tiers have experimented with different tying methods and along the way many suggestive leech patterns have been developed, none better than the Woolly Worm and all of its derivatives. Long body-length tails, slim dark body, add some palmered hackle for suggestive movement, flash if you care to, and a leech pattern is born. I have seen many different colours of leeches inhabiting the same body of water including brown, blood-red, black, olive and maroon, but I have the most confidence in blood-coloured flies with black trim like the Blood Bugger. I used to tie mine on long shank 4-X long hooks such as Mustad 79580, but more recently on 2-X long Mustad 9671, because I think the 2-X hook gives the tail a little more freedom to undulate. If you weight your leech patterns with lead (I always do), weight only the front half of the shank, which allows the leech to undulate realistically, and to drop face-first in the water column when your retrieve is paused. Fish like that movement, and often clobber it ruthlessly (see page 157).

Since this pattern came to me, I've tied it with many other colour combinations, all using black palmered hackle: tails of maroon, rust and olive; bodies of black or red-black sparkle dubbing, peacock or bronze herl, and olive chenille.

Jack Shaw came up with his mohair leech after many years of experimentation at the vise. He shared it with me in his later years, insisting this was the one to break the camel's back when it came to fishing the lowly leech patterns around the Kamloops area—it's a good one (see page 157).

Water Boatman and Backswimmer

Families: Water boatman—Corixidae, Backswimmer—Notonectidae
Sizes: Water boatman—up to 13 mm, Backswimmer—up to 18 mm
Colours: Water boatman—brown, tan, yellow-cream or green-olive body, and tan wing-case, Backswimmer—brown-olive body, and dark brown wing-case

These two insect families are cousins, very similar in nature, appearance, movement and activity as far as the fly fisher is concerned, but quite different in their sizes and colours, feeding habits and swimming actions. From a quick recognition point of view, water boatmen swim upright, usually on the bottom of the lake or streams, whereas backswimmers swim on their backs, belly-side up and are often noticed close to the surface.

Water boatmen are marked with pale tones of tan, yellow, or yellow-olive on their undersides, and tan-brown backs V-ribbed with black markings. Backswimmers are the larger insect and darker in colouration; undersides are olive-green marked with brown and a dark olive-brown wing-case topside that you rarely see. Both have long rear legs attached slightly behind their midpoints that they use for oar-like propulsion, and short front legs utilized for grasping, holding onto their air bubbles and for feeding.

Their feeding habits are different; water boatmen are herbivorous, dining on aquatic plants, vegetation and algae, whereas backswimmers are predatory and hunt their prey, which includes all insect groups and even small fish or their favourite food, tadpoles. They inflict a bite to conquer their quarry, a chomp that can be painful to humans and to feeding trout, which is why water boatmen are the preferred fish food. A fly fisher will rarely encounter either of these bugs in deep water because they inhabitat weedy shoals of less than 2-m depth, where they can find cover, foliage to cling to and the most abundant sources of nutrition.

Both insects breathe air; they must routinely surface to stay alive, and maintain a swimming pace or attach to vegetation to stay submerged. In order to breathe, water boatmen surface and carry a bubble of air back to the lake or stream bottom; backswimmers float to the surface and ingest air while travelling on their backs. When imitating the water boatman, the fly tier must incorporate this glistening air bubble "look" into their patterns (but I do it for both insects)—I like to use plastic or, more recently, Midge Flex, which I use to over-wrap the body, imparting the allure of a gleaming air pocket.

On still days any time from late August through mid-September, depending on lake elevation, water boatmen and backswimmers embark in a ritual known as their nuptial mating flights, each seeking the opportunity to breed. I look forward to this event as much as I anticipate the caddis hatches of July because for a two- to three-week period crisp, sunny, fall afternoons bring out the "hatches," or more properly termed "flights" of these insects. Trout, after several weeks of non-hatch activity, go crazy on these bugs as they chase them all over the shallow zones. After having a good time feeding on these insects, fish will often go off the feed for a week or so, requiring some time to metabolize the hard-bodied skeletons they have furiously ingested. When their bodies recover, you'll find that fish will prefer to seek "meat and potatoes" table fare such as small scuds.

I recall a crisp, bright day last September when Danie Erasmus and I decided to hike into a small lake in Crooked River Park north of Prince George. We knew we weren't going to catch lunkers like Dragon Lake might offer at this time of year, but we wanted a peaceful afternoon of fishing for average-sized trout in a wilderness setting. We arrived at the lake about 10:00 a.m. after a twenty-minute hike on a good trail, and were the only anglers to pick this lake on that day.

It was quiet, not a sign of fish rising or even a loon left from the summer, and it stayed that way for several hours, but there were clues of impending good fortune: water boatmen were active on the shoreline as we launched our float tubes, scuds were cruising round and about the weedbeds, and the barometer was rising with a warm southwest breeze.

We picked up a few nice trout of 35–40 cm on chironomids and scuds during the next few hours. Shortly after lunch, I noticed a few boatmen were beginning to move near the surface, a telltale sign of the pre-emergent restless activity that invariably precedes an afternoon "flight." Around 2:00 p.m., it came: boatmen were flying all over the lake, landing with a splat, and getting clobbered by fat rainbow trout. We fished the "flight" until 5:00 p.m., each releasing over twenty nice trout. Target fishing with surface lines and light fly rods—a splendid example of being in the right place at the right time, recognizing the opportunity at hand and capitalizing on good fortune, which was so good I took a vacation day from work and repeated the act the next day!

A fly fisher cannot overlook opportunities to fish these insects; small creeks, beaver ponds and even the backwaters of major rivers have good populations. Both insects are abundant in moving water, and mate in the same time slot: early fall. I drifted the Bow River south of Calgary with my sons last September, and did very well in the soft water below McKinnon Flats and Carseland areas on the same patterns I use in still water.

When imitating these critters on a hook, you'll find that they have many similarities; so many that methods for tying the two patterns can be successfully mingled on the tying bench. The features you must imitate include their long propulsion legs, air bubbles, and surface-floating ability. For legs, many tiers use rubber bands, but I prefer to use natural materials whenever possible and choose to tie mine with a stiff peacock herl strand that I insert through the body at mid-point with a darning needle, anchor with a drop of Krazy Glue, and clip slightly longer than the body. Herl imparts a wonderful glistening effect to the insect, and has small hairy fronds on the stem, like the legs of the natural bug.

As mentioned earlier, I use clear Midge Flex to over-wrap my body material for these patterns, but a plastic sandwich baggie cut into 2-mm strips (my choice of material thirty years ago) also works. Midge Flex, however, is available without cutting and is more flexible for a clean, tight body wrap. I also use Midge Flex for the wing-cases of my patterns—brown for backswimmers and tan for boatmen (see page 158).

Trout key on the nuptial flights of these insects either on their rise to the surface, when they plop on the lake after a 10- to 15-m flight through the air, or on the descent back to the bottom of the lake after their flight. On most occasions, I have found it doesn't matter how fish are taking them; if you can put your pattern in the vicinity of a surface-feeding trout and give it a few short strips to imitate swimming action, it will be slammed whether it's rising, floating, or dropping.

But the most exciting time is when the bug is on the surface! To keep my patterns afloat for a few brief seconds like the natural after its flight drop, I tie a piece of tan foam that is narrower than the wing-case material of Midge Flex *under* the wing-case. I have discovered that if I use a type 1 intermediate sink line, grease only the front metre of leader tippet, and use my Floater pattern during a "flight," I can fish all phases of the "hatch" with more success than by using sink-tip or floating lines, and have a lot more fun doing it.

Finally, when imitating the backswimmer floating on its back, I like to tie a few stiff fronds of pheasant or grouse barbs on *top* of the hook to mimic the insect's front legs, and impart the impression that it is swimming "legs up." All this trickery to fool a worthy adversary (see page 159)!

Terrestrials:
Ants, Termites and
Grasshoppers

Ants, termites, grasshoppers, beetles and other landlubber insects that slip or crash-land into water form only a minute portion of the lake-dwelling fish's diet, but they are the preferred "opportunity meal" for fish that reside in lush meadow streams, tree-lined creeks and big rivers. On windy days, terrestrials are incapable of guiding their flight patterns; many end up in water systems, where they are helpless against moving current and surface friction, and become a welcome change from a river trout's normal diet of caddis, mayflies and stonefly nymphs.

Trout relish the mating flights of terrestrials, and are always on the lookout for them. Grasshoppers constitute a huge meal of protein; ants and termites are a luxury item, similar to us going after a sharp-tasting treat—perhaps a dill pickle? Whatever the reason, it seems that the hottest days of the year, often the slowest fishing days, are good times to try your luck with a terrestrial because they work best during periods of low hatch activity, and being a last resort fly pattern for the die-hard dry fly fisher, can salvage a day's fishing that otherwise could have been a skunking.

Ants and Termites

Ant: order Hymenoptera (12,000 species)
Termite: order Isoptera (4,000 species)
Adult: size 8–20 mm; colours: black, dark brown, red-orange, red-orange and black, and white (termite).

Ants and termites are colonizers that live in communities and work in harmony and cooperation for survival of the colony. They are fascinating insects; I think everyone should put a few hours a year aside to visit an anthill, just to watch them work in a spirit of teamwork and unselfishness. Each has a job to do, and they pull together to get it done. Ants and termites are not related. Their reproductive cycles, size and means of survival, however, are so similar that they can be treated as one for the fly fisher's benefit. If you see a white ant-looking insect flying on your favourite lake or stream, consider it to be a termite.

Individual ants of a colony can be sterile or fertile males or females, grouped into infertile workers or soldiers, and fertile male drones or queen ants. As the colony builds a mass of insects, it expands. Queen ants lay special batches of both fertilized eggs, which become fertile drones, and unfertilized eggs, which become future queens. These *special* unfertilized eggs, tended by worker ants and guarded by soldier ants, go through a pupa stage, develop wings and go forth to mate and establish new colonies—the wind-drifted missile flying ants and termites that we fly fishers mimic with our dry fly patterns.

Mating flights of ants are sporadic during the year, with different families hatching and mating any time that conditions are right from April right through the end of September. Big, black carpenter ants are seen flying in spring and early summer, small red and black ants during July and August, and large red ants during dry weather spells of early September; whereas termites are considered to have both spring and fall flights.

It was early September 2006 on the Livingstone River, my boys, Kevin and Graham, and I were enjoying our annual week in Alberta fishing for those pretty west-slope cutthroats we love so much. The weather was hot during the day and below zero at night, perfect conditions for late-season hatches of caddis, mayflies, midges and red ants. A thermal wind came up during the afternoons, and with it mating flights of black and red two-toned ants. Trout would switch from midge to ants every afternoon, so we quickly found that we needed to adjust our thinking. I hadn't much opportunity to "ant fish" in my forty years of trout fishing; my fly box didn't have much for ant patterns. It was time to come up with a pattern while on the trip or lose out on some good opportunities—"Daddy's Ant" was about to be born!

I had limited fly tying materials with me, but enough black and orange to design a decent looking ant. I started with a Mustad 94840 dry fly hook size 16, tied a post of white calf tail slightly ahead of midpoint of the hook, which simulates wings and acts as a high visibility indicator. Next was the abdomen, which I chose to represent with a built-up ball of Hare Tron H 17 Black dubbing, which is easy to spin and correctly designed with enough sparkle to imitate an ant's glossy abdomen. I chose a thorax of burnt-orange floss, and grizzly hackle tied traditional dry style over the entire thorax section.

We were armed for action, and headed straight for the river. Kevin went downstream, and Graham and I upstream, deciding to meet in two hours. We fished Daddy's Ant and when we met later our smiles were as wide as the Old-man Gap—30–40 cutties came to the ant that afternoon, and another pattern added to the arsenal, which has become a mainstay in the fly box for those "antsy" days (see page 159).

Since that glorious fishing day on the Livingstone, I've worked on a few more ant patterns, using strips of foam for the abdomen, adding hackle tips for wings. Foam floats well, and in the design of ant patterns, forms a nice abdomen when tied as a shellback. I don't use foam for the thorax area, which is better represented with floss or dubbing because I look for a "thin" form with colour, and a place to build hackle to assist in floatation of the model (see page 159 and 160).

Grasshopper

Order: Orthoptera
Superfamily: Tridactyloidea (11,000 species)
Size: 30–40 mm; colours: underbody of yellow, tan, insect-green, olive; back a darker shade of underbody, usually brown-olive

Who doesn't love a dry, windy afternoon in July and August? Or perhaps early September before the first frosts, when the wild meadow grass along rivers and lakes crackles and has turned to hay? These kinds of days are "hopper times." When I fish hot summer days, I'm always on the lookout for grasshoppers, listening for the telltale "click-click" as they snap their wings in flight, or their singing sound coming from deep in the tall grass as they rub their hind legs against their abdomens.

To trout, grasshoppers represent the ultimate fast food meal—a Big Mac with all the trimmings, and apple pie for dessert. They take them in a hurry, afraid to let the opportunity pass without a violent slash at the offering, for surely another trout will be more than willing to take a chance at the drifting, struggling snack passing through its window.

Late July is when I begin to look for grasshoppers. The young have not yet developed wings, and seem to be a bit more clumsy and vulnerable to mishaps than mature hoppers. Trout know these things—it's survival of the fittest. Hoppers are smaller than mature adults at this time of year; you'll want to fish them with hook sizes 12–14, not the big flopper patterns in sizes 4–8 you will be fishing during late August and September.

Always fish tight to the bank with hopper patterns—sometimes even 10 cm closer than what you think is close enough will make a difference to your fishing success. Bouncing the pattern off the bank is often the tactic that the trout are looking for, as they have their sights on the bank, not the water; a grasshopper pattern being pulled off the bank is pretty realistic to a foraging trout as long as it doesn't carry a clump of sod with it!

We all love to be in love with hopper fishing but frankly, the fish don't get as many as we would like to think they do. Grasshoppers only make up 5–10 percent of a fish's diet of terrestrials, whereas ants, beetles, and termites comprise up to 30 percent. Don't waste a lot of time with a grasshopper imitation if you can't raise fish; revert to the bread-and-butter caddis, midge, mayfly and stonefly adults that make up the other 60 percent of the diet, or try a nymph out of desperation.

Spun deer-hair heads are common on hopper patterns. The hopper's legs can be imitated at the same time as the head is spun. The trick is to leave enough room, which is why all of the body and wing materials are tied behind the three-quarter-point of the hook shank. First, to imitate legs, lay a 5-mm bunch of deer hair on top and bottom of the shank in front of the wings using a soft loop, so they sweep rearward and out of the way. For the head, lay three sections 5-mm width of deer hair in front of the legs, figure-eight them in succession to the shank and allow them to spin around the shank, pushing them rearward with your thumbnail and first finger as they progress to the hook eye. Trim the head to shape with scissors, creating a bullet-shaped head that is slim at the hook eye, and tapered larger to the rear (see page 160).

Resources

Books:
Backroad Mapbook Cariboo Chilcotin Coast BC, Mussio Ventures, 2008.
Backroad Mapbook Northern BC, Mussio Ventures, 2007.
The Angler's Atlas Omineca Lakes, Goldstream Publishing, 2007
The Angler's Atlas Quesnel Backroads, Second Edition, Goldstream Publishing, 2007

Websites:
Angler's Atlas: www.anglersatlas.com
British Columbia Tourism and Travel Information: www.bcadventures.com
Fly Fishing Information: www.westfly.com
Freshwater Fisheries of BC: www.gofishbc.com
Parks of British Columbia: www.bcparks.com

Index

A

Adams Emerger—Smith's **132**
Ants **159**, 202, 203
Arctic grayling **20**

B

Backswimmer 5, **158–159**, 199
Backswimmer Floater—Smith's **159**
Batnuni Bridge 51–52
BC Fisheries 14, 17, 45, 48, 60
Bear Lake 76
Bellos Lake 44
Bishop Lake 47, 58
Blackwater Canyon 52–53
Blackwater rainbow 14, 52, 66
Blackwater River **23**, 46–47, 50, 52–54, 64
Blue-Winged Olive (BWO) 100, 124, 126, **128, 138,**
155
Bowron lakes 23, 87
Bowron Lakes Provincial Park 92
Bowron River 89, 91–92
Brook trout 21
Brown Drake 126
Brown Lake 47
bull trout 18–20, 47, 54, 69, 84, 86, 95–96
Burns Lake 60
Byers Lake 72

C

caddis 27, **146–151**, 172–184
Caddis Adult **148–149, 151**, 176, 183
Caddis Adult, Cinnamon—Smith's **148**
Caddis Adult, Grannom—Smith's **151**
Caddis Adult, Green—Smith's **151**
Caddis Adult, October—Smith's **149**
Caddis Adult, Spotted—Smith's **151**
caddis, eggs and larvae 174, **197**
Caddis Larva, October—Smith's **149**
Caddis Larva, Spotted—Smith's **150**
Caddis Pupa, Cinnamon—Smith's **148**
Caddis Pupa, Spotted—Smith's **150**
Caddis Pupa, Traveller—Smith's **147**
caddis pupae 175
Callibaetis 77, 99, 100, 117–122, **135–136**
Callibaetis Mayfly Nymph Olive—Smith's **135**
Camp Lake 72
Canadian River Classifications 40
Carp Lake 73, 83–85
Carp Lake Campground 83–84
Chan, Brian 30, 111, 114, **131, 147**
Chaoborus (Midge) Pupa **131**
Chaoborus Larva—Smith's **131**
Cheslatta Falls 58
Cheslatta River 55, 58
Chilako River 55, 62, 64, 66
Chine Falls 51, 53

chironomid 17, 44, 45, 88, 98, 103, 108, 109, 111,
112, 113, 114, 115, 179, 193, 197
Chironomid—Adult 110
Chironomid—Emerger 111
Chironomid Adult—Smith's **130**
Chironomid Emerger—Smith's **130**
Chironomid Larva 107
Chironomid Pupa 108, 129
Chironomid Pupa Translucent Blood—Smith's **129**
Chironomid Red & Silver—Smith's **130**
Cicuta Lake 58
Cinnamon Caddis 150, 182
Clearwater Trout Hatchery 14
Clisbako River 46
Cobb Lake 63, 114
Coglistiko River 52
Crooked River 72–73, **74**-76, 80, 200
Crooked River Canyon FS Recreation Site 74
Crooked River Provincial Park 75–76
Cutoff Creek FS Recreation Site 59
Cutthroat trout 22

D

Daddy's Ant—Smith's **159**
Damsel Adult 163
Damsel Nymph **143, 163**
Damsel Nymph, Marabou—Smith's **143**
Damsel Nymph—Smith's **143**
Darner Dragonfly 166
Davey, Alf 170
Davie Lake 75
Dolly Varden trout 47, 83, 93
Dragonfly **144–146**, 165–167, 169–170
Dragonfly, Adult—Smith's **146**
Dragonfly Adult 170
Dragonfly Nymph **144–145, 197**
Dragonfly Nymph, Darner—Smith's **145**
Dragonfly Nymph, Deer Hair Darner—Smith's
144
Dragonfly Nymph, Gomphus—Smith's **145**
Dragon Lake 30, 41, 42, 43, 44, 108, 200

E

Eena Lake 69–70
Elk Hair Caddis 47, **149**, 180, 184
Eskers Park 21, 72
Euchiniko Lakes 52
Euchiniko River 50, 52–53
Eutsuk Lake 59–60

F

Finger Lake Resort 56
Firth Lake 80–82
Fischer, Hermann 170
Fishpot Lake 49–50, 52
Foam Ant Black—Smith's **159**

Fourteenmile Lake 91
Francois Lake 60, 181
Fraser Lake 11, 55, 58, 60, 181
Fraser Valley Trout Hatchery 14
Freshwater Shrimp 192, **194**
Frost Lake 87

G

Gammarus 156, 192–194, **197**
Gerrard rainbow 14, 18
Gillies Crossing 50–53
Goat River 96
Golden Stone 189–190
Gomphus **144–145**, 165, 169–171
Graham, Bob 6, 165
Grand Canyon 58
Grannom 183–184
Grasshopper 160, 204
Green Caddis 172, 183 (see also Hopper)
Green Drake 125, 126
Greer Creek FS Recreation Site 59
Griffith, George 117, **134**
Griffith's Gnat 117, 134
Grizzly Lake 66
Grizzly Lake East 90

H

Hare's Ear 47, 92, 125, 126, 190
Hare's Ear Nymph 123, 186, 190
Hart Lake **28**, 76–77, 121, 179
Hobson Lake 56–57
Hopper 154, **160**
Hopper, Foam Yellow/Brown—Smith's **160**
Hourston Lake 82
Humpy 111
Hyalella 192–195

J

Junkers Lake 82

K

Kamloops Sedgefly Pupa **146**
Kamloops trout 14, 168
Kenney Dam 55–56, 58, 59
Kluskus Lake 50, 52, 54, 56
Knewstubb Lake 55, 56
Kokanee 24, 43
Kootenay Trout Hatchery 14

L

lake trout **19**, 22-23, 87, 94
leech 29, 54, 88, 91, **157**, 196, **197**
Leech, Blood Bugger—Smith's **157**
Leisering Lift 116, 127, 128
Lingren, Art 170, 178
Little Green (Olive) Stonefly 191

Little Yellow Stoneflies (Yellow Sally) 190
Livingstone Springs 74
Longhorned Case Maker 172, 179
Loucas Raptis 170

M

Mackenzie 51–53, 64
Marmot Lake 47–49, 52–53
Martin Meadow Trail 46
mayfly 5, 17, 75, 118–119, 134–142
Mayfly, Brown Drake Dun—Smith's 139
Mayfly, Brown Drake Spent Spinner—Smith's 140
Mayfly, BWO Dun—Smith's **138**
Mayfly, BWO Emerger—Smith's **138**
Mayfly, BWO Spent Spinner—Smith's **138**
Mayfly, Callibaetis Adult Spinner—Smith's **136**
Mayfly, Callibaetis Dun—Smith's **135**
Mayfly, Callibaetis Dun Emerger—Smith's **135**
Mayfly, Callibaetis Spent Spinner **136**
Mayfly, PMD Emerger—Smith's **140**
Mayfly, PMD Quill Dun—Smith's **141**
Mayfly, PMD Spent Spinner—Smith's **141**
Mayfly, Slate-Winged Olive Dun—Smith's **139**
Mayfly, Slate-Winged Olive Spent Spinner—Smith's **139**
Mayfly, Trico Dun (Male)—Smith's **142**
Mayfly, Trico Spent Spinner (Male)—Smith's 142
Mayfly Nymph, Hare's Ear **137**
Mayfly Nymph, Pheasant Tail Bead Head **137**
McLeod Lake 72–73, 75, 84
McLeod River 83–85
Meadow Lake 65
Microcaddis 172, 184
midge 112
Midge Adult 114, 117, **131**, **134**
Midge Emerger 116
Midge Larva—Smith's **132**
Midge Larvae 112, 115
Midge Pupa 113, **132**
Midge Pupa—Smith's **132**
Midge Pupae 116
Midge Spinner, Olive **134**
Mikaluk, Walter 147, 178
Mikaluk Sedge 52, 59, 64, 103, **149**, 178
Mikaluk Traveller **147**
Millionaire's Pool 61
Moffat, Blair 7
Mud River 66–67
My Adams—Smith's **133**

N

Nation, Bill 14, 168
Nazko 34, 41, 44–47, 49–54
Nazko Bridge 51, 53–54
Nazko Lake 45–46
Nazko River 45–47, 51–52

Nechako River 5, 13, 55, 68
Ness Lake 70, 72
Nithi River 60
North Cariboo 10–11, 41, 43, 45–47, 55–56, 58, 118, 177, 193
Northern Case Maker 172, 178
northern pike minnow 25, 69, 83
Nulki Lake 56

O

October Caddis 172, 179, 180, 184
Opalescent Shrimp, Shaw's **156**
Opatcho Lake 88

P

Pale Evening Dun (PED) 127
Pale Morning Dun (PMD) **126**
Parachute Adams—Smith's 133
Parsnip River 80, 82
Peace River 10, 31, 68
PED Spent Spinner **142**
Pelican Lake 53, 66
Pennask Creek 14
Pinkerton Lake 93, 95
Pregnant Shrimp 195
Pregnant Shrimp, Smith's 157
Premier Lake rainbow 14
Prince George 6, 9–13, 20–21, 23, 38–39, 44–45, 55, 60, 62–64, 66–74, 79–80, 84, 86–92, 94–96, 200

Q

Quesnel 11, 13, 41–45, 50, 89, 108, 173

R

rainbow trout 13–14, **15, 16**, 44–48
Red Ant **160**
Redfern River (Rapids) 59
Robert's Roost 42–43
Rocky Mountain whitefish 25

S

Salmonfly 185–190
Sedge 177–179
Sedge, Mikaluk Traveller 147
Shaw, Jack 6, 9, 14, 30, 101, 108, 110, 113, 121, 144–146, 156–157, 162, 164, 168–170, 174, 178, 192, 194, 198
shrimp (scud) 5, **156**, 195
Shrimp, Gammarus—Smith's 156
Skwala 153, 189–190
Slate-Winged Olive 125
Slate-Winged Olive Dun—Smith's **139**
Slim Creek 94–96
Soft Hackle Emerger 59, 116, **128, 133**, 182, 184
Spotted Caddis 172, 181–183

Spruce Lakes 93
steelhead trout 15
Stellako Lodge 60
Stellako River 55, 60, 181
stonefly **152–156**, 185, **187**
Stonefly Adult **152–156**
Stonefly Adult, Golden—Smith's **154**
Stonefly Adult, Little Olive—Smith's **156**
Stonefly Adult, Salmonfly—Smith's **152**
Stonefly Adult, Skwala—Smith's **153**
Stonefly Adult, Yellow Sally—Smith's **155**
Stonefly Nymph, Golden—Smith's **154**
Stonefly Nymph, Little Olive—Smith's **155**
Stonefly Nymph, Little Yellow—Smith's **154**
Stonefly Nymph, Salmonfly—Smith's **152**
Stonefly Nymph, Skwala—Smith's **153**
Stump Lake Damsel **144**, 164
Suspender Midge 114, 116, **131**

T

Tatuk Lake 56, 66–67
Ten Mile Lake 43–44
termites **159**, 202
terrestrials **159**, 202
Tom Thumb 111, **148**, 178
Tory Lake 64, 66, **67**
Traveling Sedge 172, 177
Trico Dun and Spinner 128
Trout Lodge Hatchery 18
Tumuch Lake 94

V

Vanderhoof 11, 55–57, 62
Vivian Lake 70–72

W

War Falls 83–84
Water Boatman 158, 199
Water Boatman, Smith's Original 158
Water Boatman Floater—Smith's **158**
Werner Shrimp 192
West Everett Lake 94
West-Slope Cutthroat 14, 17
Wicheeda Lake 78–79
Williams Lake 12
Willow River 89–90, 92
Woolly Bugger 104
Woolly Worm **146**, 174, 177, 180, 194, 198

Y

Yimpakluk Lake 53